BUSINESSMEN and REFORM

A STUDY OF THE PROGRESSIVE MOVEMENT

Robert H. Wiebe is Professor of History at Northwestern University. He is also the author of *The Search for Order, 1877–1920*; *The Segmented Society*; and *The Opening of American Society*.

BUSINESSMEN
and REFORM: A STUDY OF
THE PROGRESSIVE MOVEMENT

ROBERT H. WIEBE

ELEPHANT PAPERBACKS

IVAN R. DEE, INC., PUBLISHER, CHICAGO

FOR LONNIE

PREFACE

The early years of the twentieth century — the progressive era — served as a way station between agrarian and urban America. Into it came men, institutions, and values born on the farms and in the towns; out of it went the first practical experiments in social reorganization for an industrial nation. Although this exciting, hopeful, and noisy period contained much lost motion, it did contribute beneath the tumult several changes of lasting significance to American life. For the first time, an appreciable number of public leaders thought in terms of a society characterized by indeterminate process rather than a society of predictable motions under natural law. In response to a new sense of human relations, these leaders began constructing a government of flexible powers and continuous responsibilities, involved in the workings of the nation, which in later years rapidly replaced the older detached government of occasional intervention. Particular demands for reform came largely from a wide range of middle-income Americans whose arrival as organized, articulate, and demanding citizens reordered the social structure. As a result, the privileges of leadership were partially redistributed to accommodate the challengers.

This study examines the ways in which businessmen, weak and strong, rising and established, influenced the progressive movement and were influenced by it. Of necessity, the study is also a quest for elementary tools of description and analysis, because an abundant literature on both the progressives and businessmen has not supplied a satisfactory working definition of either. Arthur Link, for example, discusses "advanced progressives" without fixing the main body of reformers left behind or defining the goals toward which this vanguard advances. The profiles of the progressive personality which George Mowry has sketched leave the strong, but unverifiable, suspicion that allegiance to the Progressive party determined his sampling. Richard Hofstadter, on the other hand, deals with an "impulse toward criticism and change that was everywhere so conspicuous after 1900 . . . a rather widespread and remarkably good-natured effort of the greater part of society to achieve some not very clearly specified self-reformation." But no one learns why those who recorded their views in "the popular magazines, the muckraking articles, the campaign speeches, and the essays of representative journalists and influential publicists" best portray this majority of Americans.

Despite a few careful analyses of businessmen, they emerge from the main stream of historical literature in similar condition. Over the past four decades a large body of that literature has placed the business community, monolithic and undefined, on trial. Writing for the prosecution, Arthur Schlesinger, Jr., states, "The business community has been ordinarily the most powerful of [the groups competing for control of the state], and liberalism in America has been ordinarily the movement on the part of the other sections of society to restrain the power of the business community." Allan Nevins declares in rebuttal that the genius of businessmen has enabled the United States to protect the free world against fascism and communism. But who are the businessmen? Sometimes they appear to be a handful of particularly successful and powerful men. At others the community presumably includes everyone from the chairman of U.S. Steel to the corner grocer, without information on how, if at all, their thoughts and actions differ.

Traditionally, historians of the progressive era have cast businessmen as the villains. In the standard story, they move in the shadows, plotting the downfall of the reformers and reminding the reader what vested interests inspired all the commotion. But in recent years historians have rehabilitated businessmen so thoroughly that Carl Degler now maintains, ". . . progressivism, as all admit, was largely a businessmen's movement." The businessman-reformer currently so popular proves on closer inspection to be a poor representative of his occupational group. Typically he is a retired or semiretired man who finances political movements and humanitarian causes. Almost truculently independent of still-active businessmen, he accentuates the conservatism of the community he has abandoned, strengthening thereby the stereotype of the business villain.

This study attempts to bring businessmen of all types out of the shadows and trace their varied relations with progressive reform. "Businessmen" means those who combine labor and capital to realize a profit, with the following exceptions: farmers; self-employed artisans; professionals, such as lawyers and academicians; publicists; men such as Marcus Hanna who have thoroughly identified themselves with a political party; and men such as Andrew Carnegie who have retired. In the interests of manageability, the study concentrates upon the national progressive movement. Finally, it involves both the differences among businessmen and their areas of agreement.

Among the many people whose kindness contributed to this work, I wish to thank in particular Meyer Fishbein, John Garraty, William Leuchtenburg, Carl Resek, and Richard Wade. In a variety of ways, these men took precious time to point out my blunders and to open new avenues for thought and research. During successive phases of the study, the Social Science Research Council, Michigan State University's All-University Fund, and the Columbia University Council for Research in the Social Sciences contributed indispensable funds. The editors of the *American Historical Review* and *Mississippi Valley Historical Review* graciously permitted me to use material which first appeared in a different form in these journals. The greatest debt lies with Lonnie, my wife, who supplied backbone and wisdom throughout.

R. H. W.

CONTENTS

BUSINESSMEN and REFORM

A STUDY OF THE PROGRESSIVE MOVEMENT

I

A SETTING FOR PROGRESSIVISM

In the past hundred years three great waves of technological change have broken over the United States. No sooner have Americans begun seriously to reconstruct their society after one of these than another has crashed upon them. Each has swelled greatly just after a major war; each has spread confusion as it strikes; and each has carried promises of a vast increase in the nation's wealth. These are the motive forces in a century of American history.

The first wave, rising after the Civil War, covered the United States with a system of railroads which, in combination with a telegraph and telephone network, revolutionized communications. New methods of steel production, new sources of industrial energy, new devices for the extraction of minerals, and new techniques of preserving food enabled basic industries to specialize, consolidate, and multiply production for a national market. Around the centers of production and distribution clustered people from all parts of the United States and Europe, transforming town into city and city into metropolis; and to feed urban America an increasingly mechanized agriculture also specialized and consolidated. By the end of the century a grillwork of nationalizing forces lay over a society still predominantly local in orientation.

During the late nineteenth century the structural elements of the new industrial economy — large corporations and financial houses — developed far more rapidly than the rest of the nation. Not until the beginning of the new century did secondary groups achieve an approximation of what John

Kenneth Galbraith has called "countervailing power." By then organizations were congealing throughout the nation to protect their members against impersonal forces and to provide strength in a society which disregarded individual demands. These collective agencies, ranging from tightly disciplined craft unions to the loose affiliation of liberal clergymen, represented in the main a maturing middle segment of society — moderately prosperous businessmen, professionals, established farmers, skilled workers — and for a short time their balance to the magnates gave American society relative stability.

The second wave struck with full force after World War I. Another revolution in communications, driven by the radio and the motion picture, brought uniform values into the home; a revolution in mass production and distribution brought standardized products; and the automobile built mobility into the lives of individual Americans. Cities sprawled into formless urban complexes; machines and chemicals enabled farmers to supply them with far more than enough food. Where the first years of the twentieth century had been the era of the financier, the new technology marked the resurgence of the great corporation, financially independent and often lord over an empire of suppliers and distributors. And where the earlier technology had shaken the foundations of American localism, this wave overwhelmed it.

No less confused than post-Civil War America, the United States after World War I displayed greater surface calm. Despite the collapse of old values, despite the disruption in family life, despite the destruction of community patterns, Americans were indulging in the wonders of modern technology. A flood of distracting new consumer goods, presumably available to all, dulled the shock of change. Then under the spur of depression, Americans regrouped. The countervailing blocs from an earlier era had already divided, most of them rising into a broader leadership stratum, a few joining the dispossessed. This time the agents of a new order came from a lower segment of society — unskilled laborers, previously disdained ethnic and color minorities, marginal and submarginal farmers, and masses of unemployed and destitute everywhere. Although the ties which bound them together were often loose and their organizations sometimes informal, their demands, hinting at revolution, were compelling. An accommodation—primarily economic, secondarily political and social—to these lower groups again brought American society into temporary equilibrium.

The third wave—the wave of our time—has given a new mastery of distances by air, new sources of atomic and thermonuclear energy, and a new revolution in the replacement of human by electronic labor. Where an earlier technology destroyed American localism, the most recent changes have assaulted the nation state and have most immediately affected the international relations of the United States. The emergent countervailing forces in our day are rudimentary regional and socioeconomic groupings of nations largely in response to a monopoly of modern technology by a few nations. Preoccupied with a world in revolution, Americans have postponed revamping their domestic structure.

Americans have responded to each wave of technological advance in similar stages of protest and reform: diffuse criticism, attempts to patch the old order, then efforts to modernize the social and political framework. Yet each period of protest and reform has produced its own distinct attitudes toward government and society. During the late nineteenth century the most prominent critics of industrial America offered simple means of preserving a competitive, individualistic, moral society without sacrificing the material benefits from technological progress. Civil service, antimonopoly, the single tax, the earliest cooperatives, dreams of a classless America, and schemes for inflation all were presented as panaceas which at one stroke would free the individual and ensure prosperity and justice for everyone—or, as in the case of civil service, everyone who was anyone. When government was involved at all, it played the role of prime mover. A single act, properly executed or enforced, would readjust society's machinery; further tampering would only disrupt the mechanism. Even the more imaginative schemes of Edward Bellamy and the Populist party conceived of government in these terms. In the nationalist paradise which Bellamy's novels described, the state had at the outset established a collectivist system. The society functioned by perpetual motion, and the government was nowhere to be seen. Through nationalization the populists expected to take certain basic segments of the economy from the "interests" and hand them to the "people." As the populists explained it, the transfer would occur by sublimation; government as a separate agency did not exist.

The middle-class groups which hardened around the turn of the century saw before them a more complex society and demanded that the government assume long-range commitments. Through a series of laws enacted early in the twentieth century, progressive reformers sketched a new relationship between government and society which gave government continuing responsibilities to keep order, correct abuses, and preserve morality. But the tasks of the enlarged government were almost all negative — to stop undesirable acts. Only a few secondary laws suggested a positive government of assistance, and none provided substantial power for governmental guidance. The progressives, in part from a distrust of the normal processes of government, placed most of the new power in regulatory agencies which they detached from the executive and the legislature. Believing that they had accomplished a permanent revolution in civic consciousness, the progressives relied upon the right men in the right offices to complete their system of government controls. No more than a framework, the progressive system would suit many structures.

The groups which the progressive agencies were designed to control captured them during the 1920's. Leading businessmen and their sympathizers, drawing upon prestige and experience which they had acquired during the First World War, built a new system of government service upon the progressive foundation. Neither able nor willing to ignore the government as many of their predecessors had during the late nineteenth century, businessmen now used government as a mechanism for regularizing their affairs. New York financiers worked through the Federal Reserve system to guide national banking practices; members of an industry ordered their operations through the Department of Commerce and the Federal Trade Commission; the United States Chamber of Commerce voiced its program through President Calvin Coolidge; brokers legitimized foreign bond issues through the approval of the State Department; and wealthy citizens modified the tax structure through the good offices of Andrew Mellon's Treasury Department. Although the Railroad Brotherhoods and some agricultural cooperatives acted in a somewhat similar fashion, the government during the 1920's, reflecting the apportionment of power within American society, operated largely as a means for business self-regulation.

The undermining effects of the new technology did not show clearly until the depression of the Thirties. Herbert Hoover and Franklin Roosevelt responded at first by trying to save the system of self-control inherited from the 1920's. Where Hoover refused to lend the prestige of government to these efforts, Roosevelt and the New Deal, particularly by way of the National Recovery Administration and the first Agricultural Adjustment Administration, identified the government with the attempt of private citizens to regulate their own affairs. But as attacks by the dispossessed groups altered the social structure, the New Deal shifted in response, reordering the government's relationship to American society with such measures as the Wagner and Fair Labor Standards Acts, Social Security, and the Works Progress Administration. From 1935 the government made extensive commitments to provide an economic minimum below which its citizens should not fall. And as the government developed an elaborate bureaucracy to fulfill its new responsibilities, it acquired substantial power independent of the private groups which might attempt to use it. Now citizens would have to work with the government rather than through it.

Since the outbreak of World War II, the most powerful

private groups have readjusted their policies and tamed the independent power of government sufficiently to retain their dominant positions in American society. Beyond a bit of patching nothing has been done within the nation, and distressingly little outside the nation, to remake the governmental structure in response to the current technological revolution. Still, in a way totally alien to the late nineteenth century, successful businessmen and their allies in the professions have had to accommodate themselves to secondary power groups within government, among laborers, and in agriculture. That is one fruit of a century of social change and reform. Another is a distribution of our phenomenal national wealth which assures organized segments of society a more than adequate living income. Finally, a tradition of periodic reorganization suggests possibilities for a modernized social structure which we have not begun to realize.

II

The progressive movement, then, represented the culmination of America's response to the first of three waves of technological innovation. Powered by emerging organizations of middle-income Americans, it demonstrated the effectiveness of collective means to achieve reform ends, and it established a more modern social and governmental system upon which later readjustments rested. The success of the United States during World War I depended upon the accomplishments of the progressive movement. And, however much some Americans in the 1920's pined for the days of Benjamin Harrison and William McKinley, they perforce had to adapt themselves to the changes of the intervening era, and thereby fashioned a more serviceable social system.

With many voices the progressives concerned themselves with three general issues: regulation of the economy to harness its leaders and to distribute more widely its benefits; modifications in government to make elected representatives more responsive to the wishes of the voters; and assistance for the dispossessed to open before them a richer life in

America. The first issue cast the widest net. Among those prominent in the movements for a regulated economy were businessmen and farmers after greater profits, politicians in need of an issue, journalists in search of a story, a new class of economic and administrative specialists looking for ways to utilize their knowledge, and clergymen hoping to re-establish morality in industrial America. A catchall of opportunists, idealists, and harried citizens at least agreed that life would be more rewarding if the mighty in business were humbled.

Programs to establish direct lines of influence from the ordinary citizen to his government ranked next in popularity, appealing to most of those who wanted business controlled. Even before the turn of the century, many believed that spoilsmen, corporation agents, and mediocre lawyers had made politics their private domain. To save America's traditional atomized democracy, reformers wanted the voters to participate in the legislative process, hold elected officials on call, and in some instances supervise the judiciary. When corrupt or indifferent politicians refused to enact "the people's reforms," the reformers planned to streamline the government in order to facilitate action and fix responsibility, then let the people reward and punish their political servants.

A humanitarian aura surrounded large portions of the progressive movement. Appalled by a miserable spreading poverty and worried about the future of Christianity in the slums, urban Americans, particularly women, searched for ways to protect the weak, the disabled, and the very young without damaging the spirit of individual initiative. In most cases neither charity nor socialism sufficed. Humanitarian progressives needed money, and they needed legislation to define the outer boundaries of social justice; but primarily they expected better educated, better established Americans to create for the underprivileged an environment which would nurture instead of destroy the growth of moral happy individuals. Sometimes prudence went with philanthropy:

provide a more humane and more equitable society or prepare for perpetual class strife; Americanize the immigrant in
your image or run the risk of an enemy capturing him.
At the turn of the century progressive reform was primarily local, defensive, and diffuse. Broad national reform
had broken in 1896 on the rocks of populism and free silver.
After that reformers had turned inward to their cities and
states where problems were more tangible and more amena-
ble to analysis. In the early years of the progressive era reformers demanded protection against their enemies, against
the powerful corporations and the political machines which
they claimed were robbing the people, oppressing the poor,
and prostituting government. Most of the reformers had little
knowledge of parallel movements elsewhere, even of similar
movements in their vicinity, and a little knowledge led more
often to suspicion than admiration.

Studied in depth, local problems ramified into national
ones. Success, publicity, and tighter organization produced
steadily increasing confidence. With a broader vision and
greater self-assurance grew the urge to interrelate particular
reforms into an integrated program for the whole nation.
Lincoln Steffens tracked the sources of corruption from the
cities to the state capitals to Washington; Frederic Howe
translated a desire for community service into a vision of
planned urban democracy; Jane Addams discovered in settlement work the need for a directing national government;
Walter Weyl moved from institutional economics to a program to reinvigorate middle-class democracy; Robert LaFollette left Wisconsin to lead a national drive against big business; and so the story repeated itself across the nation.

The critical transition in these trends from a local to a
national orientation, from defensiveness to confident attack,
and from diffuse reform to integrated programming occurred roughly around 1908. The flow of local reformers
into Washington was quickening, progressives were intro-
ducing the full complement of their national economic programs, and theoreticians were urging them on with ambitious
guides to America's future. The culmination of optimistic

national programming came in 1912 when the voters could choose among the Progressive new nationalism, the Democratic new freedom, and the Socialist new order. A finale began in 1917 as many reformers projected their visions of progressive America onto a world they would make safe for democracy.

Although the progressives spanned the range from tough- to tender-mindedness, among them certain values predominated, providing the movement with a set of general norms. One was a passionate concern for moral capitalism, for Christianized economics. "Industrialize Society without Commercializing Souls" could have served as the era's motto. A second norm combined skepticism about the present wisdom of the people with faith in their infinite educability. Ignorance and apathy had nourished the corruptionists. Calling the roll on reactionary congressmen, tent meetings for the uninitiated, education and more education would starve them out. A third norm anticipated extending the base of democracy while rationalizing its operation. As an enlightened electorate increasingly took control of the democratic process, progressive leaders would provide them with scientific administration, efficient city planning, a rational conservation program, and like means to guarantee social progress.

Belief in a peculiar brand of strong leadership, the fourth norm, so conditioned progressive legislation that it more than any other element determined the nature of the new framework which the reformers bequeathed to the 1920's. The cardinal sin of nineteenth-century government, progressives reasoned, was control by selfish, narrow men who had twisted democracy to serve their private interests. To ensure morality and efficiency and to provide education for the masses, at the top of government must stand "public men" — disinterested, unselfish, above the struggles for advantage and gain, able to survey the whole of America and act rationally in its behalf. These men would head the reform party tickets, prepare with the help of experts the progressive program, and fill the boards and regulatory agencies

upon whose functioning hinged so much of America's progressive future.

During the 1920's the assumptions of the progressives
about capitalism, democratic government, and the people
disintegrated. Capitalism, despite its growing alliance with
public relations, still meant profits, and Protestantism increasingly became its handmaiden. Direct democracy made
politics more complicated, more expensive, and if anything
less efficient. The people seemed to respond to almost every
teacher except latter-day progressives. And the "public men"
who were to provide Olympian guidance emerged in a form
strikingly different from that which the reformers had envisioned. Instead of rational, detached leadership in the
Mugwump tradition, the "public men" of the Twenties ex-
emplified the virtues of successful business. Instead of statesmen who preached the gospel of Justice and Democracy,
these "public men," usually private citizens, promised a land
of plenty to all who would live by the values of productivity and salesmanship. Adapting the commissions and the
strengthened departments of the executive to a new set of
goals, the leaders of the Twenties built logically from the
foundation of progressive government while they destroyed
the progressive rationale.

III

On the eve of the progressive era, the general attitudes
which businessmen shared neither separated them distinctly
from other Americans nor bound them into a self-conscious
community. Almost all of them disliked labor unions, disdained politicians, and feared panics and depressions to the
extent that "stability was [their] watchword."[1] But far more
obvious and more important were the forces which divided
businessmen into rival camps.

Their rivalries were of four general types. First, businessmen separated along an urban-small town line. By habit and
self-interest they usually identified first with their immediate environment and with other businessmen they knew
there. Men from the powerful financial houses of Wall Street

automatically understood each other; so did the proprietors along Main Street; and to a lesser degree so did members of a city chamber of commerce. An important bond among urban businessmen was the conviction that while they marched in the front ranks of progress, their country cousins remained hopelessly bound to the old ways. As the prominent New York financier, Frank Vanderlip, told a congressional committee early in the century, no reform which required the modernization of country banking could possibly succeed. Businessmen from the small towns returned this haughtiness with hostility and envy. In one mood they would reply in kind. "The tangible assets of the United States are not in Wall street [sic] or in the hands of money-lenders anywhere," a small Midwestern grain dealer announced to the cities. "They are found in our agricultural resources." But more often they, like the Midwesterners whom Russel Nye describes, would rail against Wall Street, their composite urban enemy: "the moneylender, the high-tariff manufacturer, the market speculator, the railroad king, the trust holder, the mortgage owner. It might mean Minneapolis, Chicago, Kansas City, St. Louis, or Boston as well as New York, but 'Wall Street' was a living entity," the villain who held them in bondage. Theirs was the language of populism, which had appealed to so many of them in the South and West.²

A second division separated businessmen regionally. In part this reflected the different economic orientations of the sections. Where financial power, heavy industry, and a wide variety of smaller manufacturing concentrated in the East, agricultural interests predominated elsewhere: Southern business revolved largely about financing, distributing, and finishing the cotton and tobacco crops; the Midwest, despite an increasing variety in industry and finance, still depended largely upon grains and livestock; and the Far West primarily managed its diversified food industry. Because of the country businessmen's strength outside the East, expressions of sectionalism were at times no more than rephrased rural attacks against the cities and their big businessmen.

"The effete East wishes to enrich itself at the expense of the rough and rugged West," cried T. R. Frentz, an Oshkosh banker. "Beware Mr. Morgan, Mr. Keene and Standard Oil crowd! You may form steel trusts and other kinds of trusts, but you cannot lick the cream out of Mr. Frentz' own saucers in his own home."[3]

Where sectional and anticolonial sentiment predominated, parochialism also thrived. In a letter excoriating "Wall Street," a Virginia banker told Representative Carter Glass, "I want to see the Southern funds of Southern banks controlled by Southern men familiar with Southern conditions." Here also were hints of a regional *amour-propre* which characterized so many statements from businessmen of the New South. When Daniel A. Tompkins of North Carolina was nominated for president of the National Association of Manufacturers, he thanked his supporters, not for himself, but for the honor they did the South. And the *Manufacturers' Record*, a New South periodical, harshly opposed large-scale philanthropy from the North as insulting to the dignity and self-reliance of its region. In the Far West businessmen were, in their own way, equally as exclusive. The Associated Chambers of Commerce of the Pacific Coast formally expressed their preoccupation with regional matters; and a member organization, the San Francisco Chamber of Commerce, not only rejected each plea for cooperation from east of the Rockies but even hired a Washington lobbyist to counteract "the business men of the East who are more and more anxious to shape legislation to their will."[4]

But when leading urban businessmen spoke for their regions, sectionalism showed its aggressive side. Two of the Midwest's most prominent entrepreneurs, Cyrus McCormick and James J. Hill, dreamed of regional empires. To break the dependence of his section upon the East, McCormick, in company with other successful Chicago businessmen, laid grand plans in the 1870's to link Europe and the Midwest by a line of trade running from Chicago through New Orleans to London. And the vision lived on in proposals for a deep waterway from the Lakes to the Gulf. Hill naturally built his regional plans upon a framework of railroads. Three or four sectional monopolies, he thought, would provide America with the most sensible system of roads. "In this [way]," Hill wrote to a friend, "the competition lies between the producer and the railway in one locality, acting together, against the producer and the railway in another locality, competing for the business," and he never doubted that the Midwest would emerge victorious. A similar competitive ambition animated the bankers and business journals of Chicago when they forecast the rise of their city above New York as America's financial center. To hasten the day, Midwestern city bankers proposed during the Nineties a new currency based upon a bank's liquid assets, a plan which Eastern financiers strongly opposed. Promoters in both the South and Midwest publicized strikes in Eastern cities with contrasting pictures of their regions' docile and skillful workers, and they interpreted the gradual decentralization of industry as the fruits of their labor.[5]

The division among businessmen according to the size of their enterprises, which historians often cite, is the most difficult to describe. In general, businessmen below the level of magnates subscribed to some variant of the theory that "the growing power and influence of trusts" destroyed honest enterprise and stunted "the hope and ambition of the youth of the country." They shared, in other words, the widespread, ill-defined antimonopoly sentiments of the late nineteenth and early twentieth centuries. But like "Wall Street," the term "trust" was a rubbery one, covering whatever economic forces worried a particular businessman at a particular time. Depending upon his location along a size scale, a businessman usually viewed with some suspicion all who were larger and stronger than he: the smaller his enterprise, the more enemies he collected. Most specifically, businessmen reserved their sharpest hostility for immediately threatening competitors just above them on the size scale. Thus it was relatively prosperous and established businessmen from New York who in 1881 founded the National Anti-Monopoly League; and early in the twentieth century it was the well-to-do, independent industrialists in the National Association of Manufacturers who most successfully translated their dislike for large combinations into effective antitrust lobbying. According to many of these independents, bigness was a disease which the trusts were spreading to the unions. "We observe with considerable interest," an established textile manufacturer told a Congressional committee in 1904, "that the so-called organized labor and the organized capital in the shape of trusts are not antagonistic to each other, and there is naturally a feeling of alarm as to what will become of the commercial and manufacturing conditions in the United States if one class of labor gets control of all labor, and one class of capital gets control of all trade, and those two forces agree together as to what they will do with the fellow that stays outside and with the American consumer." Farthest down the scale of size, small businessmen turned their most vigorous attacks upon the slightly larger concerns and the local pools and leagues which threatened to eliminate them. In all, it was a complex, and often confusing, pattern of rivalries.[6]

The competing functions which businessmen performed in the economy accounted for a final area of conflict. Among the protean forms of functional disunity, one of the earliest pitted the railroads against those business shippers who did not qualify for the rebates given to giant corporations. In the relatively mature economy of New York City, well-to-do businessmen marched in the vanguard of the movement for state, then federal, regulation of railroad rates; and in less developed states such as California, shippers entered the battle as soon as they had grown prosperous enough to challenge the carriers. A second long-standing rivalry set the business groups interested in foreign trade against industries which profited only from a high tariff. Here size played a less important role. It was Henry Havemeyer of the American Sugar Refining Company — the Sugar Trust — who maintained, with unconscious irony, that the tariff was the mother of the trusts. Further subdividing businessmen, advocates of a low tariff fought among themselves over the type and degree of revision. For example, the New England manufacturers who desired duty-free coal, iron, and hides naturally resented the American Free Trade League, an agency of large New York importing houses which wanted a competitive tariff on New England products. A third deep-seated conflict set bankers against a variety of other businessmen. Industrialists who lived by their habits of competition repeatedly clashed with the financiers who promoted consolidation and stability. Only a dire need of credit forced John W. Garrett, president of the Baltimore and Ohio, to join the railroad pool of 1877 instead of bulling his way into the Chicago market. Only the power and prestige of J. P. Morgan kept the aggressive presidents of U.S. Steel's subsidiary companies in some semblance of cooperation during the early years of the twentieth century. And outside the realm of finance capitalism, businessmen regularly complained about the terms of credit, neither understanding nor accepting the explanations of their bankers.[7]

A background of diversity and rivalry prepared businessmen for the reforms of the progressive era. As layers of business outside the major cities, outside the East, and below the magnates grew with a maturing and prospering economy, they produced the leaders who would challenge the dominance of established businessmen. Aggressive and competitive, these new men prided themselves upon being alert to the main chance; and with one eye to their enemies and another to their balance sheets, they entered the century in a mood to fight. But to fight effectively they required organization.

II

AN AGE OF ORGANIZATION

When dissenter met dissenter early in the twentieth century, they founded a reform organization. These proliferating leagues and associations did more than reflect widespread discontent. By supplying progressivism with a practical, durable substance which late-nineteenth century reform had lacked, they determined the character of the movement.

No single formula covers these diverse groups. Some were occupational, others functional; some began and ended as local leagues, others grew into national associations; some specialized in political action, others entered politics with obvious reluctance; some represented bright new ventures, others a reorganization of older associations; and some flowed with the main stream of the progressive movement, while others operated apart, entering reform only at selected spots. In general these organizations — the backbone of progressivism — expressed a widening social consciousness and an increasing political maturity among middle-income Americans. Yet few of them tried seriously to understand lower-income Americans, upon whom success often depended. And in general these associations moved with the trends of the progressive movement toward optimistic, integrated national reform. Yet few of them willingly sacrificed a jot of their independence to cooperate with the other agencies of reform.

A sample of these organizations suggests their intimate relationship to America's broad middle layer. From the towns and countryside came a new and sturdy company of cooperatives and agricultural organizations which pressed the federal government for bread-and-butter legislation. Respectable townsfolk also supplied the Anti-Saloon League with the Protestant recruits who dried America successively from the local to the national level. At the same time young and respectable urban Protestants formed committees of social action within their denominations, finally creating the Federal Council of the Churches of Christ, a social conscience for the nation. In the cities a host of civic federations and nonpartisan leagues not only revamped local political parties and older associations such as the National Municipal Reform League, but eventually provided nucleus organizations for national reform. Professionals, particularly young lawyers, comprised much of their leadership. And the arrival of professionals in the settlement houses, transforming the National Conference of Charities and Corrections from a distributor of alms to a center for social analysis, provided another focus for local reform as well as programs for national progressivism. Women, who played so important a role in settlement work, also collected into such groups as the General Federation of Women's Clubs, the National Consumers' League, and the organizations for suffrage, which forced reforms both for themselves and for other forgotten Americans. Among their causes was labor legislation, which attracted an elite of skilled workers, now solidly organized in their craft unions, and the professionals in the American Association for Labor Legislation. Some more militant middle-income Americans preferred the rising Socialist party.

These and similar organizations were the legions which fought the progressive battles. Ranging from disciplined pressure groups to enthusiastic crusades for morality and justice, they all carried the message of collective action to save the individual. An emphasis upon social analysis and upon the political implementation of their findings explains the practical results of the era as well as its lingering modernity.

I

As the barons of nineteenth century business retired, their successors appeared to have come from a smaller mold. No one ranked William C. Brown of the New York Central with the Vanderbilts, or George Gould and John D. Rockefeller, Jr., with their fathers; nor did the fastidious Elbert Gary of U.S. Steel compare as a public personality with the driving Andrew Carnegie. Even J. P. Morgan, whose shadowy power and obscure methods frightened his contemporaries, lacked the grand qualities of public hero or public villain. The emphasis in business was shifting from the man to the company, from ingenuity to training, from an ideal of competition to a matter-of-fact belief in cooperation and stabilized profits.

In a nation of joiners, businessmen had always excelled. A burst of their organizations at the turn of the century, announcing a new self-consciousness among lesser businessmen, figured prominently in the inauguration of American capitalism's new era. "There is not a manufacturer in the country," said James W. Van Cleave of the National Association of Manufacturers, in a mild overstatement equally true of financiers and distributors, "who is not an organization man in theory and in daily practice." Where some of the organizations restricted themselves to trade agreements or to an exchange of technical information, a larger percentage sought to increase their members' influence in public affairs. "We are living in an age of organization," John Kirby, Jr., told the members of the NAM; "an age when but little can be accomplished except through organization; an age when organization must cope with organization; an age when organization alone can preserve your industrial freedom and mine." [1]

The richest growth of associations occurred in the towns and cities. From Syracuse, where the Chamber of Commerce established a permanent Boomers Committee, to Los Angeles, where traveling businessmen were reminded to " 'boost' for Los Angeles, first, last and all the time," these organizations carried the banner of civic promotion against knockers and calamity howlers and against competitors from other cities. In an appeal for new members the Chicago Association of Commerce caught the combination of local pride and self-interest which attracted businessmen to these chambers and

leagues: join, its pamphlet read, "for the *Best* that is in you
— pride of home — joy of achievement — loyalty to principle
— aggressiveness in building Chicago's commerce — stead-
fastness as a champion of Chicago's advance — confidence
in the greatness of Chicago's future." [2]

And many organizations gave substance to their boasts by
undertaking an assortment of civic reforms. While one committee from the Cleveland Chamber of Commerce drew up a
housing code in cooperation with the New York reformer,
Jacob Riis, and then sponsored it before the state legislature,
another campaigned for city ordinances to cover meat and
milk inspection. At the same time, other committees planned
to beautify the Cleveland area and encouraged health and
welfare programs in local industry. The most powerful civic
associations — the Chicago Association of Commerce, the
Boston and Cleveland Chambers of Commerce, and the
Merchants' Association of New York prominent among them
— commanded national attention, and smaller organizations
looked to them for guidance. [3]

Almost as numerous were the various trade associations,
some of which already had long histories by 1900. Bankers
enjoyed the most complete organization, built from the many
local clearinghouses and the forty-five state associations to
the American Bankers' Association. Hardware dealers had
almost as many state groups, also capped by a national organization, and food and drug retailers and wholesalers established every imaginable variety of local and national association. Lumbermen and textile manufacturers organized
regionally, canners and independent tobacco manufacturers
nationally. Only the largest enterprises, with notable exceptions among railroads, meat packers, and iron and steel manufacturers, failed to keep pace with the movement.

Smaller in number but particularly important during the
progressive era, some business organizations concentrated
upon a single objective. Hostility toward organized labor
accounted for a majority of these. As stronger unions brought
more strikes around the turn of the century, businessmen
organized special antistrike and antiunion leagues to protect

themselves and their city's reputation for docile labor. Beginning in Dayton, Ohio, and spreading rapidly through the cities of the Midwest, the impulse soon manifested itself nationally. In 1902 the NAM turned from foreign trade to the open-shop movement, and Daniel Davenport, a Bridgeport lawyer and professional lobbyist, established the American Anti-Boycott Association as a legal agency to fight unions. At about the same time the National Founders' and Metal Trades Associations declared war against organized labor in their industries, and the National Erectors' Association was organized to break the buildings trade unions. Between the local and national associations existed several state manufacturers' organizations, mostly from the Midwest, which with the exception of the vigorous Illinois Manufacturers' Association contributed relatively little to the open-shop campaign. These organizations attracted the small and the moderately prosperous employers. Magnates preferred the National Civic Federation, where they, along with conservative union presidents and civic leaders, recommended peaceful labor-management relations.[4]

Another group of organizations specialized in aspects of foreign trade. Three Eastern associations — the Home Market Club of Boston, the Philadelphia Manufacturers' Club, and the National Association of Wool Manufacturers — and two national ones — the American Protective Tariff League and the American Iron and Steel Association — guarded the nation's tariff wall. Like the open-shop associations, the protectionist organizations held many members in common, pooled information, and attempted to coordinate policy. Of the five, the Wool Manufacturers, which concentrated almost exclusively upon wool schedules, was the most narrow, and the Protective Tariff League the least representative of business: lesser Republican politicians and publicists shared power equally with businessmen.

On the other side, three organizations sought wider foreign markets. The National Business League, composed primarily of Chicago businessmen, advocated a deep-sea channel from the Lakes to the Gulf, a more efficient consular service, and government-sponsored trade exhibits abroad. Francis B. Thurber, a founder of the National Anti-Monopoly League in the 1880's, now represented big businessmen through the American Manufacturers' Export Association, which wanted exporters excluded from the Sherman Antitrust Act. And the Merchant Marine League asked for a variety of subsidies for shipping interests. None was strong, primarily because the more general business associations also encouraged foreign trade. Why should members of the Illinois Manufacturers' Association have looked elsewhere when they believed their association "responsible for the open door in the Far East"?[5]

Three trends unified this mass of organizations during the progressive era. First, they steadily broadened their activities. Although usually founded to deal with a particular list of local or trade questions, the associations committed themselves on issue after issue of reform as the interests of their members expanded. Many then took the next step and campaigned for their solutions, despite organizational rules prohibiting it. For example, the bylaws of the Detroit Board of Commerce stated that "national movements, legislative or otherwise, should not be allowed to absorb the time and energy of the Board, which should be confined . . . to local questions." But the Detroit Board still participated in every important progressive debate, even sponsoring a national conference to promote Canadian reciprocity. Usually the organizations maintained that these activities were, as the Chicago Association of Commerce put it, "absolutely non-partisan and non-political." Yet the Chicago Association advocated a central bank which the Republican President Taft had endorsed and which Democrats denounced, and in 1914 lent its name to a plan for corporation control which Republicans used to counter the pending Democratic measures. As a final evasion, groups of these associations formed front organizations through which they conducted their lobbying.[6]

Second, the desire to accomplish more encouraged associations to amalgamate locally and cooperate nationally. In city after city, civic-spirited businessmen collected their colleagues into a single, more efficient organization. The Mobile Chamber of Commerce and Business League came from three small associations, the Indianapolis Chamber from six, and the Baltimore Chamber from sixteen. In Boston a union of the Commercial and Produce Exchanges, the Merchants' Association, and the Associated Board of Trade created a Chamber of Commerce of 5,000 members, the largest local association in the nation. More united at home, they exchanged ideas and discussed regional cooperation with similar groups in neighboring cities. The movement continued naturally toward national organization. The many open-shop associations made a number of attempts to unite, as did the textile manufacturers who were organized into Northern and Southern groups. Retailers founded several national organizations, and the steel industry formed a single association in 1912 when the American Iron and Steel Institute, comprising the magnates of the industry, absorbed the American Iron and Steel Association, which had represented the smaller industrialists. The logical culmination of this trend, an organization to represent all business, led eventually to the formation of the Chamber of Commerce of the United States.[7]

Third, as their interests multiplied and their membership rose, the associations came increasingly under the control of a few dedicated men. Preferring efficiency to democracy, the members amended their charters when necessary to centralize power. With such freedom, officers at times treated their associations as private property: this was always true of the Anti-Boycott Association under Daniel Davenport and the American Iron and Steel Institute under Elbert Gary; it was often the case with the NAM and the National Association of Wool Manufacturers. Particularly in those associations where men held office for a short term or considered their posts honorary, effective power resided in the office of the secretary, who managed the organizations' daily affairs and who usually had considerable leeway in translating the members' resolutions into actual policy. A "small army" of professional secretaries, commented *Iron Age*, was "doing intelligently and with success work for which [businessmen had] neither the time nor, oftentimes, the ability." In this way Wilbur Wakeman became synonymous with the American Protective Tariff League, Ralph Easley with the National Civic Federation, and James Swank with the American Iron and Steel Association. As a general rule power was best distributed in the local chambers and most centralized in those national associations which devoted themselves to very specific goals.[8]

But the wider an association's interests, the greater the dangers of factionalism; and the deeper the commitment to a policy, the narrower the limits of cooperation with neighbor organizations. Plans to merge the Merchants and Manufacturers Association of Cincinnati, which railway interests controlled, and the Cincinnati Chamber of Commerce, where shippers predominated, collapsed each time the national debate over railroad rate regulation became intense. Moreover, the sectionalism inherent in groups such as the Southern Commercial Congress and the Trans-Mississippi Commercial Congress led them to reject almost every offer, however harmless, for joint action with associations from other regions. For all of their protestations of brotherly love, New England's National Association of Cotton Manufacturers and the American Cotton Manufacturers' Association of the South could not unite in the face of competition which enabled the South to pass its rival in cotton-goods production during these years. And the refusal of most big businessmen to join the organizations formalized an important division within the business community. Thus the test of an effective officer was his ability to balance factions within the association and to learn when and how to cooperate with businessmen outside. The histories of the three outstanding national organizations — the American Bankers' Association, the National Association of Manufacturers, and the Chamber of Commerce of the United States — illustrated how arduous the course and how different the results might be.[9]

II

Growth and dissension almost ruined the American Bankers' Association during the progressive period. As its membership increased from 3,000 to 15,000, the ABA could not decide upon a way of changing from a club into a representative national organization. Its annual meetings grew more and more unwieldy, and those who attended went home to complain about dictatorship on the one hand and inefficiency on the other. As a result, an increasing number of bankers gave their allegiance to the strong state associations. Although Secretary Fred Farnsworth of the ABA developed close relationships with a few professional officers in the state associations, the ABA never learned how to harness these energies to the national organization.[10]

Bankers divided roughly into three groups: country bankers, relatively prosperous city bankers, and the powerful financiers of the East. Men from the last group never joined the state associations and very seldom the ABA. A number of well-to-do Midwestern city bankers, however, devoted their time to the association and predominated among its officers. Country bankers, who disliked the long annual trips to New York, New Orleans, Seattle, and the like, usually did not contest the field. Only when urban and rural bankers across the nation were hotly debating an issue did the latter come in quantity to the ABA conventions and outvote their opponents. Most of the time they fought back from the state associations they controlled.

Faced with challenges from the more powerful Eastern financiers outside the association and the more numerous country bankers nominally within it, the urban bankers proved unimaginative leaders. Attempts to appease country bankers did not stop their annual threats to secede; in fact, those from ten Southern states did league together in 1915 as the Cotton States Bankers' Conference to promote interests which they believed the ABA was thwarting. Whenever the financial magnates cooperated with the leaders of the ABA, they did so outside of the ABA, in a way which lessened the association's importance. A joint effort in support of a central bank, for example, was conducted by a separate, Wall Street-dominated agency whose decisions the ABA dutifully endorsed. The association's policies remained uncertain, its lobbying haphazard. With justification, critics accused it both of evading responsibilities and of meddling in affairs beyond its proper sphere, and the prestige of the ABA steadily declined.[11]

Early in 1902 an officer described the National Association of Manufacturers to congressmen as an organization "for the purpose of extending the trade of American manufacturers in foreign countries." Under Theodore Search, its president for several years, the NAM had been a relatively quiet organization apparently content with its modest educational program and its 1,000 members. But, working quietly within the association, a minority little interested in foreign trade envisioned a new NAM which would champion the open shop. The leaders of this group were David M. Parry, John Kirby, Jr., and James W. Van Cleave, three tough, intelligent, opinionated manufacturers from the Midwest who shared an unqualified hatred of organized labor. Parry, a veteran in Indiana politics and the owner of an Indianapolis car factory, was the best-known of the three. The open-shop coteries' candidate for president of the NAM, Parry expected to use the association as his rostrum for lectures on national affairs and as a means to improve his public reputation. Meticulous work bored him, and the details of antiunionism he gladly turned over to others, among them John Kirby. Kirby, already prominent as a leader of Dayton's open-shop drive, had exalted antiunionism to a faith in an America he believed had once been but which was no longer. He won admirers — but not friends — as an implacable, often violent, critic of all reform movements, which he considered signs of national decadence. Parry and Kirby worked closely together; somewhat apart from these two stood Van Cleave, a St. Louis stove manufacturer. When his declining health allowed, he was the most able of the three, and he was always the most ambitious. Less opportunistic than Parry and more flexible than Kirby, he considered the open shop one of several means by which American business, with Van Cleave as its leader, would direct the nation's progress.[12]

The open-shop group managed to bring the 1902 annual meeting of the NAM to Indianapolis, where the association's vice-president from Indiana, David Parry, made all convention arrangements. An effective speaker and a good mixer, Parry officially greeted the delegates and later received them at his home. After the leisurely meetings, a few delegates remained to select a president, presumably Charles Schieren, a leather goods manufacturer interested in free hides, whom Search had designated his successor. When the Committee on Nominations proposed Schieren, someone from the floor nominated Parry. In their confusion — this had never happened before — other members added three more names, all of foreign trade advocates. With only 46 of 124 votes cast, Parry was elected. Minutes later the antiunion men replaced Secretary Edward Sanford, a foreign trade expert, with Marshall Cushing, formerly private secretary for Postmaster-General John Wanamaker and Senator Henry Cabot Lodge. Within a few months, the NAM had taken the open shop as its trade-mark and was deep in national politics opposing labor legislation.[13]

Foreign trade enthusiasts who resented both the convention coup and the abrupt change in policy rallied behind Daniel Tompkins of North Carolina, a prominent spokesman for commercial expansion. At the 1903 convention the new officers shouted and gaveled down the poorly organized opposition, which through Samuel "Golden Rule" Jones of Toledo managed only to register a complaint against "the monstrous doctrine . . . that labor was a commodity like brick and sand and coal, etc., to be bought and sold." The convention then endorsed Parry's revolution.[14] A second challenge occurred in 1905 after Parry had used the prestige of the NAM in a campaign against federal railroad regulation. The many shippers in the association who were working for rate regulation came to the convention that year determined to replace Parry with Tompkins or a suitable alternative. Their leaders, E. B. Pike of New Hampshire and James Inglis of Michigan, proved no match for Kirby, who conducted the fight for Parry's re-election. By 1905 most moderates on unionism had left the association, and Kirby interpreted the attacks against Parry as a mortal blow to the NAM's open-shop program. Outmaneuvered, the shippers hastily praised Parry's antiunionism and lost control of the discussion. After some delay over balloting (no one present remembered how to hold a contested election), the dissidents admitted defeat without calling for a vote.[15]

Irritating rather than disabling, these uprisings occurred against a background of steady power consolidation. Before the 1903 convention the new leaders had so thoroughly identified the NAM with antiunionism as to make a retreat very embarrassing. Also from 1903 the annual meetings were rigidly controlled: faithful officers now planned the conventions in detail; an equally faithful committee screened all resolutions before they reached the floor; and the presiding officer carefully, often roughly, regulated the discussion. In New York the officers kept a file on each member. Safe men the president placed on committees; the firmest served on the board of directors; and eventually the board was empowered to choose the president.[16]

After four years Parry passed the presidency jointly to Van Cleave and Kirby. Van Cleave held it for three years, then Kirby for four. As the old guard was retiring in 1913, it was Parry who selected the first of a new generation, George Pope of Connecticut, to succeed Kirby. (Pope's father had established America's first bicycle factory, and George, who carried on the family business, believed that destruction of the unions would bring back the labor relations he remembered from childhood.) These men in council with a few close associates determined the NAM's policies. "What does our Board, or our Association want to know about [an important new departure]," one of them reasoned, "except that there is a large plan on hand to really establish the open shop, and perhaps to destroy socialism." What indeed? The NAM, presented year after year with *faits accomplis*, trebled its membership under Parry and continued to grow toward 4,000. But attendance at the annual conventions dwindled.[17]

Bothered by few restraints, each president led the association where his particular interests dictated. Parry involved the NAM in the railroad rate controversy, Van Cleave in tariff reform. Kirby, more diffuse, set the association against every change suggested during the Taft years. Then after 1914 Pope brought the NAM back to its original concern, foreign trade. But none of these ventures altered the association's primary purpose, the open shop, which preoccupied each administration and monopolized the time of each convention. Just as Kirby suppressed the revolt of the shippers in 1905, so the leaders replied to every criticism by pointing to the NAM's record of antiunionism: "If anyone thinks that some of our positions have been too radical, why here is a branch of the work to which nobody can possibly object . . ." And whenever a secondary project threatened the association's effectiveness as champion of the open shop, as Van Cleave's campaign for a lower tariff did, the officers soon abandoned it.[18]

Conflicting ambitions among the officers created the greatest difficulties. No sooner were the leaders unchallenged at the annual conventions than they began fighting among themselves. When Van Cleave became president in 1906, he made St. Louis the association's headquarters, leaving the New York office under Secretary Cushing with little to do. Cushing, who had enjoyed wide latitude during Parry's presidency, fought to retain his power through his many friends in the association, and early in 1907 Van Cleave fired him for insubordination. As an agent trailed Cushing to make certain he did not divulge the NAM's secrets, Van Cleave spent the balance of the year convincing Cushing's admirers that the association was stronger than ever.[19] Immediately afterward Van Cleave, a tariff revisionist, and Kirby, a stanch protectionist, parted over Van Cleave's tariff policies. Bitter and very sick, Van Cleave broke the bargain he had made with Parry by trying unsuccessfully in 1909 to block Kirby's election as president. And after Van Cleave's death, two of his close friends, Ferdinand C. Schwedtman, an engineer and businessman whose knowledge of public affairs was unequaled in the association, and James Emery, its chief lobbyist, continued the battle—now for power, not principle—against Kirby and Cushing's successor, James Bird. Finally a congressional investigation in 1913 of the NAM's lobbying tactics forced a reconciliation.[20]

The prize in these contests was the most powerful of the many open-shop organizations. Beginning in 1903, presidents of the association tried to translate nominal leadership of antiunionism into effective control. Parry's address to the NAM that year, envisioning unity among the various local antiunion leagues, invited them to an organizing convention in February 1904. There the officers of the NAM first encountered the jealousy with which smaller organizations guarded their independence. When Parry suggested an appendage of the NAM with an appropriate name, the National Association of Employers, the delegates voted to keep their organization separate from its parent and instead called it the Citizens' Industrial Association. Although the CIA made Parry its president, officials of the NAM were never pleased with their unruly offspring, particularly after Parry turned over the presidency of the CIA to Charles W. Post, the cereal manufacturer, with whom neither Parry nor Van Cleave could cooperate. The CIA, always dependent upon donations from the NAM, continued as a propaganda agency until 1907. Then the NAM's board of directors stopped the subsidy with the charge that the CIA was "trying to take possession of the [NAM's] Treasury." As a participant later described the venture, the CIA "endured for three years."[21]

A year before the CIA collapsed, President Van Cleave was at work on a grander organizational scheme—at first whispered about as the "No Name Association"—which he hoped would materialize in time to influence the congressional elections of 1906. Van Cleave pictured a union of all employer associations, national as well as local, with financial contributions from the nation's richest businessmen, which would crush the unions and dominate the Republican party.

A year behind schedule, Van Cleave finally established the National Council for Industrial Defense. Again the NAM expected to command, and again lesser associations balked. When the leaders of the NAM insisted that "our way is the only way in which the task ahead of us can be accomplished," representatives of the Anti-Boycott Association lost interest, and the National Founders' and Metal Trades Associations withdrew to sponsor a second league of employer associations. "Strange to say," Van Cleave rationalized, "while we could make no headway as a federation, one organization standing next to the other, various organizations seem to be perfectly willing to follow us as leaders." In other words, as the lock manufacturer Henry R. Towne explained to Senator James Reed of Missouri, the 186 members of the NCID contributed funds for the work of the NAM as they would have to any other worthy cause:

Mr. TOWNE. We were a member of the National Association of Manufacturers, and were a contributor to the fund of the — what is the name of it?
Senator REED. The National Council for Industrial Defense.
Mr. TOWNE. The National Council for Industrial Defense.
Senator REED. When you say you were a contributor, I suppose you mean you had signed one of these declarations of principles, and subscribed a sum of money every year?
Mr. TOWNE. We subscribed the money. I do not recall the signing of the declaration.
Senator REED. I guess you were as much a member as anybody. You were a member for the purpose of contributing.
Mr. TOWNE. Oh, yes, that is quite right.[22]

In 1913 the NCID ran afoul of a congressional investigation, inspired by the half-truths which a grafting political agent, Martin M. Mulhall, had sold to the New York *World* and the Chicago *Tribune*. Subsequent congressional hearings, although proving Mulhall a liar, uncovered enough dubious practices to discredit the NAM's political tactics, and as a result the NAM in 1914 cut its annual allocation for "public affairs" from $59,000 to $20,000, allowing the NCID to languish.[23] Two years later — a decent interval — the NAM made still another attempt to organize the open-shop associations. This time President Pope wisely shared honors with William H. Barr of the National Founders' Association and several others, and in 1916 these men established the National Industrial Conference Board, with modest political goals and greater equality among its members. The National Industrial Conference Board arrived too late to affect the record of the progressive period. What coordination the employer associations did achieve came through the unofficial cooperation of their Washington lobbyists, not through orders from the presidents of the NAM.[24]

Always aggressive, the NAM alienated other business organizations as well. For years it lobbied against the Merchant Marine League because of a minor difference over ways to subsidize American shipping. Late in the progressive period it fought with the American Bankers' Association over financial reform, which the NAM feared would favor prosperous city bankers. Other organizations, such as the National Business League, were treated rudely because of their insignificance in national affairs. But officers of the NAM reserved their harshest words for the National Civic Federation, which they called "part and parcel" of the American Federation of Labor and an exponent of "the most virulent form of socialism, *closed shop unionism.*" And while the presidents of the NAM publicly attacked the "industrial doughfaces" of the National Civic Federation, the secretaries of the rival organizations carried on a private war of spying and political intrigue.[25]

The roots of hatred lay deeper than a difference over labor policies. The threat of "Socialized Industry" — big labor and big business combined — horrified members of the NAM, who believed their future depended upon an economic fluidity which the recently formed trusts and the AFL would destroy. Thus they saw the National Civic Federation as a conspiracy between the magnates and the unionists aimed directly at them. A second source of hatred combined an ambivalence among officers of the NAM toward the magnates they both feared and admired, and a keen sensitivity to

slights from big businessmen. At the same time that spokesmen for the NAM attacked Wall Street and bigness, they
were asking the executives of large corporations to support
the association's open-shop drive. Under Parry these efforts
were cursory, but Van Cleave, as an important part of his
plan for the National Council for Industrial Defense, made
a concerted appeal to big business. In a letter to Elbert Gary,
he described his reception:

> You seemed favorably impressed with the brief statement that
> I made, and suggested that I see Mr. [Henry H.] Rogers, Mr.
> [Edward H.] Harriman, Mr. [Henry Clay] Frick and several
> others. I called on these gentlemen and succeeded in seeing Mr.
> Rogers and Mr. Frick.
>
> Mr. Rogers was just a little interested, but busy as usual, and
> asked me to see one of his departmental heads, which I did, and
> found him to be a departmental machine. After that I saw Mr.
> Frick, and he took very little interest in it. I failed to see Mr.
> Harriman. I then realized that it was no part of my business to
> knock my heels together in various offices, waiting to see gentle-
> men whose interests . . . I was concerning myself with, so there
> the matter dropped, except that I saw you once or twice after-
> wards, but nothing came of the interviews.

Van Cleave took revenge by blaming Wall Street for the
Panic of 1907.[26]

The first signs of a thaw in the relations between the NAM
and big business occurred late in 1916 with the establishment
of the National Industrial Conference Board. At the outset
the largest donations to the Conference Board came from a
few powerful corporations — General Motors, General Electric, Firestone, and Westinghouse — which approved of two
policy changes which the Conference Board's program promised. First, the Conference Board reversed the emphasis of
the NCID by placing open-shop propaganda above back-
door lobbying. Second, because the Yama Conference on
National Industrial Efficiency had contributed to the founding of the Conference Board, big businessmen expected
"scientific management," especially appealing to them, to
play an important role in its propaganda. Without suggesting

a union of forces, the Conference Board at least established
a line of communication between two business groups hith-
erto at odds.[27]

After 1902 the NAM demonstrated what centralized administration and an intelligent selection of issues could
accomplish for a national organization. The leaders of the
NAM ran an aggressive organization without suffering seriously from internal dissension. But by its inability to cooperate with other associations, the NAM also illustrated the
need for an entirely different approach to unite all business
within a single organization.

III

In 1908 James Couzens of the Ford Motor Company ir-
ritably refused to join another organization. What he wanted,
he said, was "an Association of Associations. There are too
many Associations now." [28] An increasing number of businessmen agreed, as groups claiming to represent this or that
fraction of the business community multiplied. For years the
National Board of Trade had advertised itself as that super-
association — "the most forceful organization in this Country,
excepting the Federal Congress," an officer boasted. Since its
establishment in 1868, the National Board had welcomed all
business associations and had promised them desirable legislation through the services of its Washington lobby. But by
allowing its annual conventions, often poorly attended, to
determine policy, the National Board had always invited
domination by purposeful groups. During the late nineteenth
century it had served the antimonopoly program of certain
New York merchants; and early in the twentieth century it
was used in quick succession by those who desired railroad
rate legislation, by proponents and then opponents of parcel
post legislation, and by advocates of a central bank. Disdained by most other organizations, it fell into the hands of
a few uninspired Philadelphia businessmen who were barely
able to hold fifty member associations within the board. The
few who paid it much attention found the National Board a
convenient forum for discussion but helpless as a lobbyist.

Even in little matters, the officers of the board were incompetent. Appeals to Oscar S. Straus, Secretary of Commerce and Labor under Roosevelt, which were addressed "Oscar Strouse" and "Oscar O. Straus" did not even warrant a courtesy reply.[29]

The first serious attempt of the progressive period to unify the associations was made by Gustav H. Schwab, United States representative for the North German Lloyd Steamship Company and a well-known advocate of foreign trade. In May 1907 Schwab induced his friend, Secretary Straus, to sponsor a general business organization, patterned after those existing in Europe, which would cooperate intimately with the federal government to expand commerce abroad. Schwab and Straus blundered in every particular as they organized the National Council of Commerce. Straus decided that he must work initially with only a few businessmen. When a great many associations wrote of their interest, the secretary told them to wait until after the organizational meeting. The rejected associations naturally complained of exclusiveness, and the criticism redoubled when Schwab announced an annual fee of $100 for member associations. In retaliation, a rumor circulated that the new body would be "a rich man's club, with each member paying annual dues of one thousand dollars." Then in December 1907, Straus aggravated the suspicions of a government-dominated association by holding the organizational meetings of the National Council in the department's offices and demanding that Schwab be elected chairman of its Advisory Council. And Straus, not Schwab, managed the promotion of the National Council. Finally, the organizers acted as if their most serious weakness — Schwab's identification with tariff revision — were a source of strength. While Schwab packed the Advisory Council with prominent tariff reformers and hired his colleague in the American Reciprocity Tariff League, William R. Corwine, as the executive secretary, Straus, a moderate revisionist, chose this time to lecture business groups on the advantages of lower duties. Protectionist associations effectively denounced the National Council as the tool of a foreigner — Schwab was German-born — who wished to destroy American industry.[30]

Bad luck and further errors in judgment completed the National Council's short history. From an idea conceived during prosperity, the National Council was born weeks after the Panic of 1907 when relatively few businessmen cared about anything new. As membership remained close to forty associations, Schwab unwisely postponed the start of the council's work throughout 1908 in anticipation of more applicants. By January 1909, with Schwab finally ready to begin, businessmen had all but forgotten the council. Moreover, Secretary Straus, the council's last asset, now left office. His successor, Charles Nagel, who considered the council a bad debt from the previous administration, suggested that it disband. When a few officers in the council persisted, Nagel put them off until the council died of government neglect and businessmen's indifference. In 1910 all a department official could tell an inquirer about Schwab's grand design was, "It first met here in December, 1908, at the call of Mr. Charles Schwab, who was then its president, by arrangement with former Secretary Straus" — a sentence which misstated the time and method of its origin and the name and office of its chairman.[31]

One attempt spurred others to try. The most significant contributions came from the Boston Chamber of Commerce, which was guided by men such as John H. Fahey, a soft-spoken and intelligent publisher, and the liberal merchant Edward A. Filene. As early as July 1909 the Boston Chamber wrote to Nagel suggesting that he sponsor an entirely new organization. When Nagel evaded, the Chicago Association of Commerce, in cooperation with the Boston Chamber, took "preliminary steps toward the organization of a national body of commercial associations," only to abandon the project as too formidable. Now firmly convinced that a successful call to organize would have to come from the federal government, the Boston Chamber kept the idea before Nagel throughout 1910. At the same time it publicized the need for a representative association among other business groups and won promises of assistance from the nominal competitors, the almost-defunct National Council of Commerce and the aging National Board of Trade. Prompted by the Boston Chamber, the National Board even sent a delegation to Nagel to recommend its absorption into a new national organization.[32]

By 1911 Nagel was receiving letters daily from businessmen who inquired and advised about an association of associations. In May the Chief of the Bureau of Manufacturers, Albert H. Baldwin, on his own initiative joined forces with the NAM to advocate another National Council of Commerce which would promote foreign trade. By August Nagel was convinced. He decided that credit for establishing a national business organization would help the Republican campaign in 1912; and he, along with Secretary of State Philander C. Knox and his assistant Huntington Wilson, believed that such an association might also contribute to the administration's dollar diplomacy. At Nagel's suggestion, President Taft recommended a new national body that December. On February 12, 1912, Baldwin and two assistants met secretly with a business group which the Boston Chamber had shrewdly selected. Besides John Fahey and the secretary of the Boston Chamber, there were W. Mitchell Bunker of the San Francisco Chamber of Commerce and G. Grosvenor Dawe of the Southern Commercial Congress, representing sensitive sectional interests, and Lucius E. Wilson, president of the American Association of Commercial Executives, representing the powerful professional secretaries. Out of their discussions came the letter with which President Taft invited about 1,000 business associations to a founding convention. Baldwin, Fahey, and Harry A. Wheeler of the Chicago Association of Commerce then prepared the outline of a constitution. An April 22, 1912, they offered their plan to the delegates who gathered in Washington to establish the Chamber of Commerce of the United States.[33]

Intelligent planning avoided the pitfalls which had caught the National Council. To forestall charges of elitism, the organizers invited each business association which had expressed interest to the April meetings. Once there they defeated a proposal from the Cleveland Chamber of Commerce to make the national chamber "a roll of honor of American business men," and instead opened it to all business organizations, with voting rights graduated according to the size of their membership. In cooperation with Nagel, Wheeler and Fahey kept government officials in the background. And where Straus had publicly endorsed Schwab for chairman of the council, the organizers of the U.S. Chamber worked quietly through delegates to elect Wheeler the first president. Finally, Wheeler, a genial Chicago banker with few strong convictions and a great deal of organizational talent, aroused none of the enmity which had plagued Schwab and his council.[34]

The April meetings had dealt in generalities. It was left to the first two presidents, Wheeler and Fahey, to provide the new-born chamber with substance and give it direction. The two conceptions of the chamber most often expressed in 1912 came naturally from the National Board of Trade and the National Council of Commerce: one envisioned an active lobbying agent for all of business; the other an organization which, in close association with the Department of Commerce, would lead business into foreign markets. And behind any discussion of the chamber's possibilities stood the NAM, outstanding among business organizations and the rule against which the chamber would inevitably be measured. Wheeler and Fahey, both veterans of association work, not only rejected the two most popular plans but also divorced the chamber from the controversial policies of the NAM.

First, to the astonishment of government officials and businessmen alike, Wheeler placed the chamber outside of politics. An active Republican for many years, he began by setting a personal example. "I may be over careful," he wrote President Taft in July 1912, "but it seems to me that no breath of partisanship must attach to the organization, and although it is against my inclination, and contrary to my original purpose, to cut loose from participation in the campaign for your re-election, I believe you would rather have me aid in firmly laying the foundations for the National Chamber than in any service I might render in your forthcoming campaign." During the last months of the Taft administration, when Secretary Nagel begged the chamber to recommend federal appointees, its leaders refused, a policy they continued through Wilson's first term. After the Democratic victories in 1912 Wheeler, overcoming the reluctance of several chamber officials, saw to it that the chamber tendered Wilson its warmest congratulations; and through 1916 its executive committee rejected each plea to join attacks against the party in power. Ignoring as much as possible the inbred hostility of many Southern and Western Democrats, the chamber established good working relations with both the administration and Congress. In fact so many prominent Democrats, including the President, Secretary of Labor William B. Wilson, and Louis D. Brandeis, appeared at the chamber's annual conventions that the Republican NAM registered its "humiliation and protest" at such invitations. Appropriately, the chamber's second and third presidents, Fahey and Robert Goodwyn Rhett, were themselves Democrats.[35]

The chamber relied upon regular referenda to determine the views of member associations on current affairs. Wheeler and Fahey invariably phrased the questions in moderate language and announced the results in the most mild, explanatory fashion. As the NAM defended its political practices to congressional committees, Wheeler told businessmen that the U.S. Chamber of Commerce marked "the death for all time of a lobby system." A model of tact, Wheeler met each challenge with imperturbable good nature and made every public statement general and accommodating. And after 1914 Fahey quietly followed his example.[36]

A second crucial decision during these first years separated the chamber from the open-shop associations. Wheeler stated at the outset that the chamber was "not formed in any sense for the purpose of combatting organized labor. Rather, in all matters of national import, it will welcome the co-operation of organized labor." Although the chamber's referenda registered a businessmen's consensus against labor legislation, even here Wheeler and Fahey softened the wording of the questions. When the annual convention of 1914 adopted a resolution which the NAM had sponsored condemning the immunity of unions from trust prosecution, the officers replaced the harsh phrase "vicious class legislation" with "a violation of fundamental principles." To the employer associations, all this smacked of the National Civic Federation. The National Founders' Association resigned, and the NAM, after attempting to convert the chamber's executive committee, said that it would soon follow suit. Unmoved, the chamber told the organizers of the National Industrial Conference Board that "the work of the Board lies in a distinct field which the Chamber does not contemplate to enter." [37]

From their long experience in association work, Wheeler and Fahey fixed a third goal for the chamber: to avoid domination by one section or by one segment of business. The president made an annual tour among the member associations, preaching equal rights and cultivating the friendship of the professional secretaries. The chamber's board of directors represented all sections and as many branches of business as possible, and its presidents were selected specifically to overcome sectional jealousies: Wheeler from the Midwest — the safest starting point; Fahey from the East; and R. G. Rhett from the South. The last choice was vital. A South Carolinian whose name recalled memories of Southern glory, Rhett converted a number of Southern critics, including the *Manufacturers' Record,* into warm friends of the chamber.[38]

Special pleaders bombarded the new chamber. When the chamber adopted its own policy on financial reform in 1913, the American Bankers' Association resigned. At the same time Frank Vanderlip was browbeating Wheeler to align the chamber with the big Eastern bankers. "We protest [the chamber's policy of accommodation with the Democratic Congress] . . . ," Vanderlip telegraphed. "Any approval by the Chamber of Commerce of the United States that stops short of standing squarely in protest to political control of bank credit will not have back of it the best financial judgment." Wheeler pointedly replied that referenda determined the chamber's policies. Although a few inevitably resented this independence, a large majority of the membership responded with confidence in the chamber's honesty.[39]

Certain pressing problems remained. The chamber could only be as representative as its subsidiary associations allowed, and a number of these gave their members no opportunity to vote on the chamber's referenda. Moreover, too large a percentage of member associations failed to return their ballots. Enemies emphasized these weaknesses. And the chamber offered no panacea to business disunity. As was their wont, big businessmen did not join. Those businessmen who did sometimes used their right of free discussion at the annual conventions to accentuate the community's divisions.[40]

Finally, two major policy decisions, political neutrality and moderation on labor issues, created special difficulties. When the chamber asked Congress for a federal charter, Wheeler and his associates stood by as the Democrats defeated the bill. The officers then incorporated the chamber under the laws of the District of Columbia. A minor incident, it still pointed up a dilemma which Wheeler and Fahey could not resolve. Member associations expected results from the referenda. But the officers wanted to satisfy the members without turning the chamber into a traditional pressure group. Wheeler and Fahey, who realized that inaction would kill the chamber, puzzled the problem inconclusively for three years. Then the chamber elected Rhett, an experienced politician, as president, and gradually the chamber began to state its views more as demands than opinions. Rhett's election brought a second shift in emphasis as well. An ardent champion of the open shop, he had always opposed the caution of Wheeler and Fahey on labor questions. As president he used his prestige to encourage rather than check the members' hostility toward the unions. But neither change fundamentally altered the foundation upon which Wheeler and Fahey had built the most successful national association of the progressive era.[41]

The year the U.S. Chamber was founded, Arthur Jerome Eddy published *The New Competition*, a paean to business cooperation and particularly to open-price agreements. Later heralded as an introduction to the Nineteen Twenties, Eddy's book actually summarized the progressive era. Its philosophy grew directly from years of experience by businessmen in organizational work. Even the details of how to regularize costs and prices were fairly common knowledge; "This book deals, first of all, with *what is now going on*," Eddy wrote in the foreword. Employing the unique jargon of the business association and copying arguments which businessmen knew by heart, Eddy flattered his readers by presenting the familiar as if it were daringly new.[42]

IV

In one way organization accentuated those characteristics inherent in the business community. As businessmen grew increasingly aware of national issues, a variety of associations provided the stairsteps from local to national involvement. Where conditions allowed cooperation, organization supplied the mechanism for it; and where rifts appeared, organization hardened them. But more significant than that, organization offered a means for action where none had existed before. The businessman who after years of uncertainty had achieved a relative security and a moderate prosperity, and who was searching for ways to increase both, did not relish facing his world alone. He and thousands of other citizens in a wide middle-income stratum had learned enough about life in industrial America to know that even the magnates cooperated in order to survive. And the businessman enjoyed a special advantage. Operating closer to the front ranks in economic development, he sensed more quickly the national nature of his problems and better understood the practical means to his objectives. Before most progressives had caught up, businessmen were already using organization as a weapon to win national reform.

III

THE EASY YEARS

Progressivism operated on a split level during the first years of the century. By every index — enthusiasm, results, future significance — the dozens of local and state reform movements constituted its more vital segment. In these early years national reforms which required national legislation concerned comparatively few Americans. And far more important than numbers, almost no intimate, functioning relationships connected the national with the local movements.

Until about 1907 men with a specific purpose who were knowledgeable in politics dominated national reform. Within the federal government ambitious administrators whose reform plans would increase their powers and ambitious politicians who expected reforms to further their careers formed one wing of practical progressivism. Dr. Harvey Wiley, an administrator in the Department of Agriculture, led the campaign for pure food and drug legislation, and a shrewd Senator, Albert Beveridge, attached a popular measure for meat inspection to Wiley's movement. No one labored more persistently to expand the powers of the Interstate Commerce Commission than the Commissioners themselves, notably Chairman Martin Knapp. And from men such as Gifford Pinchot of the Forestry Service and Frederick Newell of the Bureau of Reclamation came most of the ideas and impetus for a conservation program which would extend their supervision over natural resources.

A second wing composed of interest groups also pressed their favorite measures. On one side prominent railroads wanted antirebate legislation; on the other business shippers, with help from well-organized agricultural groups such as the stockmen, demanded lower railroad rates through ICC regulation. While the American Sugar Refining Company lobbied for Cuban reciprocity, an assortment of exporters and importers worked fitfully for bilateral trade agreements. Over all of these movements Theodore Roosevelt kept watch, balancing and harmonizing, advocating a square deal before the public and soothing the party faithful in private.

The total of these activities would have made the Roosevelt administration busier, but not much different in kind from its predecessors. What made the difference was the excitement, locally generated, which ran as an accompaniment to these measures; the expectations, locally inspired, which called these legislative changes only a beginning; the optimism, locally engendered, which linked national legislation with the activities of community reformers. Rising, ill-defined aspirations for much more were already mixing with national affairs by 1906, to the confusion of the hard-headed representatives of special interests. A passing frenzy, some of them thought, but occasionally an asset to practical reforms. After all, above the sound and fury the veterans still held control.

I

The problem which somehow became involved with all other problems at the turn of the century was the growth of big business, popularly called the trust question. A burst of consolidations had followed William McKinley's election in 1896. In business circles the climax to these mergers came early in 1901 with the formation of the U.S. Steel Corporation, America's first billion-dollar concern; and prospects of this giant controlling about half of a vital industry even disturbed those normally friendly toward large combinations. Arthur B. Farquhar, a manufacturer who despised antitrust laws, admitted that now the health of the economy depended upon "how long an unrestrained, irresponsible power will continue its leniency." And the *Wall Street Journal*, although it accepted large business units as both inevitable and desirable, ominously pictured U.S. Steel as "a great big blind man helpless to pick out an opponent but everyone between it and its goal must get out of the way or be crushed." Where hostility to big business was already strong, cries against monopoly redoubled. Then in May 1901, before the furor over U.S. Steel had died down, the railroad interests of Morgan and Harriman settled a stock market battle by forming another giant, the Northern Securities Company, which would dominate trackage from Chicago to the Pacific Northwest. Viewing the merger movement as a whole, a Milwaukee packer wrote Senator John C. Spooner, "The people . . . are earnestly praying to be freed from this modern oppression of commercial enslavement." [1]

Since Congress had passed the Sherman Antitrust Act in 1890, the courts had construed its ban upon monopoly and restraint of trade to cover such arrangements as pooling and price-fixing. But despite the mounting concern over bigness, the law had scarcely touched the major consolidations. Where McKinley had drifted, his successor, Theodore Roosevelt, acted. Early in 1902 he instructed his Attorney General to proceed against the Northern Securities Company, and a year later he maneuvered through Congress the Department of Commerce and Labor bill with provisions for a Bureau of Corporations to investigate possible violators of the trust law. In 1904 the Supreme Court added teeth to Roosevelt's program by dissolving the Northern Securities Company.

Apparently most businessmen below the level of magnates approved. Because the Morgan-Harriman fight had caused a Wall Street panic in 1901, the Northern Securities Company was particularly unpopular. And the expectation of a Department of Commerce and Labor which would serve middle-sized business as it checked the trusts had led the National Association of Manufacturers, among others, to lobby for it in 1903. Small businessmen, especially from the Midwest and the South, showed the greatest enthusiasm. With a sweeping disregard for legal niceties, they called upon the Bureau of Corporations to destroy their larger competitors everywhere, and they cheered each move from Washington which looked like trust-busting.

Of the complaints which poured into the bureau's office, a number singled out the largest corporations: smaller refiners attacked the Standard Oil Company, lesser packers the giant Chicago meat processing houses, and the Independent Tobacco Manufacturers' Association the American Tobacco Company. But far more described little-known leagues and pools and combinations. Who had heard of the "automatic sprinkler trust"; the Tri-State Grain Association which a grain dealer from Lily, South Dakota, blamed for his bankruptcy; or the innumerable price-maintenance and exclusive-selling arrangements which druggists, grocers, lumber dealers, and even match distributors denounced as monopolies? Yet these immediate, local enemies were the most dangerous "trusts" to small businessmen.[2]

The Roosevelt administration had big business, not local pools, in mind, and the nation's magnates knew it. After failing to block the Bureau of Corporations in Congress, they pondered ways of protecting their interests. Some, such as Harriman, relaxed under the influence of Roosevelt's moderate private statements. Others, such as Standard Oil, enlarged their legal departments and hoped the gusts of criticism would pass. And a small group, including the Chicago meat packers, tried to win over the new bureau before its agents could begin an investigation. But none of these provided adequate protection. Harriman fell from Roosevelt's grace, and the government investigated, then prosecuted, both Standard Oil and the meat packers.[3]

The House of Morgan, with the most at stake, developed the most elaborate answer. As early as 1902 Morgan himself had suggested a man-to-man understanding to Roosevelt, but it was left to Elbert Gary, chairman of the board of U.S. Steel, to fashion comprehensive agreements with the executive. A cool, meticulous man with an irrepressible superiority complex, Gary irritated his associates with paternal poses. Nevertheless his legal training, his ability to articulate the case for bigness and price stability, and above all his position as head of U.S. Steel, made him an impressive public figure. Cooperating closely with Gary was George W. Perkins, a life insurance executive who had become a Morgan partner in 1901. Although at times hot-tempered, the personable Perkins had acquired a reputation as a skilled negotiator among conflicting business interests. To outsiders, he was "Secretary of State" for the House of Morgan; in the secret code of the House, he was "Footfalls." More important to Gary, Perkins had enjoyed friendly relations with the President since Roosevelt's days as Governor of New York, when the two men had agreed upon the desirability of big business, properly conducted, and of wider publicity for corporation affairs. In 1903, after Perkins had supported the controversial Bureau of Corporations, Roosevelt sent him one of the pens with which he signed the Department of Commerce and Labor Act.[4]

When Gary learned that the Bureau of Corporations was about to investigate U.S. Steel, he arranged a conference with the President through the bureau's chief, James R. Garfield. On November 2, 1905, Gary and an assistant met at the White House with Roosevelt, Garfield, and Victor Metcalf, the Secretary of Commerce and Labor. Gary offered "to cooperate with the Government in every possible way" consistent with the stockholders' "rights and property." This would include access to all corporation files. In return, he asked that the information gleaned from the files be used by the President alone and that the President arbitrate any differences between U.S. Steel and the bureau. Gary insisted that no one wanted "to bind the Government to any promises or undertakings for the protection of our Corporation," but he added that the President certainly did not desire to harm either U.S. Steel or business in general. Once Gary and Roosevelt had checked a memorandum of the conference, the first gentlemen's agreement with the administration was consummated.[5]

In December 1906, as the bureau prepared to investigate the International Harvester Company, Perkins, who had organized the corporation, and Cyrus H. McCormick, its president, wrote to the Department of Commerce and Labor suggesting a "personal conference on the subject." With a precedent established, they did not have to see Roosevelt. On January 18 and 19, 1907, Garfield and his assistant Herbert Knox Smith went to Gary's luxurious hotel suite in New York to discuss the investigation with representatives from International Harvester. Gary praised the bureau in the words of a contented customer. U.S. Steel "had been absolutely satisfied with the treatment it had received from the Bureau," and he hoped "that Harvester Company would receive the same treatment." Moreover, the magnates endorsed Roosevelt's program for the supervision of corporations as "a strong safeguard . . . to the prevention of violent attacks on private rights in general that might otherwise come." On that pleasant note, the negotiators completed a second gentlemen's agreement, identical with the one concerning U.S. Steel.[6]

During the months following, relations between Morgan's men and the administration grew even more cordial. Herbert Knox Smith, who succeeded Garfield as Commissioner of Corporations, publicly praised the cooperative attitude of International Harvester and privately confided to its chief counsel that all available evidence pointed toward the company's legality. In return Gary flattered Roosevelt on his reform record, and Perkins pleased the President with his continuing experiments in corporation publicity. Perkins could assure Morgan that, thanks to Gary's "wise and vigilant" policies, "[U.S. Steel] is looked upon in Washington with more favor than perhaps any other [large corporation]"; and, in another letter, "that we have reached a point where the National Government does not intend to attack the [International Harvester] Company's form of organization."[7]

These thoughts may have compensated Perkins for the trouble a New York state committee had created for him and other life insurance executives. In 1905 the committee's investigator, Charles Evans Hughes, uncovered serious mismanagement in the three largest companies — Equitable,

New York, and Mutual of New York — whose officers had used company funds to purchase political favors and deal illicitly with the financial houses on Wall Street. An outcry arose for strict federal regulation. Although the companies at another time would have welcomed loose national supervision as a substitute for irregular state controls, they feared it in 1905 and hired Daniel Davenport, the antiunion specialist, to explain to business groups that federal regulation was unconstitutional. Relatively few businessmen were impressed. In answer to Davenport, the Scranton Board of Trade recommended amending the constitution if necessary. "Nothing short of liquidation of these three companies will answer the demands of justice," began the editorial of a normally conservative business journal. Among those reflexly hostile to Wall Street, a Washington state banker prescribed national control over all high finance, "sick with this contagion of dishonesty," and pointedly asked his colleagues, "Has *your* New York correspondent close and fast alliances with a great trust company, a great savings bank, a great bond syndicate, a great railroad merger or a great life insurance company?" But where the critics had emotion, the insurance companies had influence, and Congress decided against federal controls.[8]

On the heels of the life insurance scandals came exposures of the food and drug industries which greatly strengthened Dr. Wiley's campaign for a pure food and drug bill as well as the demands for federal meat inspection. Earlier some members of these industries, like the insurance companies, had approved of mild federal supervision to replace the uneven state laws and had predicted that a federal stamp of approval would raise the customer's confidence in their products. Another segment considered any interference intolerable; and in the unfavorable climate of 1906 all members of the industries closed ranks along this line. "What we are opposed to," the Chicago packer, Thomas E. Wilson, told Congressmen, "and what we appeal to you for protection against is a bill that will put our business in the hands of theorists, chemists, sociologists, etc., and the management and control taken away from the men who have devoted their lives to the upbuilding and perfecting of this great American industry."[9]

Usually that appeal touched businessmen, yet a great many of them joined the cry for thorough federal regulation. Groups such as the National Board of Trade had for years advocated strict pure food and drug legislation. Others, such as the NAM, had expressed little interest before 1906. In January, David Parry wrote to President Van Cleave that the association would have to make certain the pending pure food and drug law "will not unjustly work injury to . . . [the] nearly 300 of our members that produce food products." Accordingly, the NAM's Washington agents worked to weaken the bill. But at the same time the NAM's Pure Food Committee, which was not under Van Cleave's surveillance, lobbied for Wiley's measure, later boasting that it deserved "much of the credit for the passage of the so-called National Food and Drugs Law"; and the committee demanded tighter regulation wherever scientific experts discovered flaws in that law. Despite Van Cleave's displeasure, the NAM in convention unanimously adopted the committee's report. In 1906 Van Cleave and Parry also answered the plea of the association's vice-president for Illinois, Elliott Durand, to campaign against federal meat inspection. Then to Van Cleave's astonishment, the association's board of directors, in a rare show of independence, overruled him, and the campaign died. Businessmen, after all, ate the same pickles and sausages as everyone else.[10]

Questions of regulation disclosed a remarkable range of temperaments within the business community. In 1906 George Perkins analyzed the meaning of the federal meat inspection act for J. P. Morgan in this fashion: it established a dubious precedent and would hurt the packers in the short run; but by providing a "government certificate" in foreign trade, it would reward the packers handsomely. At the same time, E. D. Titus, a Minnesota merchant who was president of the "semi-secret" American League of Commerce, explained both regulatory measures to Senator Joseph B. Foraker of Ohio: the meat inspection bill was a conspiracy between the beef trust and President Roosevelt to monopolize foreign trade and kill domestic competition; and the pure food and drug act was a plot of Secretary of Agriculture James Wilson, "an alien [who] craves despotic power," to destroy the patent medicine business.[11]

After 1905 the discussion of particular weaknesses in particular industries led naturally to talk of a general law to correct comparable weaknesses elsewhere. Here businessmen, including those who had condemned the insurance and food industries, became exceedingly cautious. An inclusive law would affect almost all of them, and too strong a measure might upset the economy. The most popular solution was silence, which came to include food and insurance regulation once the scandals had disappeared from the headlines. Others, searching for a safe answer, decided upon greater publicity for corporation affairs, perhaps voluntary, perhaps required by law. Seldom supplying details, these businessmen simply called publicity the "great safeguard." Still others supported Roosevelt's recommendation for a national incorporation law, adding that it should be permissive, not mandatory, and that public opinion would force most corporations to use it. Many of the more prosperous businessmen felt harassed by a confusion of state controls. "The only thing that works against our progress is the multiplicity of [state] laws," said one advocate of national incorporation. "I say that the day has gone by when this country is simply a confederacy of States." But as in the case of publicity, business groups purposely kept this solution vague. When the NAM and the National Board of Trade endorsed national incorporation, they commended the shell of an idea into which each member inserted his own definition: it could imply freedom from the Sherman Act's ban on restraint of trade, or it could mean a code binding corporations to a rigid concept of just practices. Nothing more concrete came from businessmen during the first years of the progressive era.[12]

II

In their introduction to the 1900 edition of *Poor's Manual,*
the editors remarked, "There was never a period in our history in which, in the construction . . . of the railroads, the
good sense of our people was so thoroughly at fault as in the
period from 1879 up to and including 1892." They went on
to estimate that by 1900 close to half of the par value of
railroad common stock was water. Cautious as they were,
these words from a professional defender of big business indicated how precipitously the prestige of the railroads had
fallen and how vulnerable they were to demands for federal
regulation. The most pressing issue concerned the carriers'
rate structure, a tangle of exorbitant charges, discrimination,
and special privilege which in 1900 satisfied neither the
roads nor the businessmen who used them. Presumably Congress had laid the foundation for an orderly, equitable rate
system with the Interstate Commerce Act of 1887, which
prohibited pools and rate discrimination and which established the Interstate Commerce Commission to implement
its provisions. But loose wording and an unsympathetic
judiciary had, as the economist William Z. Ripley put it,
emasculated the law.[13]

In November 1900 a few Midwestern grain dealers and
millers, under the guidance of Edward P. Bacon of the Milwaukee Chamber of Commerce, met in St. Louis to organize
the Interstate Commerce Law Convention. They voted to
support legislation which would enable the Interstate Commerce Commission to lower and equalize railroad rates, and
then they turned over the new association to its chairman.
Edward Bacon, a railroad agent for fourteen years before
becoming a grain dealer, was technically well-qualified for
his post. But he dreamed too much. A man of boundless energy and indifferent judgment, Bacon pictured himself leading the nation's shippers against the railroads and rising high
among the leaders of the Republican party. Called "Peter
the Hermit" by his opponents, he drew up a bill which would
empower the ICC to establish reasonable rates and con-

ducted a one-man crusade in Washington until it was introduced in 1902 as the Corliss-Nelson bill — "the Bacon bill" to friends and enemies alike. The scattered shippers did not respond as Bacon had anticipated. Although commercial organizations from the Merchants' Association of New York to the San Francisco Board of Trade endorsed the idea behind the bill, almost none of them knew about Bacon or his convention; and those who discovered him when they came to Washington to support the Bacon bill carefully avoided the ambitious, little-known Midwesterner. His one significant convert was the National Board of Trade, whose secretary, Frank Barry, doubled as secretary for Bacon's Interstate Commerce Law Convention.[14]

At the same time Eastern railroad leaders, a tight group with formidable political power, were working for a bill of their own — the Elkins bill — to outlaw rebating, which favored large industrialists at the railroads' expense. Unless they could also legalize pooling, the overwhelming majority of railroad leaders wanted no changes beyond an antirebate measure. With James J. Hill, they agreed that Bacon's bill meant government ownership and that any further government control would depress first the railroad industry, then the entire economy. Only two prominent railroad executives dissented. In April 1901 Alexander J. Cassatt, president of the Pennsylvania Railroad, had written to Roosevelt, "We believe that it is better policy to assist in framing and passing a reasonable measure now than to have a more drastic and perhaps a seriously injurious one forced upon us by public clamor." And the maverick Alpheus B. Stickney, president of the Chicago Great Western, as part of his plan for extensive federal supervision over the economy, wanted the ICC to fix a single rate schedule for the whole nation.[15]

But the railroads did recognize the appeal of Bacon's bill. As a first step toward neutralizing it, representatives of the New York Central and Pennsylvania systems invited Bacon, Frank Barry, and Robert Eliot of the Milwaukee Chamber of Commerce to a conference where they formulated a compromise measure. The revised Elkins bill included both Bacon's rate control provisions and the railroads' full program of a ban on rebating and the legalization of pooling. During the balance of 1902, Bacon worked hard for the omnibus bill and reported regularly to Senator Spooner, who probably relayed the information to his friends in the railroad industry. Meanwhile Paul V. Morton of the Atchison, Topeka, and Santa Fe made arrangements with the Senators who were handling the revised Elkins bill in committee. In January 1903 the bill was reported without either the rate regulation or pooling sections, a pure antirebate measure which became the Elkins Act. Grimly Bacon promised "to follow this up by vigorous efforts . . . at the next session of Congress." [16]

The contest over rate regulation had attracted enough attention to bring a number of prominent politicians into the discussion by 1904, an election year. Now the shippers whom Bacon had been unable to reach responded enthusiastically, and because the Interstate Commerce Law Convention was available, commercial associations flocked into it during 1904, transforming the convention into a major business organization. Another sharp increase in membership came after the November elections as Roosevelt opened the administration's drive for rate regulation. Bacon, who deluded himself into believing he was Roosevelt's advisor, was overjoyed and spoke as if he were the President's agent. In preparation for a meeting in 1905 of the Interstate Commerce Law Convention, Bacon required that all delegates pledge themselves in advance to Roosevelt's rate program. [17]

As Bacon's Convention grew, so did its opposition. The convention, always strongest in the Midwest, had by early 1905 alienated some of the most important shipper groups in the East, including the Merchants' Association, Board of Trade and Transportation, and Produce Exchange in New York and the Chamber of Commerce in Boston. Easterners distrusted both Bacon as a person and his convention, whose Midwestern members talked almost as much about outmaneuvering their Eastern competitors as they did about controlling the railroads. As a result, the prominent Eastern associations were arguing against strict rate regulation. A more militant opposition came from businessmen whose profits depended directly upon the railroads. President Parry of the NAM, who had invested heavily in railroad stock, began to organize these men with a circular letter of January 1905, which denounced Bacon's program as socialistic and proposed instead a stiffer antirebate law and the legalization of railroad pools. Behind Parry rallied New England life insurance companies, whose agent, Daniel Davenport, soon shared the leadership with Parry; a large number of lumbermen and coal operators whose interests were entwined with railroads; and manufacturers of railroad equipment, among them John Kirby, Jr., of the NAM. That spring Parry and Kirby induced the NAM to withdraw its endorsement of Bacon's program. With Davenport and N. W. McLeod, president of the National Lumber Manufacturers' Association, they then collected delegates to outvote Bacon's supporters at the forthcoming sessions of the Interstate Commerce Law Convention.[18]

On the eve of the convention's meeting, Parry and his associates, purporting to be shippers, demanded that Bacon admit all businessmen to its sessions and that free speech prevail. Bacon, who had ignored the many signs of trouble, declined, and about 700 businessmen arrived in Chicago on October 25, 1905, to fight for control of the convention. Friends of the railroads refused to sign Bacon's pledge and were denied entry. When they tried to force their way into the convention hall, armed guards turned them back. Retiring to a nearby hotel, Parry's group then organized a rump convention under the ridiculous name of the Federal Rate Regulation Association, and for two days the competing groups traded insults and passed diametrically opposed resolutions on railroad supervision. Bacon lost the battle of the conventions. Already hurt by the defection of Eastern shippers, he forfeited additional support through his mismanagement of the Chicago sessions. Newsmen treated the meetings as a farce. Because the Interstate Commerce Law Convention had been a personal venture, Bacon's eclipse ended the one broadly representative organization of shippers. And once the Federal Rate Regulation Association had accomplished its task, it too dissolved.[19]

Although most shippers retained their enthusiasm for strict regulation, they lacked a national organization at a critical time. In anger, some within the NAM retaliated by polling the membership and publishing the results, which overwhelmingly favored a strong ICC. After a brief exchange, President Parry subsided. And Henry Clay Frick, a leader in U.S. Steel, unexpectedly gave his assistance. Defying the House of Morgan, which financed much of the attack against regulation, Frick wrote Roosevelt that the ICC should unquestionably have the power to fix reasonable rates. The unreconstructed steel man could never be anything except a shipper.[20]

But the initiative had passed from the disorganized shippers to the railroads. By late 1905 they had mobilized an impressive force of businessmen behind them. In states such as California and Wisconsin where the roads had extensive influence among other business groups, hundreds of businessmen and associations sent telegrams, petitions, and letters first to the appropriate Congressional committees and then, early in 1906, to individual legislators. It was an efficiently conducted campaign. At the same time prominent city bankers toured business organizations throughout the country in behalf of the carriers, whose securities they held, while friends of the railroads from Wall Street, such as Elbert Gary, used their influence with congressmen.[21]

Through 1905 railroad spokesmen relied upon an oft-repeated conglomeration of arguments: rates were already reasonable, and if an occasional problem arose, the court could easily handle it; regulation would end progress; the power to determine rates would mean confiscation of property; and in any case the states which had chartered the roads should regulate them. But by 1906, accepting the inevitability of some law, the railroads had shifted their defense to full judicial review before any decision of the ICC took effect. This compromise pleased many businessmen who were growing concerned that too stiff a rate law would endanger prosperity. And they rejoiced when Congress passed the Hepburn Act, which balanced a broad extension of the commission's power over the means of transportation and a clear statement of the commission's right to determine reasonable rates against the right of the railroads to postpone action on rates by challenging the commission in the courts. An important step toward effective regulation, the act still offended militant shippers as well as the railroads. But it gave many others what they most wanted by 1906 — a moment of peace.[22]

III

Almost every businessman had a ready answer to the tariff question: adequate protection for home industries. Since the Civil War industrialists had induced Congress to construct a progressively higher tariff wall and, in company with Republican politicians, had convinced a large majority of their fellow businessmen that Republican protection was prosperity's first line of defense. Events in the 1890's seemingly had proved their case. A Democratic Congress had attempted to lower duties, and the nation had suffered a severe depression; then when the Republicans had returned to power and had passed the high Dingley Tariff of 1897, good times had returned. The four apostles of protection — the Home Market Club of Boston, the Manufacturers' Club of Philadelphia, the American Protective Tariff League, and the American Iron and Steel Association — arranged these facts into a tariff catechism.

But at the turn of the century an increasing number of businessmen were rethinking their definitions of adequate protection. Prices were rising, and the formation of trusts was exceptionally common in protected industries. Why, asked customers of U.S. Steel, did the corporation sell more cheaply abroad than at home? Clearly the answer was tariff favoritism, and not some mysterious function of "the natural laws of trade and commerce," as company spokesmen would have them believe. Responding to complaints of this type, a Republican banker, George E. Roberts, suggested lowering the tariff whenever it supported monopoly, and as "the Iowa Idea" Roberts' proposal spread among those hostile toward trusts. As public pressure for revisions mounted, more and more businessmen recommended prompt action. Still protectionists, they wanted changes while the tariff was "in the hands of 'its friends' — the Republican party. Woe to it if it were to be reconstructed by Democrats." [23]

A heterogeneous group of businessmen, who had long advocated tariff reforms, benefited particularly from this shift in sentiment. Roughly the group divided into exporters and importers. For years businessmen who processed and distributed agricultural products had predominated among the exporters, which despite the inclusion of certain railroads and large produce exchanges of the East, had given that branch of the revision movement a distinctly Midwestern tone. But as semifinished and finished manufactures more than doubled their percentage of America's growing exports between 1890 and 1915, an increasing number of Eastern industrialists, merchants, and financiers joined the agricultural interests. Although both groups wanted reforms in order to lower foreign tariffs, the manufacturing interests looked more toward economically backward nations than did the Midwestern businessmen, who concentrated upon European markets.

A more significant split separated exporters and importers. Each of the importers, who were particularly strong in New England, had his own program, depending upon what raw materials his factory required. Together they demanded, in the platform of the Business Men's Tariff Reform League of New England, "the abolition of duties on Hides, Sole Leather, Iron Ore, Coal, Lumber and Wood Pulp," and an important addition, the American Sugar Refining Company wanted free sugar.[24] This branch also included a few large importing houses, notably in New York, with diversified interests. Concerned only about America's free list, importers paid no attention to foreign tariffs. Two industries almost spanned all of these factions: the ocean shippers profited from any increase in trade; and the agricultural implement manufacturers sold equipment abroad, relied upon farmers who sold abroad, and desired cheap iron and leather for their factories. And one issue came close to uniting all of them: Canadian reciprocity promised traffic for the railroads, wheat for the millers and merchants, a number of the raw materials for New England industry, and an expanding market for manufactured goods.

To gain support from those businessmen who wanted moderate tariff readjustment, a dedicated revisionist had to frame his demands in a way which seemed to uphold the principle of protection. Fortunately President McKinley, an idol of the protectionists, had supplied just such a formula in 1897 by sending John A. Kasson of Iowa abroad to negotiate reciprocal trade agreements. By 1899 the Senate had received thirteen "Kasson treaties," including a major one with France. Not only did reciprocity have the endorsement of a protectionist President but it sounded to many businessmen like a painless bargain which lowered duties on American goods in exchange for concessions to uncompetitive foreign products.[25]

In November 1901 importers from the National Association of Manufacturers attempted to organize businessmen behind reciprocity by holding a National Reciprocity Convention in Washington. Theodore Search, president of the NAM and chairman of the Convention, opened the meetings cautiously by explaining that "reciprocity will not let us alone, and the only thing for us to do is to meet it fairly and squarely . . . and find out what there is in it." His colleague, Daniel Tompkins, added that reciprocity "does not involve the abandonment [of protection] . . . under which such magnificent results have been attained." Protectionists, who had come to Washington on the defensive, took these apologetics as the signal to attack. Members of the protectionist clubs and representatives of the jewelry and perfume industries (French reciprocity was then pending) one after another extolled the glories of prosperity under the Dingley tariff and warned that the slightest revision invited free trade. They carried the convention. Reciprocity, the delegates decided, should only cover "special cases . . . where it can be done without injury to any of our home interests of manufacturing, commerce or farming." [26]

To manufacturers and merchants in the Boston Chamber of Commerce, the reciprocity convention was "a great disappointment"; to a variety of revisionists in the New York Chamber of Commerce, it was "subversive of all attempts to bring about closer trade relations with our sister nations." But the next move came from agriculturally oriented businessmen in the Midwest. In protest against the Washington convention a small Kansas group, the Western Reciprocity League, called a conference for April 1902 in Chicago where sixty-six delegates founded the National Reciprocity League. National in name only, it failed to attract more than a handful of Easterners, who preferred to work through their own chambers and such trade groups as the Free Hides League and National Boot and Shoe Manufacturers' Association. Despite some assistance from the Detroit Board of Commerce and the National Association of Agricultural Implement and Vehicle Manufacturers, the new league lasted only a year. [27]

The reformers did not try again until 1905, when a prominent group of Midwestern revisionists, after courting Eastern businessmen, arranged the National Reciprocity Convention in Chicago. The very success of the call guaranteed stormy sessions. Each industry came to serve itself: shoe manufacturers asked for a resolution on free hides and lost in a fight with the Chicago meat packers, representatives for the American Sugar Refining Company talked solely about Cuba, Northwestern millers about Canada, and New York businessmen about Europe. Not one gave in order to get, and the delegates devoted their time to struggling for control of the convention. Meanwhile Albert Clarke, secretary of the Home Market Club, distributed protectionist literature among them until the harassed chairman had him ejected. In the end the convention passed innocuous resolutions favoring a more liberal tariff and formed another organization, the American Reciprocity Tariff League. Although stronger than

its predecessor because of support from Midwestern commercial associations, agricultural machinery manufacturers,
and meat packers, the American Reciprocity Tariff League
also failed to win significant backing in the East, where tariff
reformers looked to the Boston Chamber of Commerce and
the Merchants' Association of New York for leadership.[28]

Rivalry among the revisionists simplified the task of the
professional protectionists. Particularly well-organized in the
East, they also reached into the South, where the *Manufacturers' Record* warned that reciprocity meant "the admission
to this country of raw material free of duty at [our] expense,"
and from the Far West, where a number of businessmen
feared agricultural competition from France, Italy, and
Latin America. Protectionists described the tariff as a delicate fabric which, losing a single thread, would unravel and
expose the economy to ruinous competition from abroad.
The few who tampered endangered everyone's well-being,
their own included. Denying that a true Republican could
be a revisionist, the protectionists branded the reformers
"Free Traders" and Democrats — or at least Bryan-con-
trolled. That involved them in an absurd debate over political verbiage. "Reciprocity," McKinley had said, "is the natural outgrowth of our wonderful industrial development under
the domestic policy now firmly established." Where revisionists hailed this as an unequivocal endorsement, the
American Protective Tariff League, weighing each word,
replied that McKinley had regarded reciprocity only as a
means of marketing America's surplus without touching the
Dingley tariff. McKinley remained a powerful name among
businessmen. Finally, in order to break the association between monopoly and a high tariff, protectionists blamed
tariff reform upon the sugar, beef, and harvester trusts, and
claimed that only the small steel manufacturers, not the
so-called steel trust, required protection in order to survive.[29]

Yet the desire for mild revision would not die. What the
serious revisionists needed above all was a new reform plan.
After the Senate had killed the many Kasson treaties, salving

the national conscience and the American Sugar Refining
Company with a Cuban reciprocity bill, most businessmen
had lost interest in reciprocity. Then late in the prosperity
years an alternative began to materialize — a permanent,
nonpartisan tariff commission. As the reformers envisioned
it, businessmen would staff the commission, which would
have wide powers to gather data, compel the appearance
of witnesses, and recommend specific tariff adjustments. Public pressure would force Congress to act. Such a commission
was general enough to unite the various tariff reformers in
principle, and it also held the advantages of familiarity —
the scheme dated back well into the nineteenth century —
and good references, including one from President Roosevelt. And if, as the reformers maintained, the commission
would work on one schedule at a time, it would free businessmen from a standing fear, wholesale revision. In 1907
revisionists were preparing for the campaign which would
dominate the next round of the tariff debate.[30]

IV

The nation inherited an obsolete financial system from the
nineteenth century. Under laws enacted during the Civil
War period, a bank which held specified reserves and un-
derwent periodic examinations received a national charter
and could then issue currency which was backed by government bonds and protected by a prohibitive tax on local cur-
rencies. As the economy grew increasingly national and
complex, this system served no one well. Because government bonds bore no relationship to the needs for currency,
bank paper soon replaced the official currency as the main
medium of exchange. More basic, the credit regulations fitted
neither a rural nor an industrial economy: discrimination
against farm mortgages hurt the agricultural regions, and
rapid expansions of credit damaged the whole nation. By
allowing smaller bankers to place their legal reserves on deposit with city correspondents, the system gave the major
banks in a few cities, particularly New York, a large surplus

for speculation. And without means to mobilize bank reserves in a crisis, a system which was normally untidy became chaotic during panics.

Although no one understood these weaknesses better than the bankers, fears of inflation during the 1890's had diverted them from reform. Directly after the Panic of 1893 Midwestern city bankers had organized behind the plan of Charles C. Homer, president of the Second National Bank of Baltimore, for a new assets currency issued against a bank's unimpaired capital, lightly taxed, and backed by a five-percent guarantee fund. But within a year the city bankers had dropped the Baltimore plan to battle against free silver. Then after McKinley's election, a group of businessmen and Republican politicians had formed the Indianapolis Monetary Commission to revive interest in an assets currency and to suggest ways of mobilizing bank reserves. Still inflation haunted them, and their campaign narrowed to the removal of silver from the currency. Even after the Gold Standard Act of 1900 the Indianapolis Monetary Commission was lobbying for a bill to retire outstanding silver dollars.[31]

Divisiveness presented an even greater obstacle to reform. An ambitious group of Midwestern city bankers, led early in the century by James H. Eckels of Chicago and Frank G. Bigelow of Milwaukee, supplied most of the ideas for reform, hoping to improve their competitive position *vis-à-vis* the East, and to expand at the expense of smaller rural bankers. But the powerful financial centers of the East, including the House of Morgan, Kuhn, Loeb and Company, and the National City Bank of New York, thought first of protecting their pre-eminence, and despite an awareness of danger from the present system, opposed each major change. A third group, largely Midwestern, which was composed of country bankers in and out of the national banking system, joined the opposition. Complicated reforms, the small bankers thought, always originated with the "sinners" and "plutocratic combinations" in Wall Street. Although country bankers also wanted changes — ones which would recognize rural credits and loosen their dependence upon the cities — they still devoted themselves to defense. And that ironically allied them with the financiers who actually did work on Wall Street. The unquestioned leader of the Midwestern country bankers was Andrew J. Frame of Waukesha, Wisconsin, a tenacious and ill-informed man who could not accept the twentieth century. As part of his battle against big government and big business, Frame vowed never to rediscount financial paper at a city bank. That kind of independence won the deep admiration of his country colleagues, even though they would never imitate it.[32]

In 1901 Secretary of the Treasury Lyman J. Gage, formerly a Chicago banker, endorsed a bill almost identical with the Baltimore plan of 1894, and that year James Eckels reintroduced the subject of an assets currency at the ABA's annual convention. These were preliminaries to a campaign which opened at the sessions of the ABA in 1902, where Representative Charles N. Fowler of New Jersey announced the Midwestern city bankers' full program. In addition to a currency based upon each national bank's liquid assets, Fowler proposed the legalization of branch banking in order, he said, to lower and equalize national interest rates. But when the officers of the ABA moved to approve the Fowler plan, the numerically stronger country bankers, led by Andrew Frame, defeated it. Only a parliamentary trick saved the city bankers from Frame's substitute resolution, which condemned branch banking because "individualism in management would cease, local tax be evaded, no home distribution of profits, local progress retarded" and assets currency because it would "further inflate credit, drive our gold abroad . . . and help us into a panic when we are out of one."[33]

The country bankers, with Frame still directing, then retired to their state associations in Wisconsin, Illinois, Missouri, Iowa, Kansas, Nebraska, Minnesota, and South Dakota, and passed lengthy resolutions against the city bankers' program. Primarily, the country bankers feared branch banking which to them meant an annihilating invasion from the large urban centers. Assets currency was blackened by the company it kept. In 1903 when Fowler proposed only an assets currency, country bankers denounced it by references to its companion of a year before, branch banking. A few rural bankers repeated Frame's charge that assets currency was "fiatism," and noted that the liquid assets which Fowler suggested did not include their specialty, agricultural credits.[34]

While the country bankers described the Fowler plan as a plot by "a lot of those New Yorkers," James W. Stillman and other Wall Street financiers were also opposing it. Recognizing assets currency as the real issue, the big New York bankers, like Andrew Frame, called it "second-class currency." Their reply to the Fowler plan came in a bill which Senator Nelson W. Aldrich of Rhode Island introduced in 1903. The Aldrich bill, proposing a limited expansion of the currency with notes issued against selected state, municipal, and railroad bonds, formalized the conflict between New York and Midwestern city bankers. Where the New York financiers, who either held these bonds or could borrow them from affiliated trust companies, essentially asked for no change, the Midwestern city bankers, who would have to enter the market to get the bonds, wanted a decentralized assets currency to give them a relative advantage over Wall Street. The first round was a draw: Congress rejected both the Fowler plan and the Aldrich bill.[35]

The Midwestern city bankers waited until 1906 before trying again. Over the protests of country bankers from the South and Midwest, the ABA passed a resolution authorizing a special currency commission, with James B. Forgan of Chicago as chairman, to draw up a bill for the association. The city bankers who controlled the commission wrote an assets bill and presented it in Congress through Representative Fowler. Once more Andrew Frame rallied the country bankers in opposition, and the bill died in committee.[36] By 1906 many country bankers had settled upon an alternative program. Usually called the "Shaw plan" after Roosevelt's Secretary of the Treasury, Leslie M. Shaw, who had been an Iowa country banker, it combined Shaw's recommendation for an emergency currency which a steep tax would quickly retire, and the country bankers' suggestion for its distribution through their local clearinghouse associations as a defense against high finance and big government. Rarely did a country banker argue that only the national government could protect him from urban financiers and that it should have the powers to do so.[37]

At the same time New York bankers were undergoing a change of heart. Through a committee of the New York Chamber of Commerce they gave token assistance in 1906 to the bill of the Midwestern city bankers, and they also spoke favorably of the country bankers' program for an emergency currency. Behind this sudden generosity lay their growing interest in an entirely different project, a banker-controlled central bank. Its chief advocate was Frank A. Vanderlip of the National City Bank, a haughty, often narrow-minded man whose determination as a fighter and extensive knowledge of finance had already won him the respect of the nation's great bankers. By 1906 Vanderlip had converted a number of prominent New York businessmen and at least one leading Chicago banker, George E. Roberts. But for two more years the central bank remained a topic largely for private discussions. Through 1907 bankers continued to debate a multitude of currency reforms, and other businessmen vaguely asked for more flexibility in the financial system. As an observer from the Far West remarked, "The bankers are still divided, while the public and the politicians look on, and smilingly say, 'Who shall decide when doctors disagree?' "[38]

V

Around the turn of the century the cities of the Midwest came of age in an industrial economy. Many of their citizens looked first within the cities and collected about the Tom Johnsons, Joseph Folks, and Walter Fishers to order their own houses. Others, eager to break what they regarded as colonial bonds, challenged the traditional centers of power in the East on every front at every opportunity. Here businessmen predominated. Their urge to reform, strongest in the Chicago area, fanned throughout the cities of the Midwest. From them came the earliest, most active, and the greatest number of shippers who demanded railroad regulation, the most persistent advocates of tariff revision, and the bankers who forced the issue of financial legislation by offering a clear plan of reorganization. Although some Eastern businessmen did encourage reciprocity and rate control, they played a secondary role in almost all cases. And in the South and Far West, where the industrial economies lagged, businessmen participated in local and state reforms but scarcely at all in national ones.

The Midwestern cities proved their maturity by the size and diversity of their middle-income groups. It was these citizens, increasingly self-conscious and aggressive, who demanded reforms. Moderately prosperous businessmen, operating through their trade and local organizations, conducted the campaigns for rate regulation and an assets currency, and contributed more than their share to the drive for reciprocity. With few exceptions, big businessmen defended what they had. And the small businessmen in the towns and countryside offered little more to the reform movements. Distrusting more successful businessmen, they rejected most new ideas on principle because of the sponsors. Significantly, their most enthusiastic endorsement of a reform — trust-busting — resulted in part from a misunderstanding of what trusts the administration might attack.

Over all these activities shone the warm sun of prosperity. Assurances of a reasonable profit relaxed businessmen and encouraged their reform impulses, even when their own interests were not immediately involved. Recognizing that abuses did exist, a large number of them supported food, drug, and insurance regulation, and recommended a variety of vague improvements — federal incorporation, equitable railroad regulation, tariff adjustment within protection, a more flexible currency. Of course they expected that legislators would approach with great respect the economic machinery which mass-produced profits. Controversies such as the one over rate regulation became too violent for many of them, and in general other people's reforms did not long hold their attention. Still, they enjoyed the sense of progress which a combination of prosperity and reasonable reforms provided.

IV

UNCERTAINTY

The Panic of 1907 and its brief depression acted catalytically upon the trend from local, disorganized reform to optimistic, national programming. Already the currents were running fast. Muckrakers had probed the corners of business and government. The Wisconsin Idea, fully elaborated, now belonged to the nation, as did Senator Robert LaFollette. Reformers had sprung up in every major city, and Frederic Howe's *The City: The Hope of Democracy* gave them a rationale and a vision. In 1908, the same year that the Federal Council of the Churches of Christ finally materialized, Walter Rauschenbusch called militant Protestants to battle with *Christianity and the Social Crisis*. And the AFL, in response to a ground swell for political action among member unions, moved into national politics, while the Supreme Court in *Muller v Oregon* apparently sanctioned the regulation of working hours by the states. Within this ferment the panic, which roused memories of the dark days of the Nineties, seemed to many an object lesson in irresponsible plutocracy. Reformers demanded major changes at once.

In the wake of the panic, basic issues of the progressive era fell, one after another, into national view. Congress, with the Aldrich-Vreeland Act, began the legislative process toward the Federal Reserve system. Only a guarantee of prompt action in 1909 saved the tariff from immediate attack. Proposed amendments to the Sherman Act foreshadowed the Federal Trade Commission. At the National Conservation Congress of 1908 President Roosevelt gave conservation its first sweeping national publicity, and with

his messages to Congress that year laid the groundwork for
the Progressive platform of 1912. Each of these moves sharpened the debate and intensified the heat of the progressive
movement.

The amiable conservative William Howard Taft stepped
into a sea of insistent demands and conflicting claims. His
quandary typified the troubles facing those leaders who,
like Taft, had fitted well into the busy yet familiar process
of national reform during the Roosevelt administration. As
Roosevelt's successor, Taft looked forward to a time of calm
and assimilation after the recent enlargement of federal responsibilities and the subsequent panic and depression. But
the most articulate reformers wanted more in a hurry. Perhaps an improvement here, a minor innovation there, would
satisfy them. But now reformers bridled at piecemeal reform. Then, said Taft, stand pat, conscientiously administer
the present system, and preserve the basic structure of
American society.

To stand pat after 1908 meant to abdicate leadership in
the progressive movement. As the quickening pace left the
Tafts behind, more ardent and more flexible reformers strug-
gled among themselves for dominance. The new national
leader would have to reconcile two increasingly divergent
streams in progressivism: a more aggressive, urban-oriented
group who talked of social justice, real income, and a complex of government regulations to contain business without
destroying its profit potential; and less excitable, rural-ori-
ented reformers with long-standing ambitions to break up
big business, assist agriculture, and lower the tariff on manufactured goods while taxing the incomes of the rich. Among
the contestants three stood out, each with a distinct approach to the problem of unity. Where Roosevelt balanced
his personal popularity in the countryside against an urban
program of business regulation and efficient social justice,
Woodrow Wilson combined an aura of urban professionalism
with plans to save the moral, competitive individualism
which small-town America cherished. And LaFollette projected upon the nation a program which he had formulated

for his home state: three parts Wisconsin farmer, one part Milwaukee laborer and small businessman, and one part University of Wisconsin expertise. These men and many others were planning for the nation with a sense of victory close at hand. By their national vision, their interrelated programs, and their confidence, they distinguished the United States of 1912 from the United States of 1906 as clearly as 1906 had been separated from 1900.

I

Into the early fall of 1907 businessmen spoke as if prosperity would last forever. Especially those in the interior, who were proud of the economy's toughness during minor upsets in 1901 and 1903, watched rich harvests and rising new industries, and decided that panics belonged to the big speculators, "a just retribution . . . upon all of them alike." When warnings drifted out of the East that summer, the president of Illinois Steel dismissed them as a trick of the "Wall Street Bears." Late in September an Indiana banker told his colleagues, "We could not if we would stop this onward march of progress, we might as well try to stop the ebb and flow of the ocean tide"; and on October 1, James Van Cleave promised businessmen "a prolonged era of prosperity." [1]

Panic struck Wall Street in mid-October. Waves of distress spread across the nation. Holdings were liquidated, deposits frozen, credit tightened, confidence shattered; and by 1908 the economy was in depression. Despite brief periods of prosperity, it did not fully recover until 1915.

Shocked and scared, most businessmen outside the East reflexly blamed Wall Street. "The wild scenes on the street and in the stock boards in New York City were not caused by the lack of business or a cry for bread," an Arizona banker reminded his colleagues, "but by the stock speculator." Another from South Carolina pointed to "grave abuses, wrongdoing cloaked under the forms of law, the corrupt use of trust funds, unwise and unsafe business methods, which proved to be a dangerous departure from the old-fashioned

standards of business integrity and conservatism." Who
would believe Frank Vanderlip that hoarding country bankers had "put an impossible burden on the central reserve
banks"? It was self-evident that "national calamities are not
born in country towns. Panics are bred in great cities where
colossal promotions flourish." [2]

During the next few weeks businessmen also fell back
upon two other time-honored explanations. One implied a
Deity punishing the nation for its immoral habits, particularly a "general extravagance in the mode of living." [3] A
second invoked immutable economic law. "Periods of enormous business activity and expansion followed by periods of
depression" belonged with life, read a resolution of the Ohio
State Bankers Association. A Wisconsin businessman agreed:
"Panics undoubtedly cannot be prevented, because it is impossible to change human nature . . . because prosperity
and adversity follow each other as surely as the tide rises
and falls." Even here, however, some singled out New York.
Admitting that "the pendulum of business had swung to the
limit," a Washington state banker changed his metaphor for
the edification of Wall Street: "Water may be forced up hill,
but in nature its tendency is to seek its level and there remain." [4] In a few more weeks, as thoughts turned from re-
crimination toward recovery, most businessmen settled upon
a general loss of confidence as the root of the problem. A
panic, they said, was "a fear that feeds upon itself." Recovery required the proper frame of mind, and businessmen ex-
horted each other to recapture prosperity through faith in
the essential soundness of the economy. The *Wall Street
Journal* recommended Mary Baker Eddy: think good
thoughts because "all that is wanted is confidence." [5]

But why had so many lost their faith so suddenly? Those
hostile to Roosevelt's policies had the answer: the President's attacks against business had sapped confidence in the
economy. Especially appealing because it provided a tangible villain, word spread rapidly in business circles that this
was "Roosevelt's Panic," and even many of his supporters
admitted that the President's actions had disturbed the sys-

tem.[6] Judge Kenesaw Mountain Landis became a second devil. In August 1907 Landis had imposed a fine of twenty-nine million dollars upon Standard Oil for multiple violations of the antirebate law. Almost every business journal had approved: justice had caught up with an evil corporation. But by November 1907 some businessmen suggested that the fine had touched off the panic, and in July 1908 when a higher court canceled the fine the same journals which had praised Landis a year before applauded the reversal with biting remarks about the lower court's populistic bias.[7]

More often, businessmen distributed the blame among all those who had contributed to the "undiscriminating denunciation and legislation against capital and corporations." That was the theme of the most popular business organization of 1908, the National Prosperity and Sunshine Association, which Edward C. Simmons of St. Louis had founded. As the motto for the association, "whose mission it is to spread the gospel of confidence in each other and in the future of this great country," Simmons selected "Let Us Alone."[8] The passing of the easy, prosperous days ended the honeymoon between businessmen and reform. Convinced that criticism and harassment had broken the spell, the many businessmen who had smiled upon moderate changes before 1907 now set themselves against all unnecessary agitation. By necessary reforms they meant ones which promised direct benefits. And as progressivism broadened and the economy remained unsteady, these grew increasingly more difficult to find.

II

The nation's financial structure had again proved inadequate in crisis. With some reform imperative, Wall Street bankers promptly prepared their measure. After preliminary discussions with J. P. Morgan, Senator Aldrich conferred in December 1907 with several New York financiers and received a plan for a highly taxed emergency currency based upon railroad and municipal bonds. Aldrich introduced the bill in January 1908. That month the currency commission of the American Bankers' Association met in Chicago and drew up another assets currency bill. The Midwestern city bankers faced New York in a rematch of their battle of 1903. When the ABA demanded major currency reform, the large financiers of Wall Street argued against drastic changes during a crisis; and when New York bankers extolled an emergency currency, James Forgan, chairman of the ABA's currency commission, replied that the Aldrich bill should be called "An Act to Provide an Artificial Market for Municipal and Railroad Bonds." As the Chicago Association of Commerce explained, "Banks generally in the west do not possess the class of securities called for by [the Aldrich] bill, and in order to issue currency under its provisions they would have to go into the market and buy such securities, spending about $100 to get $75 worth of relief." [9]

In the Senate Robert LaFollette of Wisconsin attacked the Aldrich bill on grounds long familiar among Midwestern country bankers. The new currency, LaFollette maintained, would encourage speculation and ally the national government with high finance. Under attacks of this kind, the Senate removed the bill's provisions for railroad bonds, and George Perkins met with Aldrich, President Roosevelt, and Senator Albert J. Beveridge of Indiana to discuss tactics. "Pass the Aldrich bill with the railroad bond feature left out now," they agreed, "in order to promptly get it through the Senate, and then when . . . it goes to Committee, bring in the bond feature again in a modified form, which is to be further discussed by Senator Aldrich and Mr. [George F.] Baker." Meanwhile the House passed a compromise emergency currency measure, the Vreeland bill, meant to palliate fears of New York control: local government bonds would back a crisis currency and regional associations of national banks would distribute it. According to plan, the provision for railroad bonds was reinserted in committee, "disguised by rather obscure phraseology." LaFollette, however, anticipated the maneuver and defeated it a second time with a short filibuster. The final Aldrich-Vreeland Act of 1908 was essentially the Vreeland bill, which the powerful New York bankers regarded as a poor substitute for their original measure.[10]

While the act was evolving, Midwestern city bankers had futilely sought support for an assets currency. As usual, country bankers refused to consider it, and the fact that urban centers had recently frozen many rural deposits made their opposition particularly shrill in 1908. Their fire concentrated on Chicago, the center of the assets currency movement. "It must not and shall not be," cried H. M. Carpenter of Monticello, Iowa, "that any half dozen men unknown almost can, in their wisdom or in their folly, as a Clearing House Committee, or any other Committee, or on any pretext whatever, in Chicago or anywhere else, over night or over the Sabbath, without notice and without warning, decide and declare that we shall not have our own." Yet, as they rejected the assets bill, their arguments often attacked the original Aldrich bill. The president of the North Dakota Bankers Association, for example, explained his objections to assets currency by declaring, "I am opposed to currency based on fluctuating watered railroad bonds or the bonds of any industrial enterprise that are subject to serious fluctuations and the manipulations of the Wall Street sharks." Completing the irony, many country bankers joined Wall Street in support of the Aldrich-Vreeland bill. Its provisions for local distribution of an emergency currency coincided with their earlier reform preferences and ensured, according to C. D. Griffith of Sleepy Eye, Minnesota, that "some banks in certain large cities" would not reap all the benefits.[11]

In 1908 a new group composed of well-to-do merchants and manufacturers, mostly Easterners, entered the debate over financial reform. Distrusting urban financiers in general, they worked first to defeat the Aldrich bill. Then several of their associations, including the Boston Chamber of Commerce, the Merchants' Association and Board of Trade and Transportation in New York, and the Philadelphia Trades' League, formed a core of support for the bill of Charles Fowler, who previously had represented the ABA in Congress. This time Fowler included in a modest assets currency measure a provision for federal deposit insurance, an anathema to city bankers but appealing to the merchants and manufacturers. After the Aldrich-Vreeland Act had passed, these businessmen organized a stand-by association to defend their interests against future threats from the bankers. Harboring similar suspicions, the National Association of Credit Men, as well as a few Midwestern business organizations, joined them in the National Currency League.[12]

No one accepted the Aldrich-Vreeland Act as final. But because the act had created a National Monetary Commission to study long-range solutions, most businessmen postponed further discussion until the commission had reported. That pause fitted perfectly into the plans of the New York magnates. Senator Aldrich, as chairman of the National Monetary Commission, immediately sought advice from Wall Street financiers such as Frank Vanderlip; Paul M. Warburg of Kuhn, Loeb and Company; and Henry Davison of the House of Morgan. Moreover, their solution, a central bank, had gained in popularity after the panic demonstrated the dangers of decentralized reserves. In fact a few zealous advocates of centralization had hoped for a central bank in 1908. When Congress decided in favor of a temporary measure, Vanderlip wrote in exasperation to his associate George Roberts, "I have never seen anything that led me to think so little of the wisdom of the majority." [13]

More patient men like Davison and Warburg realized that they must first negotiate and educate. The New York financiers at once made overtures to the Midwestern city bankers. Davison told Aldrich to select James Forgan, president of the First National Bank of Chicago and chairman of the currency commission of the American Bankers' Association, as an advisor to the Monetary Commission. Through Forgan and others, the New York bankers passed the news that their recommendations would include an assets currency as well as a central bank and that the commission would confer with the ABA's currency commission before settling finally upon a plan. In 1909 the presidential address of George M. Reynolds before the ABA indicated the success of these negotiations. To the surprise of his audience Reynolds, who with Forgan dominated Chicago banking, argued for a combination of a central bank and an assets currency. But the sharp criticism which Reynolds' address brought emphasized the importance of the other half of the magnates' task, public education. While George Roberts of Chicago toured the state bankers associations, Paul Warburg, an expert on banking and an accomplished diplomat, worked from New York. After testing opinions with mild statements about a central institution, Warburg conducted a poll through the *Banking Law Journal* which showed that sixty percent of the 5,000 responding bankers would favor a central bank — if Wall Street did not dominate it. At the same time he won over the leaders of several important New York business organizations.[14]

On January 17, 1911, the National Monetary Commission announced a comprehensive reform program. That May the commission met with the currency commission of the ABA and completed what was known as the Aldrich plan. A central bank, called the National Reserve Association and camouflaged by an intricate system of fifteen branch institutions, would direct the issuance of an untaxed assets currency. Member banks would control the officers of the National Reserve Association, in some cases by selecting them, in others by holding the power to remove the officers whom the federal government had appointed. Under Warburg's leadership, the originators of the Aldrich plan moved quickly to mobilize support. By prearrangement the National Board of Trade held a Business Men's Monetary Conference on January 18, the day after the public had heard of the plan. After speeches praising the work of the National Monetary Commission, three business associations from New York, one of which, the Merchants' Association, had often criticized Wall Street, offered a resolution which endorsed the complicated Aldrich plan. Overriding a flustered opposition, the conference accepted the resolution, then appointed a committee to call upon the Chicago Association of Commerce in order to establish a "Business Men's Monetary Reform League." After a spring of hard work, advocates of the plan had formed the National Citizens' League for the Promotion of a Sound Banking System, with headquarters in Chicago and subdivisions across the nation.[15]

Warburg, who directed each step of the process, took every precaution to make the National Citizens' League appear broad-based and impartial. Merchants and manufacturers, rather than bankers, served on the committees which founded the league and then on its board of directors. The league was located in Chicago to avoid the "animosities and jealousies" which New York inevitably aroused, and no New Yorker held office in the new organization. Instead of declaring for the Aldrich plan, the league appealed simply for "an improved banking system for the United States of America." Behind this façade Eastern and Midwestern city bankers conducted an extensive campaign for their program. Business groups heard only those speakers whose homes, occupations, and prestige would impress without frightening them. At all times the powerful New York financiers remained silent. Lectures and a flood of promotional literature concentrated upon three themes. To allay suspicions that the National Reserve Association would be controlled by a few big bankers, advocates of the Aldrich plan promised "cooperation, not dominant centralization." Capitalizing upon memories of the recent panic, they guaranteed protection against future catastrophes. And, for the conservatively inclined, they stressed the plan's affinity to current banking practices. The whirlwind drive produced an impressive array of approving resolutions and statements. Along with the American Bankers' Association, twenty-nine of the forty-six state bankers organizations endorsed the National Reserve Association, as did a host of local business groups, including several from the South.[16]

Unable to check the momentum of the movement, the many businessmen who still opposed the Aldrich plan criticized it obliquely. Through the efforts of Daniel Tompkins, who privately described the National Reserve Association as the scheme of "Mr. Aldrich, the Standard Oil Company, and the Steel Trust," the National Association of Manufacturers postponed action on the "intricate problem" of financial reform. In the same fashion the Trans-Mississippi Commercial Congress promised to give the Aldrich plan sympathetic study. The National Association of Credit Men, in an obvious plea for decentralization, suggested twenty-five, instead of fifteen regional branches, and the North Dakota Bankers Association paired its endorsement with a resolution for the inclusion of rural credits.[17]

Where business critics temporized, Congress attacked in full force. The Pujo Committee of the Democratic House, investigating the "money trust," documented the incredible financial power of a handful of magnates. In the process the committee's counsel, Samuel Untermyer, exposed the partiality of the National Citizens' League and revealed the autocratic powers which city bankers wielded within their clearinghouses. Congressional attacks against the stock market brought Wall Street into further disrepute, encouraging Southern and Western small businessmen to demand regulation of the sale of securities. In such a climate bills for the National Reserve Association, still known as the Aldrich plan and still popularly identified with Wall Street, did not even get out of committee.[18]

With the failure of the Aldrich plan in Congress, the organization around it began to crumble. The American Bankers' Association withdrew its support to wait until the next Congress had expressed its views on financial reform.[19] The National Citizens' League, now without a viable issue, fell victim to a clash between the city bankers and the league's director, James Laurence Laughlin, who had taken a year's leave of absence from the University of Chicago to coordinate its work. Although Laughlin believed in the Aldrich plan, he bridled at Wall Street dictation. "New York is willing to contribute to any movement," he wrote in 1914 to a friend having similar troubles, "provided it is understood tacitly that its judgment and direction shall be controlling.

The difficulty, however, is that its policy has too often been sinuous and stupid . . ." Through 1911 admonitions from James Forgan held Laughlin in line, but by late 1912 the league had become a tangle of personality conflicts, with city bankers denouncing their coordinator and Laughlin sponsoring speeches by Charles Fowler, a prominent enemy of the Aldrich plan.[20]

Critics of the plan now offered a multitude of alternative proposals. The least imaginative came from Andrew Frame, veteran spokesman for the Midwestern country bankers, who after denouncing both central banking and an assets currency advocated only a continuation of the Aldrich-Vreeland Act. Another mediated between the Aldrich plan and the Midwestern city bankers' earlier proposals by suggesting centralized gold reserves and an otherwise decentralized banking and currency system. And for the first time two moderately prosperous New York bankers, James G. Cannon of the Fourth National and William A. Nash of the Corn Exchange, spoke out against their more powerful neighbors. Each recommended the incorporation of local clearinghouses to oversee banks in their areas and to issue certificates against their members' assets. Naturally all of these men, rebelling against the Aldrich plan, proposed a decentralized banking structure. But, foreshadowing trouble with the victorious Democrats, they also agreed in one important particular with the National Reserve Association: the bankers should control the financial system.[21]

III

In January 1908 the House of Morgan decided to translate into law the idea behind its gentlemen's agreements with the executive. It acted then for two reasons: rising criticism of big business impressed the magnates with the need for additional protection and the President seemed in a receptive frame of mind. When Elbert Gary and George Perkins had made the agreements concerning U.S. Steel and International Harvester, they had believed the understandings would cover considerably more than investigations by the Bureau of Corporations. First, they expected legal advice from the executive on the corporations' current practices so that, by making any adjustments privately, they could avoid federal prosecution. As Perkins told Roosevelt in August 1907, the Bureau of Corporations should "come to us and point out any mistakes or technical violations of any law, then give us a chance to correct them." If the corporations complied, Perkins went on to say, the government would naturally overlook past violations of the law. Furthermore, the Morgan men assumed that they could immunize their corporations from future prosecutions through executive approval of new policies.[22]

At first Roosevelt neither accepted nor denied these constructions. Then in November 1907, at the height of the panic, he twice acted according to the magnates' interpretation of the agreements. When the House of Morgan prepared to purchase a controlling interest in the Tennessee Coal and Iron Company for U.S. Steel, Gary and Henry Clay Frick discussed the matter with Roosevelt, who gave what Gary later called "tacit acquiescence." And as Gary planned the first of his famous "dinners," where iron and steel producers would agree upon prices, he made certain that the administration did not object. Combining these events with Roosevelt's well-known distinction between good and bad corporations, the magnates confidently anticipated the President's help in Congress.[23]

The task of formulating the law fell to George Perkins, who handled most of the affairs of the House in Washington. As a basis he used the resolutions for liberalization of the Sherman Act, which a National Conference on Combinations and Trusts, sponsored by the National Civic Federation, had adopted in October 1907. Perkins and his lawyers, in consultation with President Seth Low of the Civic Federation, reworked the resolutions into a bill, and then in January 1908 Perkins arranged a conference between the officers of the Civic Federation and Roosevelt. After two months of discussions, the bill went before the House with the President's endorsement as the Hepburn amendments to the

Sherman Act. The heart of the amendments empowered the Bureau of Corporations, after thorough investigation, to issue to a corporation a stamp of approval which would both "grant immunity for the past" (in Perkins' phrase) and protect the corporation's practices from later prosecution. Also, the Hepburn amendments legalized railroad pooling under the supervision of the Interstate Commerce Commission and, to appease the American Federation of Labor, loosely exempted peaceful labor and agricultural organizations from the Sherman Act. As Seth Low reported to Roosevelt, "the large interests," with the railroads and the meat packers prominent among them, supported the bill. So did Herbert Knox Smith, Commissioner of Corporations and a firm believer in the gentlemen's agreements.[24]

But moderately prosperous businessmen in the East and Midwest organized at once behind the National Association of Manufacturers, the American Anti-Boycott Association, and the Merchants' Association and Board of Trade and Transportation of New York to oppose the amendments. Because antiunionism best unified businessmen, the NAM and the Anti-Boycott Association centered their attack upon the proposed benefits for organized labor.[25] But the crucial issue was the latitude promised to big business. The New York associations struck directly at the heart of the bill, arguing that the right to approve business practices gave the executive autocratic powers over the economy, powers which constitutionally belonged to the legislature and judiciary. And when Senator Foraker of Ohio offered a similar bill which did not mention organized labor, Daniel Davenport stated that he would oppose any measure which tried to separate good big business from bad. Opponents of the bill indicated that, on the contrary, they wanted a stricter trust law. Congress, particularly sensitive to antitrust sentiment in an election year, rejected the Hepburn amendments.[26]

The House of Morgan fell back upon the gentlemen's agreements, which had functioned well, and took confidence that fall from the election of William Howard Taft. "We are going to have a more comfortable time," Perkins predicted to

J. P. Morgan, Jr.[27] In company with much of the nation, the House of Morgan misjudged the new President. Rather than continuing and enlarging Roosevelt's agreements, the new administration ignored them. In Roosevelt's time the Department of Commerce and Labor had allowed the investigation of U.S. Steel to lag and had scarcely begun the study of International Harvester; Taft's Secretary, Charles Nagel, immediately devoted the department's energies to these two projects. Earlier, department officials had talked freely with Morgan's men about corporation affairs; after March 1909 the department gave out no information. Roosevelt and his assistants had promised to complete the investigations of the two corporations before considering legal action; the Taft administration would not be bound.[28]

This coldness emanated from a general hostility of the Taft administration toward large-scale corporate organization. Although Taft gave lip-service to new departures in corporation control, his administration relied exclusively upon a vigorous enforcement of the Sherman Act. Surprised and furious, big businessmen sent word by way of the business press that they would force Taft's retirement after one term. Even the well-to-do businessmen who had fought the Hepburn amendments grew restive and uncertain. Within the NAM, for example, three contradictory solutions to the trust problem circulated simultaneously during 1909 and 1910: one faction suggested national incorporation, a second uniform state laws in place of the Sherman Act, and a third patience but no change in the law. As the antitrust suits against the Standard Oil and American Tobacco Companies moved to the Supreme Court, an increasing number of worried businessmen looked there for clarification. After several delays, the court finally ruled in May 1911 that the two corporations violated the antitrust law. But the court then stated that these companies must dissolve only because they had acted unreasonably in restraint of trade. Reasonable restraint was legal.[29]

What did these decisions mean? Businessmen did not pretend to know, and they did not hide their disappointment.

Those who had opposed the Hepburn amendments realized that, as Senator LaFollette said, "the Court has done . . . what Congress has refused steadfastly to do." Yet they did not like the Taft administration's literal reading of the Sherman Act. In their confusion they in effect called the decisions bad not because they were vague but because somehow they had been vague in the wrong way. Nor did big businessmen, theoretically the victors, find comfort in the rulings. Elbert Gary demanded an exact definition of "reasonable" and "unreasonable" restraint of trade. Without an answer, according to George Perkins, "it became clear that chaos in business was upon us." Reading these decisions as an invitation to prosecute U.S. Steel and International Harvester, Perkins in July 1911 went to Attorney General George W. Wickersham in a last attempt to revitalize the understandings. He promised Wickersham that if the Attorney General discovered practices which "in his judgment, should be corrected, we would all meet him half way in an effort to [correct them] by agreement rather than through a suit." On October 26 the Justice Department, without waiting for the Bureau of Corporations to finish its investigation, began antitrust proceedings against U.S. Steel. Shortly afterward, it brought suit against International Harvester.[30]

In its case against U.S. Steel, the government attacked the program for price stability which Gary had inaugurated after the Panic of 1907. In November 1907 during the first "dinner" to which he invited the presidents of the nation's iron and steel companies, Gary had established the principle of price maintenance and had arranged committees to regularize cooperation in various branches of the industry. At his "dinners" and after 1910 in the American Iron and Steel Institute, he had managed by threats and pleas to preserve price stability with surprisingly few defections — one major break in 1909 and a minor one in 1911. In an effort to disarm his critics, Gary pointed out that "the law does not compel competition; it only prohibits an agreement not to compete." And, he emphasized, no agreements had been made. "The movement has been simply an effort . . . to establish a basis

of friendly association and intercourse which is calculated to
enable each to obtain full knowledge concerning the affairs of
all the others and the beneficial results which naturally
follow such knowledge." "The cooperative plan," he concluded, "was largely an ethical proposition": it placed each
man under an "obligation of honor . . . even stronger than
the obligation of an agreement." [31]

By singling out the most famous of the early open price
agreements, the indictment of U.S. Steel impressed businessmen more deeply than the decisions concerning Standard
Oil and American Tobacco. From a variety of industries,
businessmen representing all sizes now defended their price
understandings. Within days of the announcement of the
U.S. Steel suit, the National Federation of Retail Merchants
was founded to lobby for such changes in the law "as will
permit merchants to make contracts and agreements not in
unreasonable restraint of trade and commerce among the
several States"; and the older retail and wholesale associations also prepared to fight for their members' rights. Two
months later bituminous coal operators and the United Mine
Workers jointly requested amendments to the Sherman Act
which would allow price agreements.

Appropriately, George Perkins gathered these businessmen
before a Senate committee which was then studying the
trust question; and Perkins, Gary, and Seth Low offered the
committee the most elaborate substitutes for the Sherman
Act. In general these men restated the advise-and-consent
formula from the Hepburn amendments of 1908. This time
an interstate trade commission, similar in status to the Interstate Commerce Commission, would investigate corporations
and license those which met its standards. It should be a
commission "that business men could be more or less in consultation with," Gary said, one that would "decide questions"
for businessmen in order "to avoid any question of illegality
in their actions." And as an added precaution, Perkins recommended a commission "composed largely of experienced
business men." Confirmed enemies of an approving government agency took this "systematic campaign . . . headed by

Mr. Perkins, to change public opinion and to repeal [the Sherman Act]," as a call to action. But early in 1913, the trend among businessmen favored the magnates.[32]

IV

The panic struck the railroads with special severity. Their finances, distended by years of stock watering and gutted by raids upon their assets, could not withstand a precipitous fall in security values. To the financiers of the railroads, the situation demanded a general increase in rates, and early in the panic they thought that despite hard times businessmen would accept the advances. The railroads were blaming their troubles on the recent "campaign of violent agitation and extravagant, unmeasured condemnation," and a number of business groups, particularly in the East, had picked up the cry, citing railroad regulation as a major cause for the nation's loss of confidence. The ubiquitous George Perkins took charge of the movement for higher rates. After several weeks of negotiation, he reported to Morgan late in April 1908 that "at last we have succeeded in getting practically all the railroad presidents together in an agreement to raise freight rates." But Wall Street had misinterpreted the temper of the shippers. Hearing rumors of the increases, businessmen from Philadelphia to Los Angeles told the roads that they must accept their share of the recession losses and called upon the federal government for help. Roosevelt, who warned Perkins that a general increase was politically impossible, threatened along with the Interstate Commerce Commission to investigate. Grumbling about people's inability to keep a secret, Perkins canceled the plan.[33]

Also as a result of the blunder, shippers now organized the National Industrial Traffic League. Founded at the insistence of Chicago businessmen, the Traffic League, like the earlier Interstate Commerce Law Convention, drew most of its strength from the Midwest. But unlike its predecessor, it included many manufacturing firms as well as commercial associations, and it relied upon all members rather than upon one man. The Traffic League served two purposes. Through it, the professional traffic managers of the member associations argued the case for the shippers before the Interstate Commerce Commission and pressed for amendments to the Hepburn Act which would enable the ICC to suspend proposed rate advances and to establish rates effective before judicial review.[34]

Early in 1910 the Taft administration recommended both of these provisions as well as the legalization of railroad pooling and a special court of commerce to expedite rate cases. Although sharply divided over pooling and only moderately favorable to a commerce court, shippers greeted the administration's proposal with enthusiasm, and the Traffic League at once became its outstanding supporter. When Congress received the measure as the Mann-Elkins bill, reform-minded legislators demanded also the regulation of railroad securities and the evaluation of railroad property as a basis for reasonable rates. Whatever the railroads might otherwise have done, they now determined to defeat the Mann-Elkins bill. Give the Hepburn Act a chance before changing it, they complained. "I believe the proposed legislation is unnecessary," said Walker D. Hines of the Atchison, Topeka and Santa Fe, "and its proposal at this time serves to stimulate an anti-railroad agitation when I think the railroads have fairly earned a respite from that sort of discussion." [35]

Unable to impress enough congressmen, the railroad executives once again listened to George Perkins, who by May 1910 had organized all but the Southern systems behind another movement for freight increases. This obvious attempt to slip in an advance before a new law took effect infuriated both the shippers and the administration, and on May 31 Taft announced that he would block the increases with a federal injunction, then prosecute the roads for collusion under the Sherman Act. The railroad presidents hastily made peace with the President. In conference with Taft they agreed to suspend the increases in return for tacit assurances of a hearing before the ICC immediately after Congress had completed the railroad bill. A few days later Congress passed the Mann-Elkins Act without provisions for pooling, physical valuation, or securities regulation. The shippers had received exactly what they had wanted: the ICC could suspend increases; and its rate decisions became effective immediately.[36]

In June the scene shifted to the Interstate Commerce Commission where hearings began on the railroads' proposed rate advance. The carriers had prepared their case with confidence, erroneously assuming that the administration would support the increases. Moreover they had again misjudged the enmity which their attempt to advance rates had aroused among the shippers.[37] By June the National Industrial Traffic League had collected business organizations from Pennsylvania to the West Coast into a special Shippers' Association to supplement the Traffic League's work before the ICC. At the same time nine of the largest commercial associations along the East Coast banded together to hire the brilliant Boston lawyer, Louis D. Brandeis, to represent them before the commission. Completing the opposition were trade groups such as the National Petroleum Association, whose members believed higher freight rates would favor their larger competitors.[38]

The shippers, unified everywhere except in the South and Great Plains, had reached their peak of organization. In heated sessions before the ICC, they claimed the need for decreases instead of an advance. And when the carriers declared that without increases they could not attract investors, Brandeis replied that "the railroads to meet any existing needs should look not without but within": greater operational efficiency would save them millions of dollars. Outside the hearings, businessmen argued just as vigorously. The carriers made exorbitant requests, said the NAM's committee on interstate commerce, because of "the unappeasable demand of the Wall Street owners for more dividends. This concentration of the railroad interests of the country in the hands of less than a half dozen men" was a national crime. In return a spokesman for the railroads called the leading shippers "professional agitators guilty of deliberate misrepresentations worthy of the cheapest political charlatans." In February 1911 the Interstate Commerce Commission, impressed by the arguments of Brandeis, ruled against the rate advances.[39]

These two major defeats within a year forced the railroad executives to reorient their policies. Now they listened to a few perceptive colleagues, including Frederic A. Delano of the Wabash and William W. Finley of the Southern, who even before the Panic of 1907 had urged better public relations. President Roosevelt, in a letter to George Perkins during the attempt to raise rates in 1908, had added his recommendations: talk less about increases and more about "equalizing" rates; and channel requests whenever possible through shippers, laborers, and ostensibly impartial public figures. After the rate decision of 1911, the campaign to win public approval became industry-wide. A Western railroad president summarized the approach: "First. We must realize, as I think we all do (after a series of very hard knocks), that the railroads are not strictly private property, but subject to regulation by the Public through its regularly constituted authorities . . . Second. To meet this situation we must endeavor to get in touch with Public opinion . . . Third. The avoidance of action seriously counter to Public opinion except for compelling reasons. Fourth. The disposition to explain these reasons through officers and employees of all grades. Fifth. Efforts to improve service in many cases without hope of reward and for the deliberate purpose of winning public approval."[40]

They hired public relations experts and established publicity bureaus under them. Particularly concerned with the "public opinion" of the shippers, railroad executives visited the large commercial associations and as many as possible of the smaller ones, preaching the same message of accommodation. The raw days of railroad building were over, they declared, and every carrier knew it. Today the keynote among railroad men was service. "We railway men of the United States have been going to school," Finley told a Southern audience. "We have learned that a railway can thrive only as a result of the prosperity of the communities that it serves." No one denied the advisability of regulation; but, they went on to say, no one wanted excessive regulation. Just as the railroads depended upon the regions they served, so the shippers depended upon regular, efficient carrier service; and a regulatory system which rejected every rate increase out of hand would bankrupt the roads and disrupt transportation. The answer to everyone's problems lay in a minimum of government interference and a maximum of private cooperation between shippers and carriers. Supporting the railroads, "manufacturers of railway materials and equipment, contractors in railway construction and dealers in miscellaneous railway supplies" organized the Railway Business Association. The new association, led by George A. Post of the Standard Coupler Company, worked effectively within such organizations as the NAM and National Metal Trades Association to which many members of the Railway Business Association also belonged.[41]

Shipper unity was always brittle. Even a common effort against rate increases had not suppressed the manifold conflicts among cities and regions over rate levels, and once past the hearings of 1910 and 1911, these rivalries intensified. The struggle, already a half-century old, among Boston, New York, Philadelphia, and Baltimore for favorable rate differentials in Western commerce entered an especially bitter phase. So did the equally traditional battle between Chicago and the Twin Cities over the grain trade. At the same time Eastern cities fought to overrule the Spokane rate decision of 1909, which had granted more advantageous rates to Midwestern cities in service to the West Coast; San Francisco and Los Angeles complained that the rate structure favored Salt Lake City and Denver at their expense; St. Louis and Kansas City competed over rates to the Gulf; and New Orleans had discovered thirty-odd rates which they called discriminatory. The railroads, with no control over differentials, sacrificed nothing by posing as the champion of each city and region in turn and watching the rivalries grow. And in portions of the South and West, they encouraged the competition

among the many communities which sought better rail service at each other's expense. By 1912 the combination of railroad propaganda and shipper rivalries had broken the ranks
of the opposition. The National Industrial Traffic League
suddenly became conservative: now it would only oppose
attempts "to abridge in any way the power at present lodged
in the [Interstate Commerce Commission]." After the fall
elections, the carriers planned to try again for higher rates.[42]

V

Attacks upon business privilege during the Panic of 1907
naturally struck the Dingley tariff, and serious revisionists
were prepared to take advantage of them. By late 1907 those
businessmen interested in tariff reform had settled upon the
new program of a permanent, fact-finding commission and
had found their leader in the National Association of Manufacturers. A year before, President James Van Cleave had
selected Herbert E. Miles, a wagon manufacturer from
Racine, Wisconsin, as chairman of the NAM's tariff committee, and with some difficulty the two men had committed
the association to a strong tariff commission. Miles, also
president of another revisionist organization, the National
Association of Agricultural Implement and Vehicle Manufacturers, charged ahead with a campaign for immediate
tariff reform. For months this brash and energetic man made
little headway. Then came the panic. Senator Albert Beveridge, who had recently rebuffed Miles, now responded to
the pleas of the NAM. In cooperation with Van Cleave and
Miles, Beveridge drew up a bill for a strong tariff commission
composed of businessmen, and introduced it in January
1908.[43]

Van Cleave committed "all the power [the NAM] controls"
to the cause. More ambitious, Miles organized an *ad hoc*
lobbying committee to press for the Beveridge bill. The
budget which Miles proposed to his committee read like a
roster of business revisionism: $3,000 each from the NAM,
the American Reciprocity Tariff League, which represented
Midwestern agricultural interests, and the Merchants' Asso-

ciation of New York, which served exporting manufacturers, importing retailers, and ocean shippers; $2,000 apiece from three trade groups — the National (New England) Cotton Manufacturers' Association, the American Meat Packers Association, and the Interstate Cotton Seed Crushers Association — and from a spokesman for exporters, the New York Board of Trade and Transportation; and $1,000 each from the National Association of Agricultural Implement and Vehicle Manufacturers, the Association of Licensed Automobile Manufacturers (interested in the Canadian trade), the Chicago Association of Commerce, and the Chicago Board of Trade. To be complete, the committee should have included the Boston Chamber of Commerce, several of whose members worked with Miles, and the National Association of Boot and Shoe Manufacturers, which never cooperated well with other groups.[44]

Several forces combined to defeat the bill. Congressmen who resented interference in tariff matters or who believed in protection fought it both in Congress and within the Republican party councils, with Senator Aldrich and Sereno Payne, chairman of the House Ways and Means Committee, their chief spokesmen. President Roosevelt preferred to equivocate in 1908, an election year, and leave the tariff for Taft in 1909. Finally, New York financiers feared tariff disturbances while the economy was still unstable. After a spirited attempt Beveridge acceded on March 15 to the persuasive George Perkins and accepted crippling amendments to the commission bill which kept full control over the tariff in Congress. The next day Beveridge wrote Miles that they would have to postpone their fight until after the elections. The Republican platform that June promised revision with proper consideration for differences in foreign and domestic production costs plus a reasonable profit for American manufacturers; it did not mention a commission.[45]

Although Miles considered himself a good Republican, he could not let his campaign rest. He vowed he would "hit Payne between the eyes." Throughout the summer and fall Miles attacked the Dingley tariff, cast aspersions upon the

Republican platform, and above all condemned the existing method of tariff-making as incompetent and corrupt. Once past the elections, Miles and Van Cleave stepped up their drive hoping to pass a strong commission bill before the Republicans could begin revising the tariff. Van Cleave, in a public letter which refused Payne's invitation to appear before his committee, declared that no self-respecting citizen could associate himself with the evils of a political tariff. Then in December Henry Riesenberg, an Indianapolis cigar manufacturer, wrote to Beveridge offering to organize "a great National body" to publicize the tariff commission. The Senator referred him to Miles and Van Cleave, and the leaders of the NAM took charge. In the name of their association, they called a national convention for mid-February in Indianapolis to mobilize businessmen behind a commission bill. The unauthorized publication of a letter of endorsement from President-elect Taft helped to attract a large gathering to the National Tariff Commission Convention, which demanded the full sweep of businessmen's reforms: a strong, permanent tariff commission; federal assistance, including reciprocity treaties, for increased foreign trade; and a generally lower tariff level. Before dissolving, they established the National Tariff Commission Association, with Miles as chairman and Henry R. Towne of the Merchants' Association of New York as treasurer. For a moment, revisionists from the East and Midwest, importers and exporters, were united.[46]

But as Democratic reformers had discovered in 1894, businessmen grew faint-hearted as soon as Congress considered specific duties. It was as if, beneath the surface of reform talk, they had believed all along the protectionists' theory of the interdependent tariff which disintegrated whenever people pulled here and there at its parts. After all, almost all revisionists were, in their own fashion, sincere protectionists who wanted to retain most of the high duties. First the moderate reformers deserted. "Can't something be done to hurry up action on tariff question?" David Parry telegraphed to Beveridge. "This protracted delay is killing business for God's sake." Then one by one the serious revisionists weakened, leaving only the most hearty, such as the shoe manufacturers, to fight against the protectionists. In a crisis, businessmen quickly forgot general principles, and a strong tariff commission, which Beveridge again introduced, was an early casualty. Even Miles and Henry Towne, president and treasurer of the National Tariff Commission Association, failed to mention it when they appeared before the House Ways and Means Committee. Miles restricted himself to the tariff on steel and Towne, who was president of the Yale and Towne Lock Company, to higher duties on imported locks. Before the Payne-Aldrich tariff bill passed, protectionist Congressmen had stripped Beveridge's commission to the weakest possible tariff board, even lacking definite authorization to investigate.[47]

And the revisionists had met effective opposition from the four citadels of protection — the Home Market Club, the American Protective Tariff League, the Philadelphia Manufacturers' Club, and the American Iron and Steel Association. From the moment Miles and Van Cleave assumed control of the NAM, these organizations dogged the "National Association of (Free Trade) Manufacturers" with accusations: when the panic struck, the NAM had caused it; when recession followed, the NAM kept the economy from recovering; when Taft faced William Jennings Bryan in the Presidential campaign of 1908, the NAM threatened a Democratic victory; and when the association's leaders criticized Congressional tariff-making, they insulted the duly elected representatives of the people. In February 1909 a hostile circular from the Home Market Club lowered attendance at the association's tariff convention in Indianapolis. At the same time those who belonged both to the protectionist organizations and to the NAM disrupted the association's tariff movement from within. From time to time a protectionist resigned with a flourish from the NAM in protest against tariff reform, and the Home Market Club followed immediately with stories of mass defections. Other protectionists, some of them highly placed in the NAM, remained inside the association, attacked Miles, and waited.[48]

Slowly these tactics brought results. The zealous Miles made his enemies' task easier by seeming to document each of their claims. A letter written during the 1908 campaign to Beveridge which said, "We certainly have given the Democrats a good deal of literature, and will give them a thousand times more if we don't get our bill," explained precisely why Republican businessmen did not trust him. Furthermore, he alienated congressmen whose votes were needed against labor legislation. Gradually protectionists, Republicans, and antiunionists joined forces to demand his resignation. As Miles single-mindedly pursued his goal, Van Cleave found he had to devote more and more of his time to defending the association and his friend from Wisconsin. Incessantly he denied rumors of a large drop in membership. By 1908 each issue of the NAM's magazine contained the president's declaration, "The National Association of Manufacturers is Unequivocally and Absolutely Devoted to the Principle of Ample PROTECTION to All American Industries." As a last resort, Van Cleave demanded that the worst enemies of Miles within the association resign. But by the time Congress was revising the tariff, all of the NAM's inner circle except Van Cleave had decided against Miles. Out of respect for their president, otherwise a popular leader, the board of directors waited until Van Cleave had left office in May 1909 before they removed Miles from the NAM's tariff committee and stopped contributions to the National Tariff Commission Association.[49]

Along with their shrewd campaign against Van Cleave and Miles, the protectionists also conducted the more familiar one in praise of a high tariff. Anticipating Senator Aldrich's notorious remark by almost a year, the protectionists at once interpreted the Republicans' campaign pledge of 1908 to mean "Tariff Revision Upward." Never defensive, they extolled the Dingley tariff throughout its revision. By the summer of 1909, they enjoyed the double satisfaction of a new bill approximately as protectionist as the last and a consensus among businessmen that the Payne-Aldrich tariff would have to do. Not even the most ardent business revisionists dared to suggest in 1909 that Congress try again: their colleagues wanted a rest. Because Congress had lowered certain duties, the professional protectionists shammed some dissatisfaction in public; but privately they thanked Aldrich for his "great service to American industry" which "[entitles] you to the highest praise and warmest gratitude of all who are interested in this legislation." [50]

Just as businessmen settled back, other Americans, particularly in the Midwest, demanded honest tariff reform. Their complaints rose with the cost of living, and by 1910 businessmen were involved in elaborate defenses of themselves and the Payne-Aldrich tariff against accusations that they had caused rising prices. Before a special congressional committee investigating prices, some businessmen in the manner of Thomas Nast's Tweed Ring stood in a circle pointing at each other: manufacturers blamed retailers who blamed wholesalers who blamed manufacturers. The more experienced protectionists located the source of trouble with the farmers, the unions, or an extravagant government. And, as usual, some offered moral explanations: a popular lecture began "Americans as a rule eat too much" and ended with strictures on the use of liquor and tobacco. Employing James J. Hill's phrase "the cost of high living" as their keynote, these businessmen conducted a sententious campaign for thrift and self-restraint. Significantly, almost every answer from businessmen in 1910 exonerated the tariff. [51]

But reform sentiment grew. In 1911 President Taft tried to redirect it toward Canadian reciprocity. Both from relief and from sincere conviction, businessmen outside of the rabid protectionist organizations responded enthusiastically to the treaty, and for a few months veteran revisionists led an exuberant campaign for adoption. Along a tier of Northern cities, including Boston, Buffalo, Detroit, Minneapolis, and Duluth, businessmen described Canadian reciprocity as the formula for unlimited profits. Eventually their excesses em-

barrassed the administration, which had presented the treaty
as a national measure. One too many public statements from
James J. Hill, who had just published a book recommending
union between the United States and Canada, led Taft to
request that the railroad magnate relinquish his campaign to
someone "not identified with the milling or railway interests"
of the Northwest. After bitter debate, the treaty passed the
Senate. Then it failed in Canada, where Hill's absorption
thesis and similar insults had rankled a proud people.[52]

For businessmen the wound festered, because discussion of
Canadian reciprocity only intensified the agitation for general
tariff reform. Congressmen, whose constituents competed
with Canadian agriculture, retaliated against the Taft administration by cooperating with low-tariff Democrats to pass
"pop gun" bills which revised the Payne-Aldrich Act schedule
by schedule. Piecemeal revision, promising uncertainty at a
time when the economy was already shaky, hardened businessmen's opposition to any reconsideration of the Payne-
Aldrich tariff. Throughout the North they joined the industries directly affected by the "pop gun" bills — textiles, iron
and steel, shoe manufacturers — in denunciations of "sectional tariff tinkering."

When Taft, in vetoing the bills, berated Congress for
ignoring the administration's tariff board, businessmen suddenly recaptured their enthusiasm for a permanent, nonpartisan tariff commission. Since 1909, as the President kept
the tariff board alive by the ingenious use of general appropriations, businessmen had paid it little attention. The
supposed champion of a commission, the National Tariff
Commission Association, had devoted itself to reminding
Americans that "the greatest eras of prosperity . . . have
been under a high protective system." When the association
revived its campaign in 1911, the purpose of the commission
contradicted the one Miles had advocated three years before.
Where the earlier commission had offered a way of bypassing
a protectionist Congress in order to lower the tariff, the new
one would bypass a low-tariff Congress in order to save
protection. As John Kirby put it, a strong commission would

enable "the legitimately protected interests of the country [to] escape from what may prove a destructive attack by extremists." Among the recent converts, the National Association of Wool Manufacturers and the Home Market Club of Boston entered the campaign as soon as Taft's board upheld the woolen goods schedule of the Payne-Aldrich tariff. The revisionist sentiment which Canadian reciprocity renewed could thrive only within a protectionist framework. And by 1912 businessmen feared that Congress would construct the next tariff up from free trade rather than down from protection.[53]

VI

Businessmen's concern with reform remained for the most part a private matter between themselves and the federal government. Through the Taft years businessmen showed very little sympathy for other people's reform problems. This the bankers discovered in their battle against a postal savings system. Although practically all of them disliked the idea, the savings and country bankers complained most bitterly. "I [am] opposed to [postal savings] from a conviction that the Government should not enter business in opposition to any class of her citizens," a banker from Paducah told the Kentucky Bankers' Association. "Such business ventures upon the part of the Government tend toward the creation of a paternal form of government which I believe to be fundamentally wrong." Another from Missouri prayed "that the dominant political party in control at Washington will not permit partisan politics to get the better of its sane and safe business judgment and enact legislation guaranteeing deposits under the guise of a Postal Savings Bank law." And out in Highmore, South Dakota, a banker claimed that postal savings was "gotten up for the benefit of the Poll [sic], Bohemenian [sic] and Italian, foreigners who are afraid of American institutions. [Americans] will not patronize it."[54]

But other businessmen either said nothing about postal savings or commended it for the very reasons bankers denounced it. Postal savings would "foster the economies of the people under Government guarantees," said the Boston Associated Boards of Trade; and it would keep the immigrants' money in the United States, added the Philadelphia Trades' League. In the postal savings legislation of 1910, the bankers won only a place within the new system for their two-percent government currency bonds, which would lose their value in any financial reorganization. These the government used as an investment for postal savings.[55]

The debate over parcel post demonstrated the same indifference. To express companies and to most small-town merchants, government delivery constituted the great threat of the day. The only beneficiaries, declared a member of the Trans-Mississippi Commercial Congress, would be "those great commercial fakirs, those mercantile mendicants, the mail-order and catalogue houses." A merchant from Mt. Vernon, Ohio, warned his fellows, "The big cities of this country have been a menace from the time Thomas Jefferson made that statement to the present time, and we do not want to build them up to the detriment of the country." While the express companies sent their agents to gather protests from the merchants of the South and Midwest, the National Retail Hardware Association and similar organizations formed the American League of Associations to encourage local enterprise and, specifically, to oppose parcel post legislation. Again other businessmen, including the bankers, did not respond. Even middle-sized urban merchants refused to assist; instead, groups such as the Merchants' Association of New York and the Los Angeles Chamber of Commerce protected themselves by endorsing parcel post only along "Rural Free Delivery Routes." In 1912 the small retailers lost in Congress to a combination of farm representatives and the powerful merchants in the Retail Dry Goods Association of New York City.[56]

VII

The moderately prosperous businessmen of the Midwest, who had ranked high among national reformers in Roosevelt's time, fell into disarray during the second phase of the progressive movement. They failed the new tests of leadership. Not only did these businessmen have no plans for general reform, they feared wide-ranging social reorganization; and as progressivism grew increasingly ambitious and optimistic, they, like President Taft, turned cautious and pessimistic. The reform movements which they had done so much to initiate had, in their eyes, turned against them. Torn between a desire for specific legislation and a hostility toward broad reform, they stalled during these critical years of progressivism.

At the same time, the furor after 1907 alerted the most powerful leaders of the American establishment. Earlier challenges to particular prerogatives had irritated; but the scope, the zeal, and the strength of the reformers after the panic posed a different and far more dangerous threat. Now everything seemed in jeopardy. And the reformers, who forecast a new society of the people, boasted that they could command the votes to realize it. A revolt of the masses pushed at the foundations of power.

That, at least, was how American society looked from the perspective of the establishment, and its leaders for the first time in the century fought back in earnest. Tightening credit squeezed the muckraking magazines. Win or lose, the Republican hierarchy grimly determined to keep the reins of the party from insurgent reformers. And beginning in 1908 magnates from the East pre-empted the business campaigns which Midwesterners had led and lost. Wall Street now conducted the movement for financial reform. From the Hepburn amendments to the plans for an interstate trade commission, Eastern big businessmen supplied the new ideas for corporation control. After 1909 the protection which almost all magnates favored dominated business discussions of the tariff. And by 1911, even the Midwestern shippers, most durable among the older leaders, had lost the initiative to Eastern railroad executives, whose experiment in public relations was well underway.

In almost all cases, the business movements became holding operations: the Aldrich plan to institutionalize the power of the most successful financiers; a trade commission to protect, above all, the large corporations; a tariff commission to defend the high tariff; and public relations to check the opposition to the railroads. The well-to-do businessmen from the Midwestern cities stood in a no-man's land between increasingly aggressive reformers and these counterattacks from big business. The dilemma paralyzed the tariff revisionists. City bankers, on the other hand, attached themselves for the price of an assets currency to the Eastern campaign for a central bank. Still others, including the organized shippers and many enemies of the trusts, fluctuated between attacks upon their business opponents and defense of a status quo which changed as they tried to define it.

Just as prosperity had set the tone for the business community before the panic, an unsettled economy conditioned its mood after 1907. Businessmen wanted peace; instead they heard the major issues of the progressive era debated incessantly. The federal government had failed them. There to insure domestic tranquillity, it could not end the discussion and decide. Year by year the tensions from political uncertainty and economic instability mounted to a climax in the elections of 1912.

V

DILEMMA AND MYTH IN POLITICS

The majority which the Republicans acquired during the political revolution of the 1890's remained to curse the party during the progressive era. In 1896 the forces behind McKinley, employing Big Lie mass publicity, so successfully branded the moderate Bryan a woolly-headed revolutionary that respectable reformers in the East and Midwest refused even to consider the Democracy a vehicle for national reform. As the reform impulse spread and deepened, most of these progressives, perhaps after a try at nonpartisanship, operated within the Republican party in lieu of an alternative. At the same time Mark Hanna was completing the interdependence of the national Republican party and a small group of wealthy, powerful businessmen. By scientific assessment of the magnates, Hanna ensured ample campaign funds for the party; the Republicans in turn presented a safely conservative national program. And the Republicans who assumed responsibility for the party's finances after Hanna continued his system.

This was the party which Roosevelt inherited in 1901 and kept in balance through 1908. As pressures within the swollen Republican party mounted after 1909, Taft could neither understand nor control them. Although the Republican split in 1912 represented both a struggle for power and a difference over program, each of these in turn related to the division which the 1890's had built into the party's structure. Would the ambitious and aggressive reformers, lately arrived, or the established professionals control the party machinery? Would aspiring reformers or latter-day Hannas determine the Republican program? By a quirk of politics, Taft led those Republicans beholden to Northeastern businessmen, whom the Ohio lawyer had always viewed with suspicion, while Roosevelt, the New York aristocrat who dealt easily with the magnates, championed reform.

The problem of discipline which a divided Republican party created was aggravated by the progressive mystique of the people. In Hanna's day standing lobbies and agents for big business provided most of the cement for party unity. These men had specific programs, jobs to dispense to politicians and their friends, the money which kept the party functioning, and some ability to influence voters. A congressman might have chafed, but he usually found the combination of arguments irresistible. Yet a reform movement which presumed an awakening of the people offered an alternative. Even if no one could precisely gauge the people's desires or measure their power, almost everyone, whether he approved or not, came to believe in them. The congressman, after devising his plan, told the lobbyists that however sensible their programs, only his would soothe the people; and if he were moderate, he often succeeded without alienating the lobbies and agents.

President Roosevelt, a master of this technique, lost almost as much as he profited from it. Major accomplishments of his administration — settling the anthracite strike, applying the Sherman Act, winning rate, meat inspection, and pure food and drug legislation — had depended upon his skill in using "the people" against lobbies and especially against the magnates' representatives. As each tactic succeeded, the sum of his victories wore down the patience of the party's benefactors. At the same time, Roosevelt discovered that reformminded legislators also enjoyed the greater personal freedom of a "people's" reform era, and many of them would not willingly make Roosevelt their proxy. When panic and depression spurred the reformers and hardened the lobbies and party angels, even Roosevelt partially lost control, as the sullen Republicans at the national convention of 1908 illustrated. Neither J. P. Morgan nor Robert LaFollette mourned his passing. But as Roosevelt left the White House, the task of disciplining the party had fallen beyond the talents of any man. The various methods of Taft, Aldrich, Cannon, LaFollette, and a Roosevelt without office all failed.

It remained for Wilson to bring back efficient party government. Where the party of Hanna was too closely controlled late in the Nineties, the party of Bryan sprawled. Without the unity which majority status supplies, without geographical or programmatic focus, and without a truly national leader, the Democrats suffered from formlessness. Also, they needed respectability. As an individual Wilson provided much of the latter, and as party leader he united Democrats with the same mystique of the people which had helped to rend the Republicans. Lacking the same close ties to the lobbies and business agents which the Republicans had formed, Democrats — some reluctantly, some in relief — rallied to Wilson's standard of the people as the one clear banner in the field.

Implicit in the struggles over leadership and goals lay conflicting definitions of a national political party. Seen in one way, the debate concerned the internal nature of a party. Aldrich conceived the Republican party as a sift into which demands from all sources fell indiscriminately. Party leaders such as he provided a mesh to hold back the coarse appeals of envious and ignorant Americans and allow only a small residue of safe, rational, and politically necessary legislation. But prominent Republican progressives considered the party a vehicle for action, powered by the people's interests and guided by public men with a program. Viewed in another way, the debate concerned a party's obligations. For Bryan, the Democratic party belonged to its most numerous occupational and geographical segment, the rural-small town elements of the South and West. In power the party should serve that majority of its constituents. For Wilson, however, the party in power was responsible to all the people and therefore had to legislate for the nation as a whole. Here as elsewhere the rhetoric of progressivism reflected substantial differences over the nature and uses of power.

I

"I know well the antipathy felt by the average business man today being mixed up in politics," a speaker told the National Business Congress in 1911. "He feels that he has no time for it, is not fitted for it, and is thoroughly disgusted with it." That truism among businessmen provided the background to one of their most perplexing problems during the progressive period. Almost all of them believed that they had time only for business. Other people managed affairs in Washington. And on those occasions when national events did require their attention, businessmen usually restricted themselves to a letter or a petition; anything beyond that took them too far afield. To explain why the National Association of Manufacturers had hired a disreputable political agent, an officer said that he and his associates "were business men and did not know the ways of reaching those in formal control of the Government, and [we believed] that this man was some sort of heeler who knew the ins and outs that we did not know." The heeler especially made sense, for businessmen considered politics intrinsically sordid. "I suppose," sighed J. P. Morgan, Jr., "that when one deals with politicians one must expect to be lied to." By its very nature, a life in politics led to venality, demagoguery, and the lust for power. Who paid? "Businessmen are in great part [the] victims of politics." [1]

Their distaste intensified at each Presidential election. "With the uncertainty in regard to the policy and character of the coming administration," ran a business maxim, "capital becomes timid, all enterprise is restricted and trade and commerce suffer." At worst this became a self-fulfilling prophecy, at best a source of persisting nervousness. A number of businessmen sought relief through a single, six-year Presidential term, for which the National Business League campaigned under the incredible slogan, "Take the Presidency out of Politics." And adding to their quadrennial jitters, businessmen extended the theory as the progressive movement developed. "We know by sad experience," said

Elbert Gary in 1911, "that when Congress is in session there is a sudden and marked hesitation, fear and doubt and distrust which enters the mind of the general business public." [2]

Considering government a servant of business, they never excused politicians for harassing them so. Even many whom Speaker Joseph Cannon had served well automatically cheered the House revolt against that epitome of the party professional. "Politics" explained any business failure, and association with politicians condemned any business opponent. Only a very few politicians received their highest praise as men who stood "above politics." Of course when a businessman suggested legislation, he termed that apolitical: "Give the country a rest from politics for awhile" and endorse the Aldrich plan for a central bank, an advocate pleaded; work for a strong tariff commission, another said, because the tariff "is a business proposition pure and simple, and not a political one." [3]

Yet businessmen could not resist progressive politics. Every year they required new favors of the government and new defenses against their enemies. They faced a dilemma: to seek their objectives, they had to deny an emotional reflex. And nothing affected their relations with the progressive movement more than this quandary.

The crudest answer, particularly common for some reason among country bankers and textile manufacturers, threatened every man and measure which the businessman opposed with a depression. As his lone argument against postal savings, John L. Hamilton, Illinois country banker and a president of the American Bankers' Association, promised that it would "close three-fourths of the country banks, starting a panic such as the country has not known before." Every four years, Arthur H. Lowe, cotton manufacturer from Fitchburg, toured New England with a brief message: "In the event of the election of a Democratic President, mills will cease running and the country will face a terrible situation." William Jennings Bryan served as the favorite target. Bryan's election, read the standard warning in 1908, "would put a stop to the present move toward recovery, it would involve the markets in another collapse, it would chill the confidence of investors, both foreign and domestic, to the point of paralysis, and it would set back the economic progress of the country two or three years." Bryan's candidacy had caused the bankruptcy of the Pillsbury Flour Milling Company, the *Financial Age* reported that same year, and more failures would certainly occur before November. In defense of such statements, the *Economist* declared that businessmen did not threaten: a Bryan victory would guarantee hard times.

The same business groups greeted Theodore Roosevelt's return to active politics in 1910 with their pat message. Widespread support for Roosevelt's new nationalism, they predicted, would "precipitate a season of industrial disturbance greater than any which has existed in say the last 30 years." But as Henry Clews of Wall Street had pointed out earlier to Roosevelt, that kind of opposition brought votes. More mature businessmen, realizing that it reinforced the image of them as unscrupulous dictators over the economy, tried their best to suppress it. Fortunately for Wall Street, few heeded the conclusion of the *Banker and Tradesman*: "If the conservative element at the center of the country's financial department makes up its mind that a discussion of the tariff would have a bad effect on business, it may be taken as more than an even thing that that is just about what will happen."[4]

At the other extreme, a small group composed mostly of magnates had long considered close relations with political leaders sound business. Some limited themselves to generous campaign contributions, which served both as insurance and as a deposit against future favors. On a few occasions these gained the donor a cabinet post, as they apparently did for Adolphus Busch, the St. Louis brewer and Taft patron, whose counsel Charles Nagel became Secretary of Commerce and Labor. At least they assured a friend at court. When the President of the United States treated C. C. Hanch with less respect than the president of Marmon Motor Cars believed his due, Senator Beveridge soon after explained to Taft the virtues of courtesy to powerful manufacturers. And when the Taft administration contemplated antitrust proceedings against the National Cash Register Company, Charles P. Taft cautioned his half brother to go slowly: the Cash Register people were "all our friends." [5]

Other big businessmen supplemented contributions to the parties with retainers for important politicians. In this way Standard Oil and Senator Joseph Foraker reminded each other of their interdependence. And during the depression of 1908, Senator Stephen B. Elkins of West Virginia asked James Stillman for a liberal extension on his loan in a letter which itemized political services recently rendered. In addition, countless little favors strengthened these relationships: some government officials still received railroad passes even after the Hepburn Act had outlawed them; others, such as Charles W. Fairbanks, Vice-President under Roosevelt, found jobs for their relatives through the magnates; even more were wined and dined — a favorite practice of Elbert Gary — when they happened to be in town.[6]

Although these businessmen never lacked an audience of politicians, they required an intelligence service to speak with effect. Because of the importance of communication between the government and big business, some politicians specialized in liaison work between the two. In 1903 one of these, Senator Orville H. Platt of Connecticut, sensed the need for a financial bill to counter assets currency and served as intermediary between Senator Aldrich and the House of Morgan in the formulation of that year's Aldrich bill. In general the Morgan firm had developed an especially fine Washington news service. A partner, usually George Perkins or Henry Davison, often covered the capital in person, and in their absence, Perkins received dispatches from his personal Washington agents. Even more valuable, strategically placed politicians — such as Platt — would volunteer information. In 1909 while Morgan vacationed on his yacht, Aldrich telegraphed news about his tariff bill, including a list of the Senators who opposed the measure. And in crisis men such as Aldrich and Roosevelt's Secretary of the Treasury, George B. Cortelyou, turned at once to the House for advice and assistance. Similarly, Henry Clay Frick gathered his informa-

tion from two Republican leaders of Pennsylvania, James
Donald Cameron and Matthew Quay. But more big businessmen by preference relied upon paid informants. Frank Vanderlip hired, among others, a vice-president of the Riggs National Bank in Washington who recounted each detail of the
U.S. Treasury's operation to his "boss." And in like fashion
other magnates carried on business as usual until an agent's
report alerted them.[7]

Although most of the magnates also disliked politicians,
they had the resources necessary to overcome the political
dilemma. Instead, they wasted their reserves. First, they
relied too heavily upon force and too little upon tact. The
attempts to raise railroad rates in 1908 and 1910, the pressure
for the high Payne-Aldrich tariff, and the formulation of the
banker-dominated National Reserve Association all demonstrated a bluntness which invited defeat. Second, they responded slowly to the shift in governmental power from
Congress to the Executive. During the late nineteenth century Congress had made the government's economic policy,
and the magnates had naturally emphasized congressional
connections. Then Roosevelt tipped the balance, which never
again fully swung back to Congress. Still most big businessmen clung to their congressional inheritance rather than
redistributing their influence throughout the executive
branch. Cordiality with a President did not by itself suffice, as
the amiable Taft proved. More promising were the close,
regularized relations which Gary and Perkins developed with
the Roosevelt administration; but the Morgan men allowed
these to lapse at the critical moment when Taft was forming
his administration. Finally, the magnates saw an increasing
number of new congressmen, who represented the maturing
middle-income groups, replace proven friends of big business in Washington. Although they remained politically
formidable, magnates temporarily suffered the acute pangs
of a declining great power.

Both the magnates and the panic threateners were exceptions. Most businessmen seeking political power looked to
their associations. They wanted an organization, on the one

hand, to shield them from personal involvement; on the other, they expected it to supply the bargaining power which they as individuals did not have. But men who lacked political confidence often led these organizations, so groups of associations sponsored special agencies to act for them, with the parents supplying money and the prestige of their names. Although these proxies — the Interstate Commerce Law Convention, the National Industrial Traffic League, the National Tariff Commission Association, the National Citizens' League, and others — played a significant role during the progressive era, they in turn usually depended upon the few permanent organizations which participated as a matter of course in political affairs. Among these, the National Association of Manufacturers stood pre-eminent.

The NAM seriously entered politics in 1902 with the election of President David Parry. Within a few weeks Parry and his colleagues had transformed the association into a pressure group which opposed all legislation favorable to organized labor. During sessions of Congress, the officers of the NAM encouraged members to write their congressmen in support of the association's political program. (Generally business organizations sent members a guide sheet for their letters, with a reminder "not [to] mention this Association.") And before elections, the association told businessmen how to vote. To assist its politically active members, the NAM hired "The Boys on the Firing Line" — agents in Washington and among local party organizations — whose instructions read: "If any member of Congress is ambitious — and he has a right to be — then it would seem that he might be brought to realize somehow that . . . the substantial and loyal business interests of his state might be the only means by which he could attain a laudable desire." As proof of its interest, the association contributed funds and workers toward the re-election of congressmen who excelled as antiunionists. And because Congress for several years rejected all of the bills which the association had opposed, the NAM soon acquired a reputation for political prowess which its leaders eagerly publicized. The association, they claimed, could accomplish anything with "centralization of power, and . . . regularity, and discipline, and devotion to a cause — and money."[8]

President Parry acted as overseer. While Secretary Marshall Cushing directed the day-to-day work, Parry, whose prominence in Indiana politics inspired rumors that he would run as Roosevelt's vice-president in 1904, provided policy statements and introductions to important political figures. Even after he left office, Parry's Indiana friends — James A. Watson, Representative and lobbyist, and Senator Beveridge — remained the association's most valued political connections. Also under Parry, the NAM concentrated upon particular bills and particular congressmen. James Van Cleave, who succeeded Parry in 1906, reoriented the association's program. Personally directing the political apparatus, he tried to establish the NAM as a primary power within the Republican party. Van Cleave, who had left the Democratic party in 1896, believed that prosperity depended upon the soundness of the Republican leadership, and although he continued the lobbying, he devoted much of the association's energies to impressing the Republican high command. First he tried to bring all employer associations and selected industrial magnates under his direction in the National Council for Industrial Defense. When the new organization became no more than a source for funds, Van Cleave used the money to hire additional lobbyists and increase election aid to friendly congressmen. Then in 1908, supported by a delegation of manufacturers, he went to the Republican National Convention to demonstrate his power. Although he helped to emasculate an anti-injunction plank in the platform, he discovered that the party professionals, particularly Speaker Cannon, made his decisions for him. That fall, instead of leading the Republicans against Bryan, Van Cleave campaigned hard under the direction of Taft's managers.[9]

The next president, John Kirby, lacked Van Cleave's vitality but retained his ambition to dictate to the Republican party. Kirby returned to David Parry's practice of allowing subordinates to conduct the association's daily affairs and used his time to lament the decline of true republicanism. In an effort to improve upon Van Cleave's technique, Kirby approached the party leaders before the 1912 convention. "What we are aiming at," he wrote Taft that February, "is to create, in advance, a sentiment among those who will participate in the June Convention, favorable to a platform so clean and free from obnoxious promises as to justify our urging the manufacturers and businessmen of the country [to support it]. We are . . . mindful of the experience we had in 1908 in freeing the Republican [platform] of the 'evil' planks which the Resolutions' Committee had injected into it and we want to avoid a repetition of that fight . . ." Kirby's arrogant letter received a cool, correct response from Taft's Secretary Charles D. Hilles. Without Kirby's assistance, the Republicans composed a platform which satisfied the leaders of the NAM, and they again gave Taft their full support in the fall campaign.[10]

The members responded weakly to the more ambitious schemes of their leaders. In particular, they resisted Van Cleave's program of reconstructing the Republican party. Although members usually wrote their congressmen upon request, they balked at the participation in party affairs which Van Cleave's project entailed. The NAM, they believed, should stand between them and the seaminess of politics, and monthly commands to "GO INTO POLITICS" did not change their minds. In addition a number of members, some of them Democrats, expected results without making the NAM an adjunct to the Republican party. At the height of his campaign for Taft in 1908, Van Cleave tried to deny the obvious: "I have said time and again that the National Association of Manufacturers is not in politics, nor am I tied to a party, nor do I believe it advisable to have business men play party politics." In 1909 after his dream of political power had dissolved, Van Cleave commented, "We require business men in politics, but there is very little inducement for business men to go into politics." Perhaps, he concluded sadly, another generation would have greater incentive.[11]

Politicians also disliked the more aggressive aspects of the NAM's policy. Regardless of their views on labor legislation, only a handful of congressmen, including Watson of Indiana and Charles E. Littlefield of Maine, identified themselves with the NAM's work. The rest remained aloof. Significantly, the association alienated both Roosevelt and Taft, who considered its antiunionism a political liability. After Parry led a businessmen's movement against railroad rate regulation in 1905, the association lost all influence with Roosevelt, who opposed its efforts at the 1908 party convention. And despite his efforts for Taft in 1908, Van Cleave irritated the Republican candidate with his boasts of remaking the party platform and his descriptions of Taft as an advocate of the open shop. When the NAM requested Watson as Secretary of Commerce and Labor, Taft appointed Charles Nagel, whom none of the association leaders knew. Soon after Taft's inauguration an officer of the NAM complained, "It is dreadful we haven't somebody close to Mr. Taft and that he is left to Seth Low, Gompers and Roosevelt influences, the 'labor trusts' and the 'steel trusts,' and no one of our old-fashioned way of thinking close by." The distance increased during the presidency of the most old-fashioned of them all, John Kirby. The American philosophy, Kirby wrote Taft in 1912, holds "that it is not a function of government to regulate private industry, and that . . . the relation of industry to government should be as remote as possible." Taft did not reply. After a decade of activity the NAM remained as far from the centers of power as before.[12]

In varying degrees other business organizations also experienced difficulties as soon as they encroached upon the private preserve of the politicians. If an association worked for limited objectives, it was generally treated with respect. But when it became loud and demanding, both its reputation and its effectiveness declined. The standing of groups such as the National Founders' and National Metal Trades Associations, erroneously considered appendages to the NAM, rose and fell with the fortunes of the NAM. The National Association of Wool Manufacturers, an example of the highly specialized business organization, succeeded as long as its tariff demands were political possibilities and its lobbying respectful. Passing those points during the late Taft years, it suffered along with the NAM from the congressional investigations of lobbying in 1913.[13]

The receptions accorded the American Protective Tariff League and the Southern Commercial Congress perfectly illustrated the importance of manners in politics. Secretary Wilbur Wakeman of the Tariff League liked to brag. His organization, Wakeman announced in 1902, had convinced President Roosevelt to leave the Dingley tariff alone, thereby killing the Kasson reciprocity treaties in the Senate. A year later when Roosevelt pressed for Cuban reciprocity, Wakeman's agents circulated the rumor that tariff agitation would defeat Roosevelt in 1904. Apologies and professions of loyalty from other members of the Tariff League did not undo the damage; an irate Roosevelt agreed with Senator Henry Cabot Lodge that Wakeman's organization "ought to have no countenance of the administration or of the party generally." Nor did this incident improve Wakeman's judgment. On the eve of the Republican convention of 1908, long after Taft's nomination was assured, the Tariff League still campaigned against him. Although the Tariff League later spent large sums in Taft's behalf, that gaucherie closed the White House door nine months before the new administration took office, and, as in Roosevelt's day, alienated the President's friends in Congress as well.[14] The Southern Commercial Congress did not leave a trail of blunders to follow. Throughout the progressive era, it worked unobtrusively for legislation which prosperous Southern businessmen desired, eschewed other businessmen's causes, and generally kept its opinions to itself. Although Democrats probably controlled the Commercial Congress, both Roosevelt and Taft invariably deferred to it. And when the reformer Gilson Gardner, who called it a dangerous and insidious pressure group, asked congressmen to expose it in 1913, the lobby investigators ignored him.[15]

Many businessmen who thought they were influencing

politics were being used by politicians instead. Usually partisanship prepared their downfall. Some limited their views to a party's platform: parroting current Republican policies made Myron T. Herrick of Cleveland a standing joke at the American Bankers' Association conventions. Other businessmen expressed their party loyalties more subtly. Before accepting new responsibilities in a business organization, Herbert Miles asked a ranking Republican for clearance. "I would not want to take [the chairmanship of the NAM's tariff committee]," Miles wrote James R. Garfield in 1906, "if there is any chance that work along these lines will be out of harmony with the views of the President and Secretary Taft, and yourself in what I feel I can properly call the Roosevelt School." A more alert Garfield would have saved his party from embarrassment two years later. Dutiful Republicans also checked with party leaders before they supported the candidates whom their organizations had endorsed. When John V. Farwell, a prosperous Chicago dry goods merchant, discovered that he had backed the Chicago Association of Commerce's choice for Interstate Commerce Commissioner against the wishes of the Taft administration, he quickly apologized and promised next time to be more careful.[16]

Softened by partisanship, many businessmen fell easy prey to the politician's skill. Roosevelt's casual flattery held Edward Bacon and his Interstate Commerce Law Convention blindly loyal to an administration railroad policy which Bacon had to follow in the newspapers. Taft, experiencing more difficulty with Van Cleave, finally managed the president of the NAM with party discipline. While Van Cleave campaigned for Taft in 1908, he was also suing the officers of the American Federation of Labor in a case important both for the open-shop movement and for Van Cleave personally. But Van Cleave's antilabor activities brought the candidate bad publicity, so Taft demanded through intermediaries — one of them the persuasive lawyer William Nelson Cromwell — that Van Cleave drop the suit until after the campaign. Over the protests of his lawyers from the American Anti-Boycott Association, Van Cleave acceded.[17]

Although it required more skill to guide an entire business organization into camp, politicians, working through partisan members, accomplished this as well. Republican pressure on the American Bankers' Association in 1908 illustrated the technique. When the Panic of 1907 frightened depositors into demanding greater security for their bank savings, William Jennings Bryan responded the next year with a proposal for federal deposit insurance. The Republicans, preferring less government responsibility, countered with a low-interest postal savings program. Bankers everywhere recognized these as matching planks, which appealed to the same widespread desire for deposit safety. Prosperous financiers condemned them both: deposit insurance invited the "rascal . . . to become a national banker"; postal savings placed the government in competition with private enterprise. Although many small bankers agreed, a number of them — perhaps a majority — feared only the direct competition from postal savings. Some already operated under state guarantee systems, and others had been requesting them. These country bankers, who had probably given Bryan the idea in the first place, welcomed federal deposit insurance as the best means of surrounding their banks with an aura of stability.[18]

In August 1908 the Taft headquarters received word from the Midwest that support for Bryan's deposit insurance was spreading rapidly. More and more country bankers, the reports said, believed that under a federal guarantee system they "would no longer be subject in the same measure to the dictation of New York and the East in currency matters." George von Lengerke Meyer, Roosevelt's postmaster general and a champion of postal savings, got in touch with A. Barton Hepburn, a loyal Republican and the only influential New York banker active in the American Bankers' Association, and the two "arranged for educational literature [opposing a deposit guarantee] to be distributed [by the ABA!] among western bankers and prepared to have speakers at the Denver [ABA] convention" who would refute Bryan. Hepburn assured Meyer, Roosevelt, and Taft that the ABA would vote correctly on deposit insurance. At the same time Meyer induced several Republican financiers to defend postal savings before the ABA. At Denver, contrary to the expressed views of most bankers, the association separated the matching planks, condemned Bryan's deposit insurance in the harshest terms, and gently chided the Republican plan for postal savings.[19]

In the same fashion Taft used the National Tariff Commission Association to buttress the administration's tottering tariff board. The President first employed it to lobby for appropriations after the association had elected an ardent Taft supporter, John C. Cobb of the Boston Chamber of Commerce, as chairman. When Congress continued to refuse money for the tariff board, Cobb and Taft decided to stage a businessmen's investigation of the board. In May 1911 Cobb and five other Republican officers of the association, consulting with Taft at each step, conducted their survey and a month later issued a eulogistic report which strongly seconded Taft's request for funds. The following year the President, who privately scoffed at the association as a "false alarm," told the organization how best to assist the Republicans in the congressional campaigns.[20]

Some moderately prosperous businessmen, deploring the politicians' independent ways, decided that they must elect masses of businessmen to public office. After Van Cleave's efforts to capture the Republican party had failed, a number of Chicago's best-known businessmen sponsored the National Business Congress in 1911 to urge their colleagues into politics. But the Congress only underlined the dilemma: a large and enthusiastic audience reflected a widespread interest in politics; and its total absence of results indicated that businessmen still did not want to participate themselves. Appropriately the most extreme plan for businessmen-in-politics came from John Kirby of the NAM. Kirby, who believed that by 1910 "class-conscious agitators" dominated both parties, called for a third party — the businessman's party. "The function of a new party," he explained in his rambling way, "would be to protect the Constitution against

the assaults of its organized antagonists who defy the law,
invent new constructions of the Constitution to meet fancied
needs which they have imagined, but which have no existence in fact, intimidate legislators, defame courts, and endeavor in every way to make the legislative, executive and
judicial departments of our government immediately responsive to every crazy, transient, popular whim and caprice,
which they themselves have created and whose object is the
benefiting of the class to which they belong at the expense
of the majority of the people and the perpetuity of Republican institutions." When the NAM publicly dissociated itself
from its president's project, Kirby, a manufacturer of railway
equipment, sought out Eastern railroad leaders. The magnates politely told him that they preferred the existing parties. Instead of easing their plight, demands for businessmen
in politics served as an excellent index to their frustration.[21]

II

Businessmen lived as satisfactorily as they did with their
dilemma because most of them considered the United States
irrevocably Republican. At each election from 1898 to 1910
they expressed ritualistic worries and then predicted the
Republican victories which followed. Unbroken Republican
administrations became a comfortable part of their lives.
Under the safe party, their need to enter politics lessened
appreciably.

Republicanism permeated the business community. Its
press and the vast majority of its articulate members spoke
as if party loyalty did not require discussion. In 1904 a
Denver broker advertised municipal bonds by celebrating
"the redemption of Denver" through a Republican victory.
"GOOD TIMES AND REPUBLICANISM," he declared,
"Always March Side by Side." "Well, the election is over,"
announced a spokesman for the railroads in November 1911
after Democrats had registered a series of local victories,
"and everybody seems to have been defeated." "The editor
of the *Magazine* has always been a Republican," began an
article in *Bankers Magazine,* and its subscribers read on.

"Our *Bulletin* goes regularly to all the Republican members of both houses," the secretary of the American Iron and Steel Association remarked, and his audience understood. A prominent tariff reformer declared in 1906, "Let the Republican President who is inaugurated on March 4, 1909," guide revision, and his colleagues nodded in agreement. It was this reflex which protectionists tried to touch with their peculiar logic: a high tariff equaled Republicanism; every revisionist must be a Democrat; and Democrat meant Free Trader.[22]

Republicanism reflected the dominance in the business community of big and moderately prosperous businessmen from the East and Midwest, who included only a few Democrats. Some of the exceptions had become Democrats in order to work with local political machines; others inherited a Democratic allegiance and, like the Belmonts and Thomas Fortune Ryan, remained because they exerted more influence there than they could within an already filled Republican hierarchy; and still others, such as Irving T. Bush in ocean transportation and the large retailer Nathan Strauss, liked the Democratic low-tariff policies. In the South the situation was reversed. Except for a few manufacturers, opportunists, and those with strong Northern connections, businessmen operated within the Democratic party, where struggles between the more prosperous businessmen, usually urban, and the smaller ones, often from the towns, explained in part the battle between Cleveland and Bryan Democrats.

Yet none of these Democrats challenged the Republicanism of the business community. The Bryan Democrats in the South and Midwest were as a rule neither well-organized nor particularly articulate. Moreover, to a surprising degree they deferred to the dominant Republican sentiment when they did speak, as if they feared ridicule for their heresy. And the better established Democrats North and South accepted Republican rule with few misgivings. Rarely — and then in private — did one of them complain as bitterly as the financier Daniel S. Lamont: "Was [the Northern Securities Company] prosecution pressed because Mr. James J. Hill and some of his associates are Democrats? . . . Is the

Steel Trust protected because its attorney . . . was Mr.
Knox [Roosevelt's attorney general] himself and because Mr.
Carnegie . . . has pledged himself to pay the republican
[sic] campaign expenses?" Whatever their particular interests in a Democratic victory, they preferred Roosevelt or
Taft to Bryan.[23]
   Even the conservative candidacy of Alton B. Parker in
1904 did not arouse much enthusiasm among well-to-do
Democratic businessmen, perhaps because Bryanism remained so strong within the party or perhaps because Parker
could not win. During the campaign, the financier Ryan
hedged his contributions to Parker with a donation for Roosevelt, symbolizing the uncertainty which still beset the
Cleveland Democrats. And in 1908, with men such as Ryan
and the Belmonts abstaining, only three businessmen contributed as much as $1,000 to Bryan's cause. Of course some,
such as Daniel Tompkins and A. B. Farquhar, missed the
convenience of political friends in power, but not until the
preconvention campaigns of Judson Harmon, Oscar Underwood, and Woodrow Wilson in 1912 did many of these prosperous businessmen again become active national Democrats. Before that, they floated with the tide of Republicanism.[24]
   Business organizations oriented their political activities
around Republican administrations supported by Republican majorities in Congress. Naturally attracted to the party
in power, they followed even more the dictates of partisanship. The major associations advocating rate regulation
never considered working through Democrats nor did any
of the important tariff reform leagues. These biases enabled
James Van Cleave in 1908 to ask his fellow businessmen
in "an impartial, non-partisan way . . . to aid in burying
Bryan and Bryanism under such an avalanche of votes . . .
that the work will not have to be done over again in 1912,
or ever." The officially nonpartisan NAM appealed only to
Republicans — "our party" as the leaders called it — just as
the officially nonpartisan American Protective Tariff League,
which promised the Republican National Committee $200,-

000 in 1908, stated that its work "must succeed or fail with the Republican party." In 1912 when a prominent member of the NAM prepared to serve as chairman of a committee for the Progressive party, President Kirby telegraphed, "Such action on your part repudiates a fundamental principle of the association . . . I beseech you to preserve your integrity by standing inviolate for the party that preserves the sacred right of industrial freedom and personal liberty." Even most magnates failed to prepare for the day when the Democrats would win. Like most articulate businessmen, they accepted Republican government as an essential American tradition.[25]

Businessmen's Republicanism did not preclude criticism of their party. Treating the Republican party as they might a family affair, they expressed constant concern about its welfare and particularly about the President, their party's leader. During the optimistic years before 1907, a large majority of articulate businessmen judged Roosevelt a marvelous leader. He was accomplishing things too long postponed, they felt, and despite his impetuous moments, he unified and elevated American society. Businessmen liked his moral tone, which made each speech "a splendid sermon." The saying went, "President Roosevelt is always sound when he strikes out on morals." And wherever he went, he charmed. After a flashing visit to Little Rock, Roosevelt's host for a few hours recounted the event with obvious worship: "'I am delighted,' said the President, just exactly as he is quoted in the illustrated papers, adding the words 'to meet you.'"[26]

Ordinarily when businessmen mentioned a politician by name in an association meeting, they did so to attack him. Praise, rare and grudging, was almost always generalized. But Roosevelt as a prosperity President shattered the rule. His victory in 1904, a time for rejoicing among most businessmen, led the Chicago Board of Trade to report: "The election of President Roosevelt by an overwhelming majority and a widespread confidence in a conservative yet aggressive national policy . . . imparted to business a strong impetus and revived many industries which awaited the result of the national election . . ." Businessmen paired his name with "the great American," "the most democratic" leader, and "our clever and capable President." James Van Cleave, accustomed to speaking his mind, said in 1906 what many businessmen must have thought: "Gentlemen, I do not re-nominate Theodore Roosevelt for President again in 1908; he is already re-nominated in the hearts of the American people." In such an atmosphere, Roosevelt's business enemies had somehow to attack his actions without mentioning his name.[27]

Panic and depression broke Roosevelt's spell. As under-currents of criticism became the dominant themes, even his defenders admitted that the times required a calmer man. Businessmen from Wall Street to Savannah welcomed the election of Taft, self-controlled and "thoroughly conserva-tive," and, except for a few professional protectionists, ex-pected the new President to continue the best of Roosevelt's policies without such disruptive methods. One journal told it all in a title: "Hail to President Taft, with the Olive Branch and Promise of Prosperity and Peace — No More Industrial Disturbances." But the United States did not recapture pros-perity and peace, and in the troubling times which followed, businessmen talked as if Taft had cheated them. During the ordeal of the Payne-Aldrich tariff, protectionists called "the Taft tariff . . . a long step toward free trade," while revi-sionists found "nothing good in Prest. Taft's attitude." His statements concerning organized labor bothered the NAM. His uses of the Sherman Act disturbed a wide variety of busi-nessmen. According to a spokesman for the railroads, the administration's rate regulation program suffered from "Roo-seveltitis." By 1910 prominent businessmen were demand-ing firmer, safer leadership. To their distress, that was an unfavorable year for conservative Republicans, and they de-voted most of their time that fall to opposing Bryan Demo-crats, Republican insurgents, and above all Theodore Roo-sevelt, who had returned to politics calling for a "New Na-tionalism." The Democrats gained appreciably in the No-vember elections.[28]

Only a small group composed of the NAM and leading

business journals, which would monopolize the discussion of politics for two more years, offered an interpretation of the off-year elections. Already prisoners of wishful thinking, the analysts agreed unanimously upon the meaning of the Democratic success. "The business men of the country," they began, "when justly aroused, invariably become an invincible power." Business votes had elected Taft in 1908, they continued, and now those who had given were taking away: businessmen and their friends had punished the Republicans by electing conservative Democrats. "The salient fact which emerges from the [election] . . . ," read one account, "is that the sober thinking element of the business community control [sic] the situation." Or, "Reduced to simplest terms, conservatism has won a signal victory, while in addition the Republican party has received at last a good and sufficient warning . . ."[29]

After 1910 these business spokesmen set themselves the task of ridding the Republican party of its corrupt elements, known collectively as the "Insurgent Prosperity Wreckers." In particular they concentrated upon Senator LaFollette, never a good Republican by most businessmen's standards, who in 1911 was campaigning hard for the Presidential nomination. "This talk of LaFollette's about 'the people's money,'" said the *Commercial West* in a typical comment, "is about the limit of financial twaddle and what one might expect from a populistic walking delegate." When the La-Follette boom collapsed in February 1912, the analysts cheered the health of the party.[30]

Their next, and more formidable, opponent was Theodore Roosevelt. This one they approached more gingerly, wondering what kind of candidate he would become. Weighing his qualities of leadership and his appeal to the voters against the radicalism he championed, all but one of the analysts decided against him, eventually claiming that he had dictatorial ambitions and would, if necessary, ravage the economy for personal gain. To meet Roosevelt's challenge, they completed the rehabilitation of Taft, which had been underway since late 1911. A few alert businessmen had already warned their colleagues that the President offered the only hope for "a conservative ticket next year." By March 1912 Taft had returned as the stable progressive. After explaining away Roosevelt's popularity that spring, the analysts had a moment of elation in June when Republican leaders secured Taft's nomination. A sane man would lead the safe party to victory in November.[31]

The analysts lived the myth of America's perpetual Republicanism. Neither a national preference for a reforming President nor a split in the Republican party had entered their calculations. Then Roosevelt led his Republicans into the Progressive party, destroying the vital illusion. The commentators excoriated Roosevelt, of course. Bryan and organized labor, one reported, had participated actively in the rebellion. But now for the first time the analysts had to give serious attention to the Democrats, whose candidate had all but won the election.

Two months before, the *Wall Street Journal*, followed by two business weeklies, had amiably endorsed Eugene N. Foss, a renegade Republican who was Governor of Massachusetts, for the Democratic nomination. Who cared that Foss was a political impossibility? His mention fitted the tradition of using conservative Democrats to remind the Republicans of their duty. Once sobered by Roosevelt's revolt, the analysts could only pray that the Democratic convention in July would reject Bryan and any close associate. They received Woodrow Wilson's nomination with evident relief. Disregarding his record as Governor of New Jersey, the analysts fashioned a picture of the Democratic candidate similar to that of Taft. Wilson, a scholarly man with great strength of character, would stand above his party, yet control the lunatic elements within it. (The NAM violently dissented: "To stand for Wilson," it declared, "is to stand for Gompers.") With that they drifted through the campaign.[32]

In contrast to the full record which the small group of analysts left, the large majority of businessmen remained exceptionally quiet in 1912. Between the Republicanism of Taft and the Republicanism of Roosevelt, almost all of them probably selected the former. Their silence, so inappropriate in the Progressive party's crusade, suited Taft's almost non-existent chances of re-election and the general lack of enthusiasm among businessmen for his administration. An uncertainty which the President either encouraged or could not stop had most distressed businessmen about the Taft administration. In particular they had complained about continuous agitation which unsettled the economy. Roosevelt's platform, promising extensive economic and social changes, could not have calmed them.

Those businessmen who followed Roosevelt apparently did so for some combination of three reasons. To men such as B. F. Harris, the banker from Champaign, Illinois, who dreamed of revitalizing rural America, the Progressive party offered a respectable home for the ardent Republican reformer. This presumably explained why the Chicago *Economist*, which called Roosevelt's acceptance speech in August "the most impressive political document since the emancipation proclamation," became the one business journal to support the Progressives. Second, some businessmen desired to contain reforms which they considered inevitable and, in moderation, even desirable. The publisher Frank A. Munsey, a financier of the party, regarded Roosevelt as the restraining force: "while splendidly progressive," he wrote the candidate, "you [are] at the same time amply conservative and sound." Herbert Miles, on the other hand, wanted broader controls. "I felt," he explained afterward, "that it would be exceedingly helpful to [the NAM] and the manufacturers of the country for such men as believe in the Progressive movement in its main purposes and need, to get together equally for constructive purposes, and to steady the movement, and later, instead of appearing individually with little influence before the Progressive men in Congress (whether in the majority or not is immaterial) be able to say that they went sponsor for the movement, and that they had to do certain constructive and reasonable things, and avoid excesses, etc." Finally, Roosevelt's preference for business consolidation and cooperation under government supervision attracted those who considered Taft's use of the Sherman Act regressive. Primarily for that reason George Perkins committed himself and a piece of his fortune to the Progressive party.[33]

These were weak incentives for the business community of 1912. Ardent reformers were scarce. Disliking political involvement as much as they did, few businessmen volunteered to restrain a third party. Certain magnates might have, just as they might have supported Roosevelt out of antagonism to Taft's antitrust policy. Yet contrary to the rumors of 1912 that Wall Street backed Roosevelt in order to stop Taft, big businessmen seem to have feared the Progressives. The leaders of International Harvester and U.S. Steel, who had good cause to hate Taft, reacted sharply against the activities of their associate, George Perkins, in behalf of Roosevelt. With great pains Cyrus McCormick dissociated his corporation from Perkins, personally supporting Wilson and privately assuring Taft that International Harvester did not oppose him; and members of the board of directors of U.S. Steel, led by J. P. Morgan, Jr., tried during the fall of 1912 to purge Perkins from the Steel corporation for his political work, relenting only after the elections had passed. Perhaps an absence of enthusiasm for Roosevelt explained why the Progressive party displayed so prominently the businessmen who did join the movement.[34]

Sweeping Democratic victories in November made the choice between Taft and Roosevelt Republicanism irrelevant, a fact which the dominant figures in the business community had not yet assimilated. A day after the elections one of them could only say, "The expected has happened, only perhaps more so." Even a number of the prosperous Democrats whom Wilson had drawn back to the party found the change in parties unsettling after years of tacit Republicanism. Shattering the illusion of indefinite Republican government and sharpening the dilemma of political participation, the election of 1912 left irresolution and dismay in its wake. The analysts who had seen Wilson as conservative and nonpartisan told the President-elect that a minority leader must act very cautiously. The panic threateners, badly shaken, hastened to deny the inevitability of economic disaster. But frightened optimism did not convince men of John Kirby's stripe, who spoke from the South as well as the North and Midwest. They talked as if the depression had already arrived. Kirby grimly announced that America had reached the crossroads: it would have "self-controlled democracy" or "radicalism"; and he predicted, in an unconsciously revealing figure of speech, that "once we cut the gordian [sic] knot [of the Constitution] our course will be toward chaos." A very few businessmen recommended cooperation with the new administration. When these attitudes mixed together, as they did in January 1913 at the annual convention of the United States Chamber of Commerce, they neutralized each other. Unable to attack a President-elect, yet unwilling to congratulate him, the delegates finally tabled a resolution of "cordial greetings" to Wilson as the "other party" took control in Washington.[35]

VI

THE DEMOCRATS

The domestic climax to progressivism came with Wilson's first administration, not because of it. Given the maturity of the various movements, an administration could guide, but not deny reform. And given the pressures of 1913, another administration would probably have selected models very similar to those of the Democrats. For several years the major alternatives in tariff, banking, and trust legislation had lain before the public; and most organized, powerful groups, whose views a legislator could not avoid knowing, had already determined their positions.

Wilson's leadership combined force, clarity, and the art of the possible. Thus he and his associates made intelligent use of patronage, of an esprit de corps which followed the victory of 1912, and of a new and respected President's eloquence. To guard against a dissipation of energies, they focused congressional attention upon one major issue at a time. And in every important instance, the Democratic leaders traded and balanced to find viable compromises, tipping slightly in favor of the South and West. Congress enacted a moderately low tariff; an income tax of modest intent; banking and currency reform which measured public against private control and centralization against decentralization; legislation to control corporations which linked specific prohibitions to a commission of general powers; and comparable mediation in rural credits and the regulation of produce exchanges. Naturally committed groups complained bitterly; rigidity characterized much of articulate America by 1913. But through 1916 the administration continued to seek com-

promises among organized groups in domestic affairs, just
as it sought a middle road between the power-oriented and
the peace-oriented in foreign affairs. Democratic victories in
1916 confirmed the Wilsonian balance.

I

Businessmen who had hoped that the new President
would proceed slowly were quickly disabused. Immediately
after his inauguration in March, Wilson called a special session of Congress which settled down to a year and a half
of intensive work. Tariff revision, the Democrats' most popular appeal the previous fall, appeared first on the agenda.
Most businessmen, despite their traditional fears of Democratic tariffs, accepted the prospect with unexpected calm.
This more than any other question they believed the November elections had decided. Six months before, when the
professional protectionists had declared the issue "Protection
vs. Free Trade," many other businessmen had joined in
warning that the party of Bryan must not touch the tariff;
now even the high tariff organizations had spent most of
their energy. Some moderate protectionists, who regarded
uncertainty as the greatest evil, welcomed prompt action.
And a number of Eastern and Midwestern exporters and
importing merchants along the Atlantic Coast, generally
quiet since 1909, gambled that a new bill would improve
upon the unsatisfactory Payne-Aldrich tariff.[1]

Of course the usual mass of special pleaders descended
upon Washington, following the advice of the American
Protective Tariff Association: "Above all, don't apologize!"
But hampered by the absence of many familiar Republican
faces and by the President's sharp attack against lobbyists,
they won relatively little in the Underwood tariff of 1913.
The dissatisfied industrialists exploded: "The eager band of
importers" had constructed "The Worst Tariff Bill Ever
Passed," declared the Home Market Club and the American
Protective Tariff Association; the Democratic bill, read a
resolution of the Philadelphia Board of Trade, "threatens
disaster to many of the city's most important industries";

Congress, said the National Association of Wool Manufacturers, had broken the economic law that any tariff "shall give American mills a fair, living chance to operate their machinery." Yet the opposition lacked depth. Although the Underwood Act appreciably lowered most duties, it did not approach free trade, and revisionists from New York, Boston, and the Midwest, congratulating the Democrats on the first honest tariff in memory, predicted that it would benefit the nation. In the South political loyalties tempered the criticism of cotton-goods manufacturers, who took their sincere disappointment with good grace. Above all the economy, which had prospered since 1912, held relatively steady as the bill passed in September. The most common business response claimed, "we shall adapt ourselves to the tariff changes without serious results."[2]

Banking and currency reform, second on the Democrats' list, remained a far more open question as the Democratic Congress convened. Three major problems were unresolved. Should the new banking system be centralized, as the Aldrich plan had proposed, or decentralized in one of the ways its opponents had suggested? What should be the nature of the new currency: if an assets currency, as almost all articulate bankers maintained, backed by what assets; and regardless of its basis, ultimately guaranteed by whom, the bankers or the government? Who should direct the operation of the new system — the bankers, the government, or a combination of the two?

Very generally businessmen responded to these questions in four groups. The financial magnates of New York, and with them most other big businessmen, insisted upon a banker-controlled central bank, emphasizing each half equally. Lesser city bankers, predominantly from the Midwest, although agreeable to a central bank, cared more about the new system's controls. Both in banking and currency they wanted maximum leeway. Most country bankers approached banking reform negatively: no big banker domination and preferably not much government control. On the other hand, as to currency they demanded the inclusion of both short- and long-term rural credits. Other businessmen, usually confused and vague about financial affairs, tended to favor limitations on the power of Wall Street, perhaps of all prosperous bankers. If no program could possibly unite all of them, almost any program would gather some support from the business community.

In June the Wilson administration announced its solution which after certain minor revisions became the Glass-Owen Act of 1913, father of the Federal Reserve system. By proposing a number of regional banks, eventually twelve, under the loose supervision of a Federal Reserve Board, it took a middle ground between the Aldrich plan's central bank and its enemies' schemes for local clearinghouse autonomy. At the outset the currency was exclusively urban, based upon commercial assets and gold, and was ultimately the obligation of the government. And it divided control of the system in a way which seemed to favor the government: where bankers would dominate the regional branches, the government appointed the Federal Reserve Board, whose members could not become active bankers until two years after their terms ended.

The compromises in the Glass-Owen bill temporarily rearranged the divisions of the banking community. Because the bill neither contained a central bank nor allowed full banker control, almost all prominent New York financiers flatly rejected it. In July their spokesman, Frank Vanderlip, opened the assault with a public letter to the chairmen of the House and Senate Banking and Currency Committees, Carter Glass and Robert L. Owen. After insisting upon centralization, Vanderlip asked, "Shall the control and domination of the banking business of the United States . . . be surrendered unconditionally into the hands of a board of seven members appointed by the President?" The new system, he declared, must be run by practical bankers and "be beyond the reach of politicians and without the bounds of political intrigues, ambitions or entanglements." Another financial magnate, disdaining argument with Democrats, reportedly said that Congress should "go ahead and pass a bad bill and let the results teach a lesson from what it would cost." On the fringes of the New York group stood A. Barton Hepburn of the Chase National and Paul Warburg of Kuhn, Loeb and Company. Hepburn, already exceptional as the one magnate active in the American Bankers' Association, grudgingly sought compromises from the Democrats that summer. Warburg, much more conciliatory, remained in communication with Glass throughout the development of the bill and, although an outspoken advocate of centralization, won the Congressman's admiration for his intelligence and relative moderation.[3]

The prosperous city bankers who had united earlier behind the Aldrich plan now split into opposing camps led by Chicago's two most powerful bankers, James Forgan of the First National and George Reynolds of the Continental and Commercial National Bank. Forgan's group, which included Arthur Reynolds, George's brother and acting president of the American Bankers' Association, and E. F. Swinney of Kansas City, chairman of the ABA's legislative committee, matched New York in violent denunciation of the bill. Like the magnates, they wanted to kill it. "Unworkable, impractical and fundamentally unsound," snorted Forgan. That fall Arthur Reynolds told the ABA, "We are facing proposed legislation which I can hardly regard as less than an invasion of the liberty of the citizen in the control of his own property, by putting under government management enormous individual investments and a branch of the country's business which should be left to individual effort." Caviling at every section of the bill, they objected primarily to the Federal Reserve Board and the various regulations of the bankers in the new system.[4]

Approximately an equal number of city bankers, including Festus J. Wade of St. Louis and Sol Wexler of New Orleans, agreed with George Reynolds that they faced "a condition and not a theory" and "that if [they] could not get a whole loaf [they] should take half a loaf." Because they also believed the Glass-Owen bill contained too much government and too little centralization, their statements often irritated the Democrats. Apologizing for himself as well as for the more rigid bankers, Reynolds wrote Glass, "You must realize by this time that almost everybody with whom you confer regarding a matter of this kind is more or less unyielding in his attitude and feels that unless he can get incorporated in the bill everything which he thinks should be there he does not regard the bill with favor." Reynolds might have added that a traditional disrespect for politicians led even the conciliatory bankers to exaggerate and abuse. Yet, carefully distinguishing his associates from the intransigents within the ABA, Reynolds convinced Glass that moderate bankers would accept much less than they requested in public and, barring a few moments of bad temper, cooperated well with Congressional leaders throughout the formation of the bill.[5]

The Glass-Owen bill fragmented the country bankers, whose unusual vigor exasperated both their fellow businessmen and the Democrats. A majority liked the general outline of the bill. According to the Oklahoma Bankers Association, it should have specifically banned the "un-American and monopolistic" practice of branch banking, but at least the system seemed free from big-banker domination. The importance of this emerged in the error-ridden explanation which a prominent Kansas country banker, William Mac-Ferran, gave Wilson of why he and his colleagues supported the bill: "We have needed [financial] reform for at least twenty-five years [which] less than one hundred banks in this country . . . have refused to allow Congress to pass . . . Their machine has been the American Bankers' Association with a strong lobby at Washington, and a strong and alert lobby in attendance at every session of the legislature of every State in the Union." The president of the Wisconsin Bankers Association stated it positively: "We are more willing to take our chances with the Government." In fact some country bankers sought additional powers for the government: a few recommended a nationalized central bank; more argued for federal deposit insurance.[6]

At the opposite extreme a group of country bankers, mostly from the Midwest, considered the dangers from big govern-

ment as great as the threat of big bankers, and they opposed
any legislation. Their spokesman Andrew Frame, maintaining that no fundamental problems existed, told congressmen
that almost no banks would enter the proposed system and
suggested instead minor changes in the Aldrich-Vreeland
Act. As Carter Glass wrote to the banker from Waukesha,
his home "was the only spot on earth where the people were
all so well-to-do that none of them found it necessary to
borrow money." Through these diverse reactions ran one
common theme. Country bankers wanted rural assets recognized and reserve requirements liberalized so that they could
invest in agriculture at home and in commercial enterprises
by way of their city correspondents.[7]

Small and moderately prosperous businessmen outside the
banking community, although shy of concrete suggestions,
expressed much interest in the bill. They talked mostly about
protection from powerful bankers. Even the NAM, which
on principle opposed all Democratic proposals, demanded
that Congress make it impossible for any "men or set of men
acting in unison . . . to create a currency famine." A small
businessman from Georgia just wanted to see "J. P. Morgan
and his crowd of 'Buccaneers' . . . squirm." These indeterminate attitudes might have helped or hindered the Glass-
Owen bill, and President Harry A. Wheeler of the United
States Chamber of Commerce deserves most of the credit
for holding them to a moderate course. With assistance from
Wallace D. Simmons, St. Louis hardware dealer and chairman of the chamber's currency and banking committee,
Wheeler ingeniously polled the chamber's membership so
that its official opinions were accommodating and toured the
country preaching reasonableness toward the bill. To the
disgust of its bitter opponents, the chamber endorsed portions of the bill — among them the Federal Reserve Board
with an Advisory Council of bankers — which almost no
banker publicly supported.[8]

Taken together, these reactions separated businessmen
into two groups. A minority of intransigents included most
Wall Street magnates, James Forgan's followers who held

strategic positions in the ABA, and Andrew Frame's country bankers. The majority were conciliationists, a more random group whose outstanding spokesmen were George Reynolds and Harry Wheeler, and whose opinions ranged from the small bankers who accepted the Democratic measure to men such as A. Barton Hepburn who still longed for a central bank. Because most conciliationists asked for major changes in the bill, some Democrats, including the President, did not differentiate between them and the unyielding opponents. But Representative Glass, Senator Owen, and Secretary of the Treasury William G. McAdoo recognized the importance of the conciliationists and worked to incorporate them in the fight for the Glass-Owen bill. Although Glass relied most heavily upon the economist Henry Parker Willis, he listened to George Reynolds and his colleagues from the early days of the bill's development, and later included others such as Wheeler and Paul Warburg in his correspondence. Owen, in what proved a futile gesture, sent advance copies of his bill to Vanderlip and Benjamin Strong of the Bankers Trust Company of New York. Then that fall he joined Reynolds in an appeal for moderation among businessmen. McAdoo, the most active of all, first recognized the value of Wheeler's efforts and encouraged them. During the summer and fall, he soothed countless bankers with conferences and flattering letters. When the relatively moderate magnate Jacob Schiff admitted that the Democratic proposal had some good features, McAdoo promptly wrote, "You are rendering a public service in helping the country to realize and understand that the efforts of the Administration to enact a financial reform bill are, in the opinion of eminent bankers like yourself, based upon sound fundamentals, even though we may not be in entire accord on some of the details. Your sound and helpful attitude cannot fail to produce a beneficial effect." [9]

Heartened by the cooperativeness of leading Democrats, the conciliationist city bankers called a conference for August 22 in order to convert the intransigents. At the meeting in Chicago delegates from the ABA, forty-seven state bankers associations, and 191 clearinghouses fully represented both sides. After a somewhat harsh opening address by Hepburn, James Forgan, whose rich sideburns symbolized a nineteenth century spirit, demanded that Congress scrap the Glass-Owen bill and start again. The delegates argued. Then George Reynolds, smooth-shaven and suave, stepped forward to deliver the critical address of the conference. As he presented the conciliationists' plea for moderation, he carefully interspersed warnings that the Wilson administration considered the Chicago conference a test of the bankers' willingness to cooperate and that obduracy would mean the end of their influence. The delegates, who knew that Reynolds had seen McAdoo the day before, adjourned to make their peace in private. The following day, they announced a truce which the conference unanimously accepted. A full list of the city bankers' grievances came primarily from the intransigents. The conciliationists wrote the preamble, which stated that "the pending measure has many excellent features and recognizes certain principles fundamental to any scientific banking system." And the conciliationists controlled the committee which presented the conference resolutions to Congress, an act which by itself committed their opponents to negotiation.[10]

Reynolds, who was "fairly well satisfied with the result of the conference," and his followers devoted the next few weeks to gathering endorsements from businessmen for the Chicago resolutions. But as their campaign got underway, an attack from country bankers diverted it. At Chicago the city bankers, intent upon reconciling their own differences, had ignored their sensitive country colleagues, who carried their complaints to the Senate Banking and Currency Committee. "[That] was the coldest deal I ever went against in my life," one of them told the committee. "We were invited there simply and solely to set the stage, to have a crowd, to carry a spear and sing a song and dance around, so that the stage would be full while the bigwigs could have the spot lights played on them . . . [A] committee was to bring in their [sic] resolutions in the afternoon, have them adopted, and they would give us a banquet at night and send us all home drunk and happy." More important than damaged pride, the country bankers wanted rural credits in the Glass-Owen bill. Although the conciliationists partially pacified their critics that October with a special country bankers session at the American Bankers' Association convention, they were fighting "corn tassel" currency until the bill passed in December. And despite their efforts the final measure included short-term agricultural paper.[11]

At the annual meetings of the ABA the conciliationists defeated a last effort by the intransigents to harden the bankers' opposition. Then, on October 23, Frank Vanderlip astounded the business community by proposing a government-operated central bank. Vanderlip, who was simultaneously preparing a bitter denunciation of the Glass-Owen bill's political controls for the New York Clearing House, hoped that his plan would block all financial legislation, and momentarily opposition Senators did rally behind it. The conciliationists, above all desiring less government regulation, placed themselves at the disposal of Glass, for whom they organized an impressive write-in campaign against the Vanderlip plan. The New Yorker's scheme failed; but so did the resolutions of the Chicago conference, which the conciliationists had not had time to press. With the banking community once more divided along familiar lines — New York magnates, Midwestern city financiers, and country bankers — no faction had the leverage to force all of its views upon Congress.[12]

Despite these disappointments, businessmen warmly welcomed the act. Months of diplomacy by both conciliationists and Democrats, and a measure which offered something to every group led businessmen to emphasize the advantages of the Glass-Owen Act. "One of the greatest pieces of constructive legislation ever enacted," cried a jubilant supporter from South Carolina. "It will decentralize the aggregation of money and resources and assist in their more equal distribution throughout the country." From the Midwest conciliationists thanked the Democratic leaders for avoiding extremes, and even James Forgan admitted that the act would benefit the bankers. The advocates of centralization were also quite mild: Warburg congratulated Glass with muted reservations; and both Hepburn and Vanderlip encouraged bankers to enter the new system.[13]

By April 1914 the administration had solved with a minimum of commotion the ticklish problem of determining twelve reserve districts and locating the twelve reserve banks. A month later came the announcement which urban financiers everywhere considered basic to the new system, the nominations for the Federal Reserve Board. For two major reasons they received Wilson's list with enthusiasm. It contained no Bryan Democrats, and it did include Paul Warburg and Harry Wheeler. Warburg and Wheeler were exceptionally shrewd selections: Warburg, the most moderate of the New York magnates, would act as liaison between the new system and vital bankers in Wall Street; and Wheeler, immensely popular among businessmen, would win the confidence of those who distrusted bankers as a group. Although Wheeler declined, Wilson's first slate had already facilitated the acceptance of the new system.[14]

Corporation control came third on the agenda. Here a majority of businessmen considered the Democratic party particularly dangerous, and during 1913 they had gloomily watched congressmen prepare a number of definitions of monopolistic business practices. In April 1914 most of these rules were combined into the Clayton bill, a comprehensive measure which tried to be precise where the Sherman Act had been vague. By covering a wide range of subjects, the bill touched several long-standing business feuds. Where powerful bankers and industrialists vehemently attacked the sections which prohibited interlocking directorates and interlacing stock ownership, almost all smaller businessmen approved. Militant shippers in particular demanded the decentralization of the nation's railroads. But method confused the less powerful businessmen. Although a United States Chamber of Commerce referendum showed more than

ninety percent opposing centralized finance capitalism, only
a few suggested remedies, and these contradicted each
other.[15]

The Clayton bill's ban on price discrimination which
tended to lessen competition aroused even more heated debate. If this provision referred only to price-cutting and
would protect the usual price-maintenance agreements, a
great many businessmen large and small would happily endorse it. That was the plea of the American Fair Trade
League, an organization of retail associations, and the preference of about three-fourths of those voting in a U.S. Chamber referendum. If, on the other hand, the ban included all
price policies which lessened competition, the large New
York merchants and mail-order houses, who opposed any
kind of price maintenance, would support it. Large industrialists, certain that the congressional Democrats would not
knowingly underwrite price agreements, argued consistently
against that portion of the Clayton bill. "Is it wise," complained one of them, "for the Government to devise and
enforce regulations that tend to make us a nation of hag-
gling, deceitful bargainers . . . ?" But, indicative of the
confusion which the Clayton bill created among businessmen, both large New York merchants and small retailers
supported the price discrimination sections. This uncertainty
eventually turned almost all businessmen, regardless of their
views on particular sections, against the bill as a whole. And
their rebellion against "a strait-jacket upon American business" did materially weaken the measure.[16]

Still, most businessmen did not want the Sherman Act as
it stood. Instead of the precision of the Clayton bill, they
preferred elasticity, and that attracted them to the companion Democratic measure for a federal trade commission. Big
businessmen had sought such an agency since their battle
for the Hepburn amendments in 1908, and many more manufacturers and retailers had come to accept it after the prosecution of U.S. Steel threatened their trade agreements. During the spring of 1914 the commission won a host of new
converts among relatively prosperous businessmen in the

East and Midwest who looked to it as a counterbalance to the rigid controls of the Clayton bill.

Initially the Democrats proposed a weak investigatory commission, similar to the Bureau of Corporations, which would help to administer the Clayton Act. In order for the commission to serve their purposes these businessmen had, first, to separate the commission as far as possible from enforcement of the Clayton bill; and second, to strengthen the commission so that it could pass upon the legality of current and prospective business practices. In 1914 the magnates wisely remained in the background, restricting their work for the most part to quiet pressure upon Congress. The National Association of Retail Druggists and the National Retail Hardware Association, who spoke for the small merchants, and the Chicago Association of Commerce and the Merchants' Association of New York, who represented more prosperous businessmen, led the public campaign for a strong commission.

All of them sounded the same note. "Now legislation is needed, not to amend the Sherman Law, but rather to provide the method and means, the *mechanism*, for applying it effectively," declared Henry R. Towne of the Merchants' Association. Because any precise definition of monopolistic practices would soon be outmoded, Towne recommended to congressmen, "Why would it not be better to anticipate that inevitable time and while defining in your [commission] bill the broad principles which shall prevail, to vest the decision . . . in the proposed interstate trade commission?" But, because these advocates insisted, as their predecessors had done, that they suffered most from the vagueness of the Sherman Act, they experienced some difficulty explaining why their ill-defined commission would serve better than the Clayton bill, modernized from time to time. Their most publicized proposal, the Chicago Association of Commerce's "Chicago Plan," opened with the theme, "nothing hampers business like uncertainty." Then it rejected the Clayton bill's "detailed definition of 'restraint of trade,' or unfair practices," and advocated a government agency, "to which we can submit business practices," with "large discretion . . . [to] decide in advance as to the propriety of such proposed arrangements, each upon the merits of that particular case." The hidden logic, of course, was the security and freedom they anticipated under a friendly commission.[17]

During the spring of 1914, while the Democrats were still sponsoring a weak commission, these pleas for an advise-and-consent agency aroused relatively little antagonism within the business community. But early in the summer when Congress greatly increased the commission's discretionary powers, an opposition sprang to life. The National Association of Manufacturers and the Illinois Manufacturers' Association, both veterans of the fight against an alliance between the government and big business, served as leaders. At the first meeting of the NAM's board of directors after Congress had strengthened the commission bill, President George Pope described how, on his own initiative, he had overruled the association's earlier endorsement of a trade commission and called businessmen to battle against the new Democratic measure.

An odd assortment either answered or simultaneously reached the same conclusion. Those small businessmen who also feared cooperation between the government and bigger business and who disliked trade and price agreements kept the U.S. Chamber of Commerce from supporting prejudgment powers for a trade commission. And several established Eastern commercial organizations, including the New York and Providence Chambers of Commerce, which apparently rejected federal investigatory rights on principle, joined the manufacturers associations that summer in a drive to "Urge Congress to Adjourn." Opposing both the Clayton and federal trade commission bills, these businessmen demanded a postponement of all regulatory laws "until," as the NAM put it, "their workability is more clearly demonstrated." "Quick action on important legislation is dangerous," added John Glenn of the Illinois Manufacturers' Association. The Democrats sought a middle ground between the two camps of businessmen. The Clayton Act, although weakened from the original bill, did extend the government's control over monopolistic business practices whenever an executive and the courts wished to use it; and the Federal Trade Commission Act, although far stronger than the original bill, did not authorize the FTC to advise and immunize as many businessmen had requested.[18]

A fourth problem, railroad rates, principally involved the Interstate Commerce Commission. The railroads turned away from a hostile congress which had enacted physical valuation of railroad property and had refused to legalize pooling and appealed instead to the ICC. By 1913 the railroads had softened their business opposition sufficiently to try again for increased freight rates. Astutely the roads asked each group of shippers not to oppose a *general* rate advance. If each association fought only the specific increases which affected it, the enemies of the railroads would diffuse their energies and entangle themselves in countless intercity rate rivalries. Before the rate hearings opened, railroad executives, individually and in teams, visited the leading commercial organizations, and one after another their former antagonists yielded: Frederic Delano of the Wabash convinced the Chicago Association of Commerce to withhold judgment on the question of general increases; Samuel Rea of the Pennsylvania actually won the Philadelphia Board of Trade to the carriers' side; and groups of railroad leaders converged upon the Boston and Cleveland Chambers of Commerce, the Chicago Board of Trade, and the Illinois Manufacturers' Association with similar successes. Outside of the East, most shipper organizations acceded with noticeable reluctance. The Chicago Association of Commerce regarded "this proposed advance in ALL RAIL rates as experimental," and others reminded the ICC "to investigate the question fully." But grudging or not, the shippers were fragmented. Without a mandate from its most powerful members, the National Industrial Traffic League — the core of the shipper's organization — decided "after protracted discussion" that each organization would determine its own rate policy.[19]

The hearings before the ICC proceeded as if the railroads

had written the script. Although hundreds of manufacturers and shipper associations complained about this or that exorbitant freight rate, only a handful of stalwarts — the smaller oil companies and a group of city chambers from Indiana and Michigan — opposed all advances. At the same time the carriers and their friends emphasized general considerations. Railroad executives maintained that their credit structure would collapse without a five-percent advance, and the Investment Bankers of America mass-produced briefs on railroad poverty. In chain letters inspired by the New York brokerage firm of White and Kemble, trust companies and savings banks described how rate increases would benefit "widows and orphans" and the "horny handed wage earner." And the Railway Business Association declared that the alternative to the advances was depression.[20]

The ICC found the show too smooth, and insulting as well. In language characteristic of the successful businessman addressing a politician, one New York broker wrote Commissioner James S. Harlan, "There never was a subject before the country, upon which the masses were so unanimously in accord, as to the justice and wisdom of granting the railroads the relief asked for. You may be very certain this is the truth, and we thought, perhaps, the commission might desire to know this." The commission stated tartly in its report that in spite of "the express statutory obligation of affording a full hearing . . . there appears to have been a set purpose to convince us that the people were of one mind respecting the very important questions involved in the case, and that, in order to satisfy every public requirement, there remained nothing for the commission to do but to register this consensus [immediately]." Instead, the ICC followed the reasoning of Louis Brandeis, whom it had hired as counsel for the unrepresented shippers, and in July 1914 ruled against any increases.[21]

Efficient reforming under Wilson had overcome much of the initial hostility among businessmen. Harsh criticism remained respectable, but now a combination of tariff revisionists, conciliatory city bankers and organization leaders, Midwestern shippers, and numerous, scattered small businessmen tempered it with a qualified praise. From the distraught pessimism of November 1912, the tone of the business community had changed to tentative acceptance, an almost reluctant confidence. Only a prospering economy could sustain it.

By the summer of 1914 the economy had entered a recession which lasted through the following winter. A reaction swept across the country which temporarily destroyed the administration's relations with the business community. Against a background of hard times, the enemies of the New Freedom — professional protectionists and professional Republicans, intransigent bankers, railroad executives, and opponents of all new corporation control — turned the most powerful argument in the businessman's arsenal upon their colleagues: the government's "crusade against business" had wrecked prosperity. Now advocates of a high tariff had only to point in order to prove their equation between Democratic revision and depression, and no businessman dared defend the Underwood Act. The Democrats, declared Arthur Reynolds in his presidential address before the ABA in 1914, "are seeking to turn back the tide of progress . . . [and] plunge us into the sea of socialism." Because of the "hysteria of criticism against big business," Frank Vanderlip told the Southern cotton manufacturers, "business success is looked upon as a crime." That fall, under the direction of Vanderlip and several others, the elect-businessmen movement, a good gauge of businessmen's political discontent, reached new heights.[22]

With far greater vigor than they had shown after the Panic of 1907, businessmen demanded an end to reform. "Many untried economic theories are now being advanced and urged for trial," lamented the president of the New York State Bankers Association. "The *discussion* even of these theories, in the present state of the public mind, causes *unrest* and *disquiet.*" "What the country needs more now than anything else," read a widely circulated letter from the Simmons Hardware Company, founder of the National Prosperity and Sunshine Association in 1908, "is a quiet time — an absolute rest from the agitation of politics, and assaults upon business — it does not make any difference whether it is big business or little business. Nine-tenths of the business of this country is thoroughly honest, but because one-tenth of it may be questionable in character or method, the whole ten-tenths is made to suffer by this agitation which is doing so much damage." On stickers distributed to all applicants, the National Association of Manufacturers printed: "Political Turmoil Means Industrial Depression"; "Free Business from Political Persecution"; "The Country Is Suffering from *Too Much Law*." Capitalizing upon the revulsion to reform, the NAM and other opponents of a federal trade commission expanded their campaign to adjourn Congress into a national business movement.[23]

After the Panic of 1907 the distaste for reform had caused the businessman to reject all changes — except the ones he had advocated. These he had demanded with even greater force. In 1914 a number of businessmen on the verge of success gave up their favorite reforms. Beginning in 1906 the American Cotton Manufacturers' Association had directed a movement for federal regulation of the New York and New Orleans cotton exchanges. Led by Lewis W. Parker, a North Carolina textile manufacturer, it had gathered momentum in the South and a few sections of the Northeast through 1913. But in 1914 when Congress passed the Cotton Futures Act, which met their demands for an official system of cotton grading, the movement outside of the Deep South had collapsed, with Southern cotton manufacturers exceptionally quiet.[24] For many years the smaller millers and grain merchants of the East and Midwest had requested federal grain inspection to provide uniform grading at the grain exchanges. In 1914 as Congress prepared what would be the Grain Standards Act, almost all of its previous supporters disappeared, leaving the defense of the measure to the congressmen who proposed it. Also after the Panic of 1907 businessmen had mixed their criticism of politicians with exhortations to each other on self-confidence and right-thinking; now with few exceptions they traduced Wilson for suggesting that their troubles were in any way "psychological." This was a Democratic recession. The Wilson administration, which prosperous businessmen had predicted in 1912 would be the enemy, had become just that by 1914.[25]

II

In August 1914 war broke out in Europe, and alert businessmen scented profits. Scattered words of horror ("Civilization will be retarded," the *Nation's Business* mourned) gave way almost immediately to the call for expansion. "This is not our trouble," the New York financier A. Barton Hepburn wrote to an Atlanta banker, "it is our opportunity. All the sea trade of Germany is at the mercy of the nations who can and will take it and handle it, and this is largely true of the other great Powers engaged in this war. This is the time for optimism; it is the time for big business." What Hepburn stated privately, the president of the NAM preached publicly: "Markets of the world heretofore largely supplied and commercially controlled by the nations now at war must be supplied," and no self-respecting American entrepreneur doubted who would capture them. The U.S. Chamber of Commerce filled the issues of its magazine with descriptions and suggestions concerning world trade. In the midst of recession, the magic words were "foreign commerce." [26]

An expanded trade required ships. As the percentage of the nation's foreign commerce carried in American ships declined from over sixty in 1860 to ten by 1914, businessmen eager for world markets had demanded a subsidized merchant marine just as they had requested lower tariffs, an improved consular service, and an enlarged information agency within the Department of Commerce and Labor. But they could not agree upon a subsidy: shipbuilders, ship operators, and railroads which wanted to acquire ocean lines all asked for assistance; and specific exporting industries added their appeals for subvention. Because the Merchant Marine League, which might have coordinated these interests, advocated tariff reductions for goods imported in

American-owned bottoms, protectionists banded together
and neutralized its efforts. Simpler plans for an expanded
ocean mail subsidy failed to arouse much enthusiasm. Then
the European war transformed what had been a minor, divi-
sive issue into a subject of immediate concern to businessmen
everywhere. "I took no very special interest in the question
of a mercantile marine [before the war]," a manufacturer of
heavy machinery told congressmen, "except that I felt it was
very essential for the support of our Navy. Since then I have
seen plainly that we are suffering very much in many ways
by not having a mercantile marine of our own." He spoke
for a majority of businessmen who, lacking a plan, simply
demanded action.[27]

The Wilson administration hastily prepared an answer that
August: the government would purchase and operate any
available vessels. The reflexive business response was outrage.
Bitter about the New Freedom, they flooded Congress with
protests against this vicious extension of government into
business. But by the turn of the year, as the bill was dying,
a significant number of businessmen had second thoughts.
The National Lumber Exporters Association telegraphed
that it would not oppose any feasible measure. A few days
later almost forty percent of the delegates to the U.S. Chamber of Commerce annual meeting, disregarding the official
pressure against them, voted in favor of the administration's
bill.[28]

The shift in sentiment continued through the year as an
economic revival softened businessmen's attitudes toward the
administration, and their desire for trade became acute. In
the search for alternative solutions, the government always
figured prominently. In the summer of 1915 a U.S. Chamber
referendum reported a majority of its members in favor of
government ownership, through stock purchase, of a private
Marine Development Company. Also, eighty percent supported federal regulation of ship rates. Although ship interests, led by P. A. S. Franklin of the International Mercantile
Marine Company and Robert Dollar of the Dollar Steamship
Company and supported by the New York and Boston Cham-

bers, still demanded unrestricted government grants, an increasing number of businessmen asked for ships at any price in federal control. In November the National Industrial Traffic League, many of whose members were exporters, stated that private capital could not build ships and resolved "itself in favor of the upbuilding of the American Merchant Marine under the authority of the United States Congress"; and a normally conservative business journal declared, "if we cannot have ships without government ownership, by all means let us have government ownership, bad as it is." By 1916 businessmen were ready to accept an administration bill which would have infuriated them two years before. The Shipping Act, eventually passed that August, allowed optional public or private operation of ships acquired by the government and established full rate control by a shipping board. In an atmosphere of general business approval, even the shipping concerns did not directly oppose federal rate regulation.[29]

With the war and returning prosperity also came a change in business attitudes toward corporation control. Those who had failed to write advisory powers into the Federal Trade Commission Act tried, as soon as the FTC was formed, to do unofficially what they had not accomplished by law. First the United States Chamber of Commerce, then the Boston Chamber of Commerce, the Merchants' Association of New York, and other business groups, set up special committees to cooperate with the new commission. As the chairman of the U.S. Chamber's committee emphasized, his body did not intend to fight the FTC but rather "to exert quietly repressive influence within the field of its responsibility. Neither can such a committee make public many of its activities without endangering much of its influence, for it occupies a confidential relationship [with the FTC]." Individual businessmen also talked with the commission to offer, and receive, advice. From the outset, the FTC responded in kind. Led by Commissioner Edward N. Hurley, a former president of the Illinois Manufacturers' Association who became chairman in 1916, the commission invited close relations with businessmen, particularly by way of their organizations, and praised those with whom it dealt.[30]

The FTC proved especially cooperative in the campaign to exclude export combinations from normal antitrust supervision. This had long been the goal of the American Manufacturers Export Association, which had received some support along both the Atlantic and Pacific Coasts. After August 1914 it became an integral part of the drive for foreign markets, endorsed by almost every important business organization. In February 1915 Secretary of Commerce William C. Redfield, a former member of the American Manufacturers Export Association, recommended such a law to President Wilson, but it was the FTC, primarily Commissioner Hurley, which most effectively encouraged the measure within the administration. As the Webb bill to immunize export combinations moved through the House in 1916, with support from the administration and the FTC, businessmen everywhere showered the commission with compliments.[31]

With a lull in reform after 1914, many businessmen hoped for increases in the Underwood tariff levels. Professional protectionists, whose confidence rose during the recession, predicted catastrophe after the war from massive dumping of cheap European goods, and some of the more moderate protectionists also wrote administration leaders in support of this theory. Advocates of a high tariff unfurled the banner of patriotism. "The doctrine of America first," said Elbert Gary, "applies with peculiar force to the idea of sufficient protection to American industries." More sharply, wool manufacturers accused the Democrats of placing "some other country first and America afterwards" in their tariff policies, and spokesmen for the chemical industry, which thrived in the absence of German competition, alluded to alien influences among low-tariff congressmen. But a much larger number of moderate protectionists and revisionists returned to the familiar plan for a permanent, nonpartisan tariff commission to guard against excessive foreign competition yet encourage international trade. The United States Chamber of Commerce first organized businessmen behind a commission. Then late in 1915 a group of powerful businessmen formed the National Tariff Commission League, whose list of officers read like an honor roll — James J. Hill as president and Cyrus H. McCormick, George Perkins, George Reynolds, James Forgan, and Henry Towne among its board members. Combining forces, the U.S. Chamber and the Tariff League claimed 700 endorsements from business organizations by the end of the year.[32]

In 1916 the Democrats made concessions. That January, President Wilson, apparently convinced that wartime conditions required a new policy, recommended a tariff commission, and a few months later Congress passed the Rainey Act which created a board to study all tariff levels and suggest changes. Also, an antidumping amendment was attached to the Revenue Act of 1916. Although rabid protectionists, led by the American Protective Tariff League, denounced these as evasions of an over-all adjustment, a far larger number of moderates saw the measures as signs of growing Democratic reasonableness.[33]

Bankers first felt the effects of the war and were the first to receive assistance. The European conflict, by disrupting international finance, upset American security values and frightened the New York Stock Exchange into closing. A decision to meet the exceptionally heavy European demand for payments with gold drained the nation's supply of precious metal. To avoid a panic, the bankers needed immediate relief. On appeal from Frank Vanderlip, Comptroller of the Currency John Skelton Williams lowered the gold reserve requirements for big banks — without specific authorization from Congress — and enabled Wall Street to fulfill its obligations unmolested. To alleviate the general crisis, the Treasury Department used the Aldrich-Vreeland emergency currency act of 1908, which Congress had extended another year until the Federal Reserve system could begin operations. By early 1915 the crisis had passed. Bankers of all sizes from every part of the country praised the Treasury Department for its prompt action, admitting that without it the nation "would unquestionably have suffered a complete financial breakdown." [34]

Twice more the Democrats mollified the bankers. In 1916 after intensive lobbying by George Reynolds, Congress passed the Kern Act which eased the Clayton Act's restrictions on interlocking bank directorates. That same year the Democrats successfully compromised on the issue of long-term rural credits. Country bankers, assisted by a few city financiers, were still trying to insert farm mortgages into the Federal Reserve system. Most city bankers, unhappy with the short-term rural credits already recognized, argued strongly against the addition of mortgages as well. Under Myron Herrick's guidance, one group of urban bankers suggested instead private credit cooperatives among the farmers, a plan the country bankers rejected. Other city financiers pretended that they saw no problem. "The American farmer," declared a spokesman for the American Bankers' Association, "is a man of independence. He does not need the stimulation of cooperation with his neighbors." The Federal Farm Loan Act, which provided government funds to finance farm mortgages either through cooperative farm-loan associations or through private joint-stock land banks, did not satisfy any faction. Country bankers had desired a clearer field for themselves, the Herrick group deplored the government's interference, and other urban financiers wanted nothing done. But neither did it arouse much opposition because, while it promised greater rural prosperity, it kept farm mortgages out of the Federal Reserve system. [35]

The new system itself continued to be the Democrats' most popular reform. Quietly inaugurated during the financial crisis in November 1914, it soon proved its value to an expanding economy. Although advocates of centralization asked for fewer reserve districts and ambitious financiers requested more liberal reserve requirements and the legalization of branch banking, no prominent banker suggested replacing the Federal Reserve system. Thus when Charles Fowler and two financial journals tried to manufacture a rebellion against it in 1916, member bankers, defending it as their own, ignored the agitators and repeated in speech after speech, "This system . . . is here to stay." [36]

Of all business groups, the railroads had least cause for satisfaction after 1914. Their only victory came shortly after the war began, when European sales of railroad securities rocked their shaky financial structure. On September 9 a committee of railroad executives, headed by Frank Trumbull of the Chesapeake and Ohio and Daniel Willard of the Baltimore and Ohio, appealed to Wilson for help to avoid bankruptcy. The following day the President generalized: "We must all stand as one to see justice done and all fair assistance rendered ungrudgingly"; but the Interstate Commerce Commission, to whom the railroads were actually appealing, responded by reopening the five-percent rate case. In the midst of the financial crisis, the ICC reversed itself and allowed the Eastern roads the full increase. [37]

Trying to push their advantage, certain railroad leaders demanded a relaxation of the rate laws. "All this regulation which has been working on your business and our business," Howard Elliott of the New York, New Haven and Hartford told one group, "has had the effect of reducing little by little the earning power of this great railway machine." Only free enterprise, he concluded, would bring back prosperity. A shrewd argument in 1914, it lost much of its impact with the economic revival of 1915. Many shippers were embarrassed that they had "been divided by an arbitrarily created false sentiment" the year before, and they reunited to oppose five-percent advances for the Western railroads, a decision which the ICC had postponed when it granted the Eastern roads their increase. After the commission had refused the Western roads almost all of their requests, shippers warned the railroads not to try again. "It is to be hoped," said the St. Louis Merchants' Exchange, "that there will be a little period of quiet now in the matter of general increases of rates so that business can settle down and accommodate itself to a stable rate basis." Most emphatically the shippers refused to consider changes in the existing system of rate regulation. "Any amendment to the law," the National Industrial Traffic League resolved, "might disturb" the entire structure of shipper protection.[38]

A final defeat for the railroads occurred in 1916. When the Railroad Brotherhoods asked for higher pay and a base working day of eight hours, the executives begged Wilson to stop the threatened strike. The President did intervene, but in favor of the unions instead of management. The Adamson Act, which Wilson drove through Congress early in September, legislated the Brotherhoods' major demands. "A pitiful exhibition," one spokesman for the railroads said in disgust. Cleveland would never have surrendered to labor, remarked another, but then "Grover Cleveland was a man." All that the railroads salvaged was a burst of business sympathy.[39]

III

During the Presidential campaign of 1916, most articulate businessmen accepted Charles Evans Hughes as their candidate. Still largely Republican and believing the nation the same, they expected their party to return to power. "Tested in the calm and dispassionate judgment which the atmosphere of the campaign makes quite possible," announced the Home Market Club in September, "there can be no doubt that Hughes, not Wilson, will be the choice of the country." Equally smug, the *Wall Street Journal* reported a month later, "It is doubtful if the stock market, as representing the barometer of public opinion . . . was ever really wrong in its forecast of a Presidential election. It is saying now that Mr. Hughes will be elected." [40]

Yet after four years of Democratic government, their Republicanism was notably mild. Although many businessmen still disliked Wilson's domestic policies, as a whole or in part, renewed prosperity and political concessions had blurred their earlier line of opposition. One index to their discontent, the elect-businessmen movement, had dropped far below its 1914 level. Another sign of moderation was their general indifference when Wilson in January 1916 nominated Louis D. Brandeis, the great antagonist of business privilege, to the Supreme Court. In part the silence reflected the businessman's distrust of lawyers, many of whom campaigned vigorously against Brandeis' appointment. Small and relatively prosperous businessmen had repeatedly complained about the deviousness and dishonesty of the legal profession and had blamed it as well for many of their political woes. Businessmen in politics, they liked to believe, could clean up the "unsatisfactory, involved, demagogic methods resulting from a usurpation of politics by the legal fraternity." But besides disinterest in a lawyer's cause, a large number of businessmen simply did not fear Democrats as they once had. A November rumor that Hughes would scrap the Federal Reserve system recalled the benefits which the New Freedom had brought. Businessmen had learned a valuable lesson: they could do business under a Democratic, as well as a Republican administration.[41]

Probably more important, influential businessmen cared as much about international affairs as about domestic, and Wilson's neutrality appealed to a great many who had prospered under it. In April, Elbert Gary, who a year earlier had expressed satisfaction with Wilson's wartime diplomacy, refused to support Theodore Roosevelt for the Republican nomination because, Gary wrote George Perkins, "he is bellicose." Numerous businessmen who since August 1914 had stated a similar preference for continued neutrality must have listened to Roosevelt's aggressiveness and Hughes' equivocations during the 1916 campaign with considerable alarm. Even a thoroughly unpopular measure such as the Adamson Act did not seem to affect many businessmen's decisions: those who had chosen Hughes were more convinced; and those who stood with Wilson winced and remained. "A serious blot" on the administration's record, admitted the New York *Journal of Commerce and Commercial Bulletin,* which backed Wilson because of his foreign policy. "Still that is not by any means the greatest issue to be affected by the result of the election, and it should not be the decisive one." If Wilson's foreign policy did not produce wholesale business defections from the Republican party, it did entice some strange followers into his camp. On election eve, a group of Republican industrialists, including Henry Ford, the railroad executive F. C. Underwood, and the shoe manufacturer H. B. Endicott, ran a newspaper ad to publicize their support of Wilson on the peace issue. Businessmen elsewhere had already done the same thing.[42]

Wilson's re-election created no crisis comparable to 1912. Surprised and disappointed when late returns from the West held the administration in office, business journals counseled caution to the President as they had four years before. Some also expressed concern about further reforms. But this time there was no obvious loss of poise, no bewilderment about the future. Businessmen could return to work remembering that they had survived, even thrived, under the Democrats.[43]

IV

During the first decade of the century, the important struggles within the business community had pitted moderately prosperous men, primarily from the Midwestern cities, against the big businessmen who concentrated in the East. The maturing of Midwestern business had marked the arrival of the section, and its leaders had sparked the early economic reforms of national progressivism. After the panic, it had been these well-to-do businessmen whom the Eastern magnates, in counterattacking, tried first and most conscientiously to accommodate. Elsewhere businessmen had reacted sporadically, often negatively, to national reform. Yet beneath the battle they were also maturing. As industry slumped after 1907, the agricultural economy continued to do relatively well. Prosperity and improved organization made the businessmen from the South and West and from the towns of the Midwest increasingly assertive. Active first in their states, they arrived nationally in 1912. Nothing better reflected this, nor encouraged it more, than the establishment of the United States Chamber of Commerce. Although founded and led by moderately prosperous urbanites, the chamber depended upon medium and small businessmen outside the major cities for much of its size and elan.

As Wilson had promised in his campaign that year, the reforms of his first administration catered to "the man on the make," many of whom lived in the sections coming late into national progressivism. Of course no party would ignore the established, traditional powers. But for the first time in the progressive era, the Democrats included the full range of middle-income groups in their compromises. Now the conservative unions received their portions through such measures as compensation, child labor, and seamen laws and the Adamson Act; and the organized farmers, particularly from the South, fared even better through a variety of legislation to assist agriculture.

Previously neglected businessmen also shared in the broadening of progressivism. A lower tariff appealed to many distributors and agricultural brokers. Country bankers participated in the horse trading of the Federal Reserve Act and rural credits legislation. Both the Clayton Act, whose restrictions on finance capitalism particularly pleased businessmen from the newly arrived sections and income groups, and the Federal Trade Commission, which most smaller retailers wanted, demonstrated this wider business base. And although many of the millers, the grain and cotton merchants, and the Southern textile manufacturers had grown fainthearted at the last minute, attempts to regulate the agricultural exchanges embodied their long-standing desires. On either side of the recession, many of these men thanked administration leaders for an attentiveness which dominant Republicans had never shown. If voting by income in 1916 remains a mystery, the recently arrived sections did clearly express their gratitude that year by returning President Wilson for a second term.

Moderately prosperous Midwesterners wavered about a middle position. Partially won over by Eastern magnates during the Taft years, many Midwesterners still appreciated the benefits from tariff, financial, and corporation legislation. Partially in sympathy with the antitrust sentiments of the new business arrivals, many of them also recognized that the smaller businessmen were attacking them as well. Caustic toward Wilson during the recession, they had mellowed under the influence of rising prosperity and administrative concessions. On balance, they had not gained enough from the Democrats to love them nor suffered enough to hate them. The magnates, on the other hand, despised the Wilsonian compromise which they believed had in each case sacrificed their interests. Big businessmen did not yet know how to use the modernized structure the New Freedom had outlined.

War conditioned all of these attitudes. The recently arrived businessmen, usually from areas least responsive to internationalism and benefited least directly by the economics of neutrality, had not completed their challenge; and with the unions and farm organizations they pressed the administration for more concessions, several of which came late in Wilson's first term. Still, returning prosperity gave them the confidence to demand these reforms. The better established groups in the Midwest and East saw 1914 as a turning point. Although still interested in amending (rarely in abolishing) the earlier reform legislation, they responded eagerly to prospects of foreign trade as well as to Wilson's intimations of domestic peace. "Business has now a time of calm and thoughtful adjustment before it," the President said late in 1914. Established businessmen anticipated an end to reform and the beginning of profitable international enterprise. Most of them, despite appreciable cooperation from the Democrats, had hoped that Hughes and the safe party would hasten the new era's arrival. Ironically, relief came before a new administration could have taken office.

VII

LABOR

The poor relations among the progressives were the trade
unions in the American Federation of Labor and the railroad
industry. Lowest on an economic scale among the middle-
income groups who engineered the progressive movement,
least certain of their social role, and most sensitive to slights
involving prestige and position, labor leaders hid many ambitions behind a façade of vague class consciousness and
bread-and-butter unionism. They wanted the assurance of
being established — economically, socially, politically — and
they would gladly make all manner of concessions to obtain
that assurance. Economic security meant a union shop, with
control over jobs; social security the recognition of unions as
valuable American institutions and their leaders as spokesmen for wage-earners everywhere; and political security a
place in the decision-making councils of the major parties.
With reason, labor leaders considered the better established
progressives dubious allies in the struggle for acceptance.

If most progressives admitted the need for unions, they
could not say precisely what the unions should do or how
they should do it. Defending collective bargaining as both
legal and just, most progressives felt that the closed shop
violated individual rights, the boycott the canons of decency,
and violence during strikes the elementary principles of social order. Although an arbitrary use of injunctions expressed
the class bias of the judiciary, the United States did require
some shield against European-minded unionists. And where

a sense of justice demanded protection for the workers against sweating and industrial hazards, a reflexive caution suggested that reforms should come to the workers, not through them. "I don't like Labor Day, except as a holiday," one reform mayor remarked. "These parades of working men seem to proclaim a difference between them and the rest of us which ought not to exist." A political party led in part by union officers verged upon a class instrument, one far less likely than a party of public men to view justice for the worker in the context of justice for all. Perhaps the unions would concentrate upon assimilating immigrants who otherwise fell into antisocial habits, hatreds, and ideologies. After all, some of the stanchest Americans whom the better established progressives knew were union leaders.

Labor leaders did not enlist in reform movements with these premises. Susceptible in their own fashion to sweeping moral principles, the unionists did not want to be patronized and rationalized. Sometimes assisting and sometimes embarrassing other reformers, the leaders of the AFL unions worked on the periphery of the progressive movement. They willingly cooperated in attacks against the IWW and the Socialists; and by disparagement and union rules they carefully distinguished themselves from newly arrived immigrants. They talked industrial peace and openly despised scientific management. They often saw Machiavelli in other people's programs for labor and just as often issued extravagant claims of success when the programs were enacted. Far more than other progressives acknowledged, organized labor helped itself to reform legislation in such states as Massachusetts, Pennsylvania, and Ohio. Far more than Samuel Gompers acknowledged, unionists such as the Republican James Lynch of the International Longshoremen and the Democrat John Frey of AFL headquarters ensconced themselves within the major parties. But like organized business, their antagonist at the other end of the progressive's economic spectrum, organized labor participated in reforms selectively and suspiciously.

I

In May 1902 the United Mine Workers struck in the anthracite fields of Pennsylvania. Prominent businessmen in the National Civic Federation and the New York Board of Trade and Transportation immediately asked for a peaceful settlement. Not understanding that the union above all wanted recognition, they argued that employers should always mediate differences over wages and working conditions. A far larger number of businessmen, spread through the East and Midwest, responded with their customary hostility toward organized labor. The arbitration which Senator Mark Hanna and the Civic Federation suggested clearly did not apply, they declared. Two years before, Hanna had forced the mine operators to grant concessions to the workers, and now John Mitchell, the UMW's president, aspired to become "the dictator of the coal business." As the aging entrepreneur Abram Hewitt put it, you did not arbitrate about the "right of a man to his own home." Send troops into the fields, they said, and honest workers would soon be operating the mines again.[1]

The miners stayed out all summer. Mitchell, who had held the strikers at peace, relinquished his demand for union recognition and continued to request arbitration, whereas the anthracite operators, led by George F. Baer of the Pennsylvania and Reading Railway, not only refused to compromise but even claimed God as an ally. That arrogance incensed businessmen wherever antitrust sentiment prevailed. And as fears of a winter coal famine gripped the seaboard, spokesmen for Eastern business also demanded a settlement.[2] President Roosevelt completed the isolation of the coal operators on October third at a White House conference for the operators and the UMW. The operators, feeling the intense pressure for concessions, promised in desperation to mine coal with ample police protection. The numerous businessmen who had welcomed Roosevelt's intervention now declared that the operators must produce or settle. Failing to reopen the mines, the operators conceded. The House of Morgan, which financed the operators, and the Roosevelt administration arranged an Anthracite Coal Strike Commission which would arbitrate all outstanding questions except the central one, union recognition. Mitchell accepted. As the crisis dissolved, almost all business spokesmen praised Roosevelt for his invaluable public service.[3]

It had been a confusing experience. The businessmen who had originally suggested arbitration never realized that the major issue was recognition; many others had drifted from the side of the operators to that of the compromisers; and almost none had thought about the role of the federal government before Roosevelt acted. Neither Mitchell's moderation, the operators' obduracy, nor a shortage of coal explained their muddle. Most businessmen simply had not settled their minds about organized labor in 1902. The trade unions, retaining a skeleton organization during the depression of the 1890's, had grown along with industry in the prosperous years which followed. At the turn of the century the American Federation of Labor approached two million members. The number of strikes and strikers had tripled between 1898 and 1902, and the strength which the United Mine Workers displayed nationally had already been demonstrated many times at the local level. Strikes upset a community's peace and prosperity, giving it a bad reputation. New industries did not locate there; and established industries threatened to move. In 1903 the president of the Denver Chamber of Commerce told his colleagues that an important "home industry" would transfer its plant unless they solved the city's labor problems. Shortly afterward the National Cash Register Company issued the same ultimatum to the citizens of Dayton.[4]

The president of the Denver Chamber recommended a local board with representatives from labor, management, and the public, patterned after the National Civic Federation. As long as enough businessmen believed that the unions, in exchange for better wages and working conditions, would follow management toward industrial progress, these leagues multiplied. During the late Nineties, the National Founders' Association, the National Metal Trades Association, and bituminous coal operators had arranged industry-wide agreements with the unions on such an assumption, and after 1900 the National Civic Federation served as the educational center for cooperative capitalism. But the cooperative capitalism of 1900 assumed a sense of common cause between unions and employers which seldom existed: where labor organizations wanted independence and job security, management expected full freedom in alloting favors and establishing production policies. Of the three agreements, only the labor-management conferences in bituminous survived a brief trial period, and these almost collapsed in the first decade of the new century. Although the anthracite settlement did give mediation and arbitration momentary prestige, the conciliation agencies dissatisfied most employers, who by 1902 were already seeking alternative solutions.[5]

The anthracite strike highlighted another issue as well. Employers had long taken for granted the assistance of both local and national government against the unions. Roosevelt's actions in 1902 disturbed them. At the time many businessmen had applauded the President when he unbent the imperious operators, but they certainly had not wanted a precedent of favoritism for organized labor. And employers relied even more heavily upon the good will of Congress and the courts. How would they respond to the unions, which already showed signs of political ambition?

II

In March 1903 the Anthracite Coal Strike Commission issued its report. Besides compromising the specific disputes between the operators and the miners, the commission pronounced certain general rules for organized labor. "The union," it declared, "must not undertake to assume, or to interfere with, the management of the business of the employer." Because all men are free "to work upon what terms and at what time and for whom it may please them to do so," the union must never coerce nonmembers. "The right to remain at work where others have ceased to work, or to engage anew in work which others have abandoned, is part of the personal liberty of a citizen, that can never be surrendered, and every infringement thereof merits, and should receive the stern denouncement of the law." For good measure, the commission added that the "cruel and cowardly" boycott lay "outside the pale of civilized war." [6]

Out of an embarrassing strike had come a set of business truths which employers proudly quoted throughout the progressive era. These principles belonged to a theory about labor which the business community accepted in much the same thoughtless way it adopted the Republican party. Directly reflecting the views of almost all manufacturers, it apparently satisfied most other businessmen as well. "Labor," the theory began, "is a commodity which the worker has the right to sell and the employer has the right to buy under such conditions as the market offers." The worker's wage depended upon his productivity, for which piecework usually provided the best gauge. If a worker was dissatisfied with his market price, he had two legitimate options. Assuming he was not under contract, he could seek another job. Otherwise he had to increase his productivity through greater skill or by harder work. "Labor," said one employer, "is a blessing to humanity — as a rule, the more work we do, the better it is for us" and, in practical terms, the higher the laborer's wage would be.[7]

"Strikes at best are an unnatural and unnecessary evil of the body politic," the theory continued. "They are forceful attempts to secure something unattainable through natural evolution, and they engender bitter hatred and strife where from the nature of things a harmonious unit should exist . . ." Reasonable men could always settle differences without a work stoppage. Whenever employees did choose not to work, they must stand aside and see whether or not others would accept the employer's terms. If replacements came, the strike failed; if not, it succeeded. Yet some illegality accompanied every strike. Personal violence and property destruction, boycotts and sympathetic strikes, all proved that idlers were demanding what they could not win through fair competition.[8]

Most laborers, the theory's exponents declared, would work in peace if they were left alone. But walking delegates who "thrive on other peoples' troubles" came "from remote headquarters" and deluded the workers into demanding "ten hours pay for nine hours work." Sam Parks, extortionist in the New York buildings trade, epitomized the walking delegate's morals. The McNamara brothers, who confessed to dynamiting the Los Angeles *Times* building, demonstrated his techniques. Behind these troublemakers sat men like Samuel Gompers, president of the American Federation of Labor, who mapped the strategy and gave the orders. Confronted with a national conspiracy, respectable Americans had to defend themselves with "the police, the troops, the jail and the electric chair." Strikebreaking by public or private means was a social service.[9]

The theorists warned that the unions would end America's prosperity. Dedicated "to do as little work as possible for as high wages as possible," labor organizations promoted featherbedding, encouraged slowdowns, and fought scientific management. Their uniform wage scales hung "the one-dollar man about the neck of the ten-dollar man like a millstone." After supporting minimum hour legislation, the unions struck rather than accept a natural reduction in wages for less work. As a result, productivity declined and prices rose. Add a few disturbing strikes and a panic followed. Then when employers tried to liquidate "watered labor," men like Gompers dared to oppose wage reductions.[10]

Fortunately, the theory concluded, a large majority of the workers despised the unions. An honest laborer wanted no restrictions upon his hours of work or his chances of rapid advancement. But duped by a walking delegate and then intimidated to remain in the union, workers needed assistance in breaking the grip of organized labor. Businessmen must champion the cause of free labor by installing and defending the open shop. An ill-defined term which might mean unorganized labor or optional union membership, the open shop always included the employer's control over personnel, wages, and working conditions and his protection against any union pressures which he deemed illegal.[11]

A sprinkling of businessmen dissented from particulars in this theory, especially the view of the laborer as a commodity. Usually these men advocated instead a spirit of benevolence among employers. Committees from the Cleveland Chamber of Commerce discussed sanitary plant facilities and safety rules with local industrialists, and one of its presidents, the cloak manufacturer Morris A. Black, even commended the unions for reminding employers to treat their workers decently. Recognize the laborer's legitimate aspirations, they warned, or strikes necessarily followed. The trade journal *Cotton* chided Southern textile manufacturers for complaining about labor troubles when they imposed "small wages, unpleasant social and school surroundings and long hours" upon their workers. "When the cost of living is increased," said the president of the Chicago Board of Trade during a rash of strikes in 1902, employees naturally demand their "proper and fair share in the common prosperity." That same year George H. Barbour, a stove manufacturer from Michigan, after suggesting that employers delete fifteen minutes from the working day each year until they had established the eight-hour day, told David Parry, "What I want to see is the employer and employee getting closer and closer together, getting rid of strikes and other difficulties, and if the [NAM] can bring this about, it will have a great amount of influence." [12]

Others took issue with the standard theory by differentiating among unions and praising the conservative ones. In 1907 the chairman of the board of the Big Four Railroad, Melville E. Ingalls, who spoke for several other railroad executives as well, congratulated the Railroad Brotherhoods for stabilizing an industry once beset by militant unionists and wildcat strikes. Because unions came inevitably with big business, Ingalls argued, it paid to encourage the peaceful ones. Bituminous operators in the East and Midwest invited the United Mine Workers to help them regularize a highly competitive, dangerously overproduced industry, and, ironically, by the end of the progressive period anthracite outdid bituminous in supporting the conservative UMW. Scared by the success of the IWW in the Lawrence textile strike of 1912, the Boston Chamber of Commerce joined AFL unions in Massachusetts to lobby for a state Industrial Relations Board and a more effective workmen's compensation law. And elsewhere a variety of businessmen favored arbitration laws which they expected to contain the unions and end strikes. As in the case of the humanitarian dissenters, these proponents of conservative, limited unionism wanted management to retain effective power over the workers. Almost all businessmen could still endorse the open shop, an elastic slogan which became increasingly popular as the progressive movement developed.[13]

III

When businessmen turned from theory to practice, they showed considerably less agreement. The most notable difference separated big businessmen, often financiers, from the moderately prosperous industrialists whose lives were imbedded in their factories. The magnates, ignorant of the details of industrial management, devised policies to protect profits and security values and, if possible, to win public approval as well. Smaller employers, whose pride and habits depended upon full control over their companies, thought first of protecting a way of life.

Elbert Gary and George Perkins, who so often pioneered for big business, evolved one answer to the labor question by making U.S. Steel a showcase of open shop paternalism. Their program carefully blended coercion, inducement, and public relations. First, U.S. Steel cleared the unions from its properties. The Amalgamated Iron, Steel and Tin Workers, which never recovered from the mismanaged strike of 1901, disappeared entirely in 1909, and in 1907 the Western Federation of Miners was driven from the corporation's Minnesota ore fields with assistance from "the Mayor of Duluth, the Sheriff and other [local] authorities." Second, Gary and Perkins, over the opposition of the subsidiary companies, centralized the corporation's labor policy. They rebuked the presidents of the subsidiaries for making public statements on labor matters and discouraged them from experimenting in labor-management relations. Third, U.S. Steel introduced a series of welfare projects which began with an employees' stock-purchase plan and came to include a pension plan, some company housing projects, and a variety of shop devices for improved safety, sanitation, and worker convenience. The financial benefits covered those employees who stayed with U.S. Steel a period of years and who showed "a proper interest in [the corporation's] welfare and progress." Fourth, whenever practical, the corporation avoided wage reductions during recessions, preferring more moderate raises in good times to an erratic wage pattern. Finally, through membership in the National Civic Federation, the steel magnates gave lip service to the principles of conciliation.[14]

To the presidents of the subsidiaries — and for the benefit of the public — Gary gave the rationale of the corporation's policy. Labor organizations exist, he said, either because an employer foolishly recognizes them and "the men cannot get employment except by joining the unions," or because the workers feel abused. Therefore, he told the presidents, "make it certain all the time that the men in your employ are treated as well, if not a little better, than other men who are working for people who deal and contract with unions . . . and, so far as you can, cultivate a feeling of friendship, and influence your men to the conclusion that it is for their interests in every respect to be in your employ."[15]

The business press acclaimed U.S. Steel the exemplar of benevolent capitalism. Most popular was the stock-purchase plan: its widespread application, predicted the *Wall Street Journal*, would restrict unions to their rightful function as insurance societies; it would "prevent the Country drifting into Socialism," Myron Herrick wrote Perkins; and a Denver businessman saw a future without strikes. Although a num-

ber of companies already had stock-purchase and profit-
sharing programs, U.S. Steel's plan received special attention
because of the publicity which Perkins gave it and because
of the corporation's importance. Each year more large corporations, envying the labor peace which U.S. Steel enjoyed,
introduced similar plans, and each year, despite indifference
to the plans among laborers, more businessmen forecast the
extermination of the unions. An even wider range of companies adopted pieces of the steel corporation's welfare program, for which there were several other models including
Standard Oil and the Baldwin Locomotive Works in Pennsylvania. And some industrialists, in the spirit of the steel
corporation's system, enlisted employees and renegade union leaders to preach the identity of labor-management interests among their workers.[16]

Toward the end of the progressive era, a few magnates
were extrapolating from the steel formula. In January 1914
Henry Ford announced an eight-hour day and five-dollar
minimum wage for all employees, a plan too radical for the
business press which called it unscientific and demoralizing
to workers elsewhere.[17] More indicative of a trend, John D.
Rockefeller, Jr., announced in 1915 an elaborate program of
employee representation and company and community welfare, all carefully controlled by management, for the Colorado Fuel and Coal Company. Developed by the young
Canadian, William Lyon Mackenzie King, as Director of Industrial Relations for the Rockefeller Foundation, this "industrial democracy" presumably compensated for the company's brutality in suppressing a miners' strike in 1914, and
an enthusiastic reception by the business press suggested its
significance for the years following.[18]

But a large majority of employers lacked the capital and
convictions for the labor policies of big business. Although
some of them utilized profit-sharing's poor relation, the annual bonus, and others introduced portions of the welfare
and safety programs, moderately prosperous industrialists as
a rule regarded the destruction of unions an end in itself. To
achieve this, they fell back upon antiunion techniques which

had served employers for decades. What they added was better organization. Early in the century local employer associations mushroomed in the Midwest, then spread to other parts of the United States. Formed at first to combat specific strikes, many of them remained to oppose unionism generally in their areas, and businessmen elsewhere, profiting from their example, organized in anticipation of labor trouble. In 1902 their fervor brought national results. According to his own account, Daniel Davenport discovered upon traveling about the country that year such an overwhelming sentiment in favor of an antiunion legal service that he formed the American Anti-Boycott Association, which argued and won two of the most significant labor cases of the progressive period, *Lawler v. Loewe* and the Buck's Stove and Range Company case. And, by distributing samples of a model yellow-dog contract, the association struck the unions at their source.[19]

The new spirit also infected established organizations such as the National Metal Trades Association. After its peace agreement with the unions failed, the Metal Trades Association turned to strikebreaking. The association's labor commissioner described its services to a member whose employees balked at the introduction of piecework: "The combatting of this strike was placed in charge of one of the Association's special representatives, Mr. Frank Cheske, who within a very short time filled the places vacated by the strikers with competent men." The commissioner also managed the organization's whitelist. "If our members would make it an invariable rule," he pleaded, "not to engage a man unless he could show one of the cards furnished him by one of the Association's labor bureaus, the danger of labor disturbances would be reduced to a minimum."[20]

The National Association of Manufacturers was the most important convert to the militant open shop. In 1901 President Theodore Search, a charter member of the National Civic Federation, stated that "questions involving the relations between manufacturers and their employes have never been regarded as one of the [Association's] proper functions." Search's close associate, Charles Schieren, even wrote Samuel Gompers to endorse a moderate extension of the eight-hour day on government contracts. A year later, as Davenport founded the American Anti-Boycott Association, open-shop advocates elected David Parry president of the NAM and gave the association a new labor philosophy. The NAM did not oppose "organizations of labor as such," its officers explained, but the employer must have complete control over hiring, firing, apprenticing, paying, and every detail of production. Moreover, the NAM denounced strikes, picketing, boycotts, union blacklists, and any wage agreement made with a labor organization. According to the association's leaders, almost all workers sided with them against the union conspirators.[21]

Among its bans, the NAM included any form of third-party interference in labor disputes. "We do not want any more national arbitration tribunals," announced President Parry shortly after the Anthracite Coal Strike Commission had reported, "to higgle with labor trusts as to the terms upon which they will consent to allow industry to proceed in this country." The NAM's natural enemies were the National Civic Federation and the magnates who supported it. Whenever employers uphold their rights, sneered John Kirby, big businessmen "stand there trembling and shaking with fear that this stock or that stock would be affected." Such cowardice, he said, avoided the fundamental question of the day: "Shall labor unionism or Americanism rule?"[22]

After 1902 the NAM never wavered. Where Parry equated the unions with "mob-power," his successor, James Van Cleave, identified their leaders with "the hired thug and assassin." Next came Kirby who defined unionism as "treason, pure and simple," followed by George Pope, who called the unions "lawless organizations . . . and because they are lawless, they must go." Aside from assistance for a boycott of publishers and printers who recognized unions, the NAM left the specifics of antiunionism to individual employers and trade organizations. Instead, consistent and articulate, it provided moderately prosperous industrialists with a headquarters for strategy and propaganda.[23]

With men like Davenport, its leaders also strengthened the note of fanaticism which the local strikebreaking leagues had first sounded at the turn of the century. At times their abuse of organized labor reflected the certainty of the crusader, at others the pettiness and absurdity of the obsessed. In his 1911 presidential address, Kirby offered as "a fair illustration of the extremes to which labor leaders will go" the fiction that William B. Wilson, chairman of the House Committee on Labor and formerly secretary of the UMW, had wrangled government jobs for every member of his family, including "his wife . . . [who] is janitress of the room of the House Labor Committee." And Davenport's peculiar logic confused even the witness whom he had selected to appear before a Senate committee:

Mr. DAVENPORT. [The eight-hour bill] would make it impossible for the Government to build ships and promote the general peace of the world?

Mr. KEEN. Yes, sir.

Mr. DAVENPORT. It would bring about disarmament in the United States pretty soon, would it not?

Mr. KEEN. Well, I don't know about that; the Government could build the ships, of course.

Those magnates whose social standing and sense of respectability required a more measured tone found the NAM offensive. By silence and through the editorials of the business press, they condemned the early excesses of the militant open-shop advocates. Only after the first generation of zealots had left office and George Pope had moderated the propaganda of the NAM did the magnates associate in any way with this representative of smaller businessmen.[24]

Soon after the NAM's conversion to antiunionism, the AFL expanded its state and national political campaigns. Leaving the state battles to the local employer associations, the NAM led the opposition to labor legislation in Washington, where after 1902 Congress always had before it bills to extend the eight-hour day on federal contracts and to limit the applicability of court injunctions granted without jury trials. As Marshall Cushing of the NAM wrote in 1904, "The Anti-Injunction fight is comparatively easy": many congressmen who did not particularly dislike organized labor placed too much faith in the judiciary as the defender of law and order to limit its independence. A broader eight-hour bill, on the other hand, seemed both reasonable and expedient to many of the same politicians, and these annual struggles taxed the resources of the antiunionists. At first the officers themselves represented the NAM before Congress. Soon the leaders of other employer organizations reinforced the NAM. Within a few years these groups — the NAM, the National Founders', Metal Trades, and Erectors' Associations, the American Anti-Boycott Association, and a few local organizations — had turned over all lobbying to professionals. Year after year the same lawyers appeared before the same committees with the same arguments. Where earlier opponents of eight-hour legislation, mostly large corporations, had emphasized economic hardships, the open-shop associations stressed general considerations: any restrictions upon employers or encouragement to organized labor undermined American institutions.[25]

Although the employer associations bore the brunt of these battles, they received valuable support from all parts of the business community. Firms which held government contracts continued to lobby against the eight-hour laws, and big businessmen in general condemned labor legislation, occasionally reminding congressmen in private of their duty. Finally, a host of business organizations whose members had no direct stake in the bills contributed annual memorials to Congress which denounced all laws which the American Federation of Labor had endorsed. Until 1912, these efforts sufficed.[26]

IV

Behind the challenge of labor legislation lay the threat of the labor vote, a subject so upsetting to businessmen of all varieties that they discussed it in contradictions. Would the workers vote as union leaders directed? Most businessmen, committed to the theory that the officers of a union represented only themselves, had to dismiss their claims to political leadership as a "gigantic bluff." Yet the numbers involved were formidable, and no sooner had business spokesmen ridiculed the idea than they were rallying citizens to counteract "the powerful labor vote." [27]

One popular explanation claimed that timid office seekers kept the myth of the labor vote alive, and the NAM decided to prove to those men who were "playing politics for the labor vote" that they had much more to fear from organized business. In 1906 when the American Federation of Labor called for the defeat of its arch-enemy, Representative Charles E. Littlefield of Maine, Van Cleave sent agents of the association to Littlefield's assistance, and Littlefield won. Unable to believe his own statement that the "very antagonism [of the AFL] undoubtedly elected [Littlefield]," Van Cleave declared a year later, "This problem [of the AFL in politics] threatens to be still larger and still more dangerous in 1908." That year, when the Democratic platform at the behest of the AFL recommended limitations on the use of injunctions in labor disputes, Van Cleave turned the NAM's political power against Bryan, the Democratic candidate, and Bryan lost. Again after the 1910 elections the NAM announced that it had defeated the unions.[28]

Always the Presidency was the most important office to defend, and after the anthracite crisis businessmen anxiously watched Roosevelt for further signs of friendliness toward the unions. Several had reminded Roosevelt, as they praised his solution to the coal strike, that he had actually exceeded his powers. The President somewhat mollified them a year later by reinstating William A. Miller, a nonunion worker, to his job in the organized Government Printing Office, with a ringing statement against the closed shop. But in 1908 he shocked employers by advising the railroads to maintain wages during a recession, an act for which the business press never forgave him. Although President Taft's labor policy gave businessmen little cause for alarm, they could not relax as they once had under Cleveland and McKinley.[29]

Nor could the apparent victories of the NAM compensate for the spread of labor legislation among the states and the mounting pressure for it in Congress. By 1910 every employer association had placed politics first on its agenda. In an address that year on employer liability laws, the president of the National Metal Trades Association spoke with nostalgia of the period when the association had "breathed the old militant feeling, the strike-fighting idea. It is interesting to observe how your thoughts have been turned away from strike-fighting [to labor legislation]." Also, despite the repeated failure of anti-injunction laws in Congress, the judiciary did not appear as secure as before. In 1905 business spokesmen had hailed the Supreme Court for striking down a New York ten-hour law. Only three years later the same Court sustained a minimum hours law for women. And rising demands for the recall of judges, even of judicial decisions, threatened the entire fabric of legal defense: the labor vote — if it existed — would have direct access to the upholders of property rights.[30]

The Democratic victories of 1912 brought all of these fears to a head. The party's record on labor explained in part the Republicanism of the business community. Now, after supplying the votes which passed an eight-hour bill in 1912, the Democrats came to power with a platform which criticized labor injunctions. Although the business press insisted that the labor vote had played no part in the elections, businessmen were obviously shaken. Who could predict what a Democratic President and a Democratic Congress would do? John Kirby dourly suggested revolution.

President Wilson began by appointing a union member, William B. Wilson, Secretary of the new Department of Labor. *Iron Age* prayed that Chicago would have no crisis comparable to the "Debs labor riots" of 1894 because this time the President's labor cabinet would surely let the city burn. Then congressional committees delved into the NAM's political past, forcing the association to retire for a time

from politics. At the same time, the President received a
Sundry Civil Bill with a rider which denied the use of funds
for the prosecution of labor and agricultural organizations
under the Sherman Antitrust Act. As Wilson studied the
measure, a United States Chamber of Commerce referendum
condemned it 669 to 9, and many prominent members, including the Chicago Association of Commerce and the Merchants' Association of New York, added individual appeals
to the President. Although Wilson disapproved "restrictions
of that sort in an appropriation bill," the contrast was plain:
Taft had vetoed the same bill a year before; now Wilson
signed it. With ill-concealed bitterness, the Merchants' Association asked the President to support a constitutional
amendment authorizing an item veto.[31]

Late in the spring of 1914, as Wilson accepted a similar
rider on that year's Sundry Civil Bill, Congress considered a
permanent exemption for the unions in the pending Clayton
bill. No portion of the antitrust measure aroused businessmen
as this one, for it jeopardized the heart of judicial control
over the unions. As David Parry had reminded the NAM in
1903, "A strike that is otherwise lawful and peaceable may
be in violation of the conspiracy law and the Sherman law,
if it is held to be in restraint of trade." Since the use of the
Sherman Act against the Pullman strikers of 1894, courts
had liberally granted injunctions during labor disputes on
just such grounds. In addition the employer associations,
which referred to unions as "labor monopoly" and "labor
trust," had tried for years to force labor organizations to
incorporate so that they would fall more fully under state
and federal antitrust laws. The NAM and the U.S. Chamber
of Commerce, for once in agreement upon a piece of legislation, led businessmen in an impressive display of opposition. Despite a compromise which left the labor sections of
the Clayton bill at the mercy of the judiciary, businessmen
maintained that Congress was leaving the nation defenseless
before organized labor. Once the bill had passed, the NAM
and the American Anti-Boycott Association assured employers that "the changes made [by the Clayton Act] are of such

slight importance as to be practically negligible." But businessmen still regarded the Clayton Act as an ill-begotten victory for organized labor.[32]

The LaFollette Seamen's Act of 1915, following so closely behind the Clayton Act, was anticlimactic, although by materially improving safety regulations and working conditions for American seamen it constituted a more substantial success for organized labor. Again almost all business groups disapproved: a U.S. Chamber of Commerce referendum showed ninety-nine percent against the bill. This time, however, the only forceful opposition came from commercial interests eager to expand America's foreign trade. Particularly active in Boston, New York, Philadelphia, and Los Angeles, these businessmen argued that, with one blow, Congress had destroyed the possibility of an American merchant marine. "It will make conditions 'safe' indeed for the American seaman," the *Wall Street Journal* commented. "It will keep him on land." Although more subdued than the opposition to the Clayton Act, the attacks against the Seamen's Act continued throughout the debate over shipping legislation.[33]

If businessmen required a final contrast between the Taft and Wilson years, the Commission on Industrial Relations provided it. Originally conceived to investigate union violence and industrial warfare, the idea had pleased the employer associations, especially when Taft's list of nominees showed a majority suspicious of organized labor. But Congress delayed approval until Wilson had taken office, and in 1913 the new President offered a slate with Frank Walsh, a reforming Democrat from Kansas City, as chairman and a majority friendly to the union movement. As the commission traveled about the country, it left a trail of employers bemoaning its bias. The open-shop organizations, through a Joint Committee of Associated Employers, tried without much success to undermine the commission's work while the hearings were in progress, and the business press followed them with a bitter commentary. Under Walsh's vigorous direction, the commission condemned in detail employers' current labor policies and even attacked the philanthropic

foundations of big businessmen. Here, said a business spokesman, was "truckling to organized labor" at its worst. By 1916
nothing in the New Freedom had relieved the gloom over
the open-shop movement.[34]

V

During the summer of 1915 rumors circulated that the
four major Railroad Brotherhoods would demand an eight-
hour day with time-and-a-half for overtime. By early 1916
the railroads had launched a campaign denouncing the
eight-hour day as subversive to the nation's preparedness
drive and the wage increases an impossible burden under
the present rate structure. Every sign portended a grim fight.
Professional antiunionists told the railroads to stand firm.
But a large number of businessmen feared a paralysis in
transportation more than they disliked the unions. Commercial shippers in particular urged a peaceful settlement to
avoid "a national calamity." [35]

The setting bore a close resemblance to the coal strike of
1902. But fourteen years and a new cast of characters had
altered the plot. This time management endorsed, and the
unions refused, arbitration, and businessmen of all types
moved solidly behind the railroads. Even the NAM, whose
attacks upon third-party settlements were notorious, joined
the cry for arbitration. Many businessmen, forgetting their
strictures against executive interference, demanded that the
President in the national interest compel the unions to yield.
But Wilson had less success at a series of White House conferences than Roosevelt had had in 1902, and a strike seemed
inevitable.[36]

At the last minute Wilson proposed an eight-hour day and
arbitration of the secondary issues. Now the unions agreed
and the railroads refused. A few shippers, in panic, were
pleading for any settlement, and the President, taking advantage of the sentiment for a peaceful solution, pushed his
answer through Congress: the Adamson Act legislated the
eight-hour day and established a commission to study all
remaining problems. Businessmen everywhere — including

the recently distraught shippers — exploded in wrath. The President, in an open bribe for labor votes, had imposed "peace without honor." What a contrast, they exclaimed, between Wilson's flagrant bias and Roosevelt's impartiality in 1902. Fortunately, the *Wall Street Journal* added, the unions had not captured the Supreme Court, and "in a sporting phrase, the chances are twenty or even fifty to one against the validity of the Adamson law." [37]

In reaction against the railroad crisis and its settlement came a flood of proposals from businessmen to outlaw strikes in transportation. Henry R. Towne, the cool, resourceful lock manufacturer from New York who had pioneered in scientific management, offered the most popular one. The Towne plan would place employees in the public service industries on "a quasi-military footing," bound by contract to remain at work unless "misconduct" or "slack business" necessitated their discharge. Union membership would have no bearing on employment, and management would determine advancements on the basis of each worker's "service record." A neutral arbitration board could manage leftover problems. Eventually, Towne said, this formula could apply to all vital industries. [38]

If the progressive era did not alter the basics of the open shop, it sharpened businessmen's ideas about labor. A Towne plan did not belong to the fumbling days of the anthracite strike. As they hardened toward organized labor, employers and their many sympathizers in the business community increasingly separated themselves from that strand of urban progressivism which advocated recognition and concessions for the unions. No movement which promised benefits for organized labor could draw more than nominal support from the business community; and any man who identified himself with the rights of labor usually drove businessmen from the other causes he championed. Guilt-by-association also diminished their trust in the Democratic party. Articulate businessmen agreed that the Adamson Act climaxed a series of gifts to organized labor which had undermined a sound economy and safe society. Experiences with labor legislation reinforced a conclusion which many of them had drawn from the reform era as a whole: there was no substitute for the right men in office.

On the other hand, as the battle against organized labor stretched out year after year, businessmen's antiunionism lost some of its earlier stridency. More calm and more grim, employers drew closer together. In 1916 the NAM discussed company unionism, while a few powerful industrialists contributed most of the funds for a new agency of the employer associations, the National Industrial Conference Board. Seeming moderation also laid a bridge toward the many progressives who worried about unions, foreigners, and a class-ridden society. So inclined, a reformer could equate scientific management and benevolent capitalism with the general progressive goals of efficiency and humanitarianism. At the very time that the open shop alienated the most ambitious reformers of the Wilson years, employers were preparing the way for cooperation with a larger number of middle-income Americans in the more prudent era which followed the war.

VIII

PREDISPOSITIONS AND PROGRESSIVISM

Never in the American past had so much been demanded in the name of so many whom so few could locate. Early in the century, almost no one doubted that the people had created the progressive movement, and almost no one explained who the people were. If you trusted the spokesmen for reform, the people were hard-working and thrifty, honest and kind-hearted — citizens who looked with pride upon their local community, their state, and their nation. Although still naïve about the ways of the interests, they learned rapidly. Instinctively they chose the good, but their instincts seldom provided the means for accomplishing the good. According to Bryan, you would find the people among Western farmers and townsfolk. Gompers directed you to the neat row houses of the skilled workers. LaFollette's people always sounded like Wisconsinites, and Wilson's like an educated, moral middle class after a profit. Whoever the guide, he almost always steered you from the very rich — "the interests" — and the very poor. In the main the lowest groups did not do things for themselves. You did things for them, and you did things for recently arrived immigrants, for Negroes, for Orientals, not for the people.

Some reformers left you with such a description; more took the next logical step. Although fine raw material for democracy, the people required leadership. A government of broad duties and independent power served as the means, and at the center of government sat the executive, peculiarly the people's office. Educator in morals, in political realities, and in national purpose, the President was simultaneously the representative of the people and their mentor. And upon the President fell the responsibility of selecting exceptionally talented, selfless men to serve as his assistants and to fill the commissions and boards of progressive government. Thus for a large number of reformers the people and the government stood as twin pillars of the good society: the people elected public men who educated and guided a responsive citizenry who in turn re-elected their leaders.

I

When a businessman delivered a speech, he invariably embellished it with maxims about man and society. Taken together these comprised a set of first principles in which most businessmen concurred or acquiesced, much as they accepted the Republican party and the open shop. Yet contrary to the use they made of their Republicanism and anti-unionism, businessmen regularly contradicted their social principles in reacting to specific events. At first glance they seemed either unable to reason or without any convictions whatsoever. Actually the maxims expressed not dogma but a predisposition about what American society was, or ought to be. Whenever businessmen could, in justice to more pressing interests, they applied these principles to particular situations. When their principles proved inconvenient, businessmen shelved them, and after the awkward moment had passed, brought the maxims out again. Countless businessmen executed this maneuver thoughtlessly, effortlessly, and often, without lessening their respect for the first principles. These insulated beliefs served as their protective ideology, a source of security in a world of perverse change. Under the circumstances, it did not matter that the sum of their responses to the progressive movement bore little resemblance to their predispositions.

America's greatness, the maxims said, depended upon a classless society of freely competing individuals whose merits determined their rewards. The people as a whole decided issues of general concern. In private matters, by far the larger and more important area, the individual exercised his own judgment. During moments of stress the businessman usually began by paring down "the people." As soon as he stood with the minority on a public question, he would explain that "the people" did not mean "the mob," an excitable mass which swarmed to the call of the demagogue. Defeated in Congress, an enemy of railroad regulation announced in disgust that the United States was ruled by "the Divine Right of the Multitude. The Crowd is enthroned." And as Congress debated financial legislation, a business journal warned that the mob "should have nothing to do with it; we know what popular sentiment is worth in relation to banking matters — we have a photograph of the crowds lined up at the doors of several banks and trust companies [during the Panic of 1907]." Properly considered "the people" were, as Irving Bush put it, the "thinking" members of society, the "better citizens" whose "natural and patent superiority" qualified them for public leadership.[1]

Moderately prosperous and big businessmen opposed a more direct democracy precisely because it would not distinguish between better citizens and worse. A violation of the principles "ordained by the authors of our constitutionalism," declaimed John Kirby. "Populistic," cried the American Protective Tariff League. The initiative, referendum, and recall, said the National Association of Manufacturers, jeopardized America's "tested, self-controlled representative democracy." To another business spokesman, they meant nothing less than "lynch law." More mildly prominent businessmen also criticized direct primaries for catering to the emotional masses. And although the threat of direct election of senators had served early in the century to chasten the haughty upper house, it too in the final analysis transgressed the tenets of good government. One spokesman summed it up in characteristic business idiom: "We have faith in popular opinion, when it is expressed through the forms of the constitution; when it is instructed, sober, moral, true. But we have no faith in popular opinion when it is rash, passionate, unjust, prejudiced and ignorant."[2]

Excluding particular groups from participation in public

affairs further delimited the people. Women, although seldom mentioned, received almost no public encouragement from businessmen in their fight for equality. Occasionally a journal commented with exasperation about noisy suffragettes; more often someone would remark upon "the instincts and impulses of women, far truer and far nobler than those of men," which required the shelter of the home.[3] Negroes, another group not often discussed, were invariably treated as inferiors. "Notoriously the negro workman of the South is spoiled by prosperity," explained one Northern spokesman. "Advancing his wages has generally the tendency to make him more of an idler, since at higher wages his wants are supplied by fewer days of labor." Politically the Negro was hopeless. "The North gave the black the ballot . . . ," the *Commercial West* reminded its Midwestern readers. "It was the one wrong action of the war." The railroad executive William W. Finley, surveying a half-century's experience, called "the attitude of the South toward the negro not one of race prejudice but of race knowledge."[4]

Business had much more to say about a third group, the immigrant, and on one point all of them agreed: "our immigration does not come from as desirable sources as in earlier times." Many small and moderately prosperous businessmen extended their remarks to class the newcomers from Southern and Eastern Europe with the "Hun, Goth and Vandal" and to reject the possibility of democracy "in a city with a large proportion of foreign element — Bohemians, Pollacks, etc." A resolution from the Scranton Board of Trade, not untypical, characterized the immigration of 1904 as "the most ignorant and vicious of European population, including necessarily a vast number of the criminal class; people who come here, not to become good citizens, but to prey upon our people and our industries; a class utterly without character and incapable of understanding or appreciating our institutions, and therefore a menace to our commonwealth."[5]

Yet only a few commercial and manufacturing groups supported even a mild literacy test to restrict immigration, while businessmen outside of the East, particularly from Alabama, Georgia, the Carolinas, Wisconsin, Minnesota, and the Pacific Northwest, did their best to entice immigrants into the factories and farms of their locality. Disregarding the sources of twentieth-century immigration, these hopeful businessmen lived with an unresolved conflict between social disgust and economic ambition. Southern businessmen, whose longing for immigration seemed at times a sectional obsession, felt the strongest aversion to the Italian and the Slav. The many associations which they established to encourage immigration welcomed only the "better class" of newcomers and disappeared as rapidly as they were founded. In 1914 the Seattle Chamber of Commerce was devising ways to attract immigrants westward at the same time that it complained about the European undesirables who came to the Far West by way of the Panama Canal. When the Detroit Board of Commerce publicized its city abroad, it distributed literature only in England. As the immigrants continued to pour in from Southern and Eastern Europe, steamship lines and railroads argued against these prejudices in vain.[6]

Two supposed answers to this problem received serious attention during the first half of the progressive era. A wide assortment of Eastern businessmen and a few from the Midwest recommended that the federal government either guide the new arrivals from New York to the South and West or route immigrant ships directly to South Atlantic and Gulf ports. Through the National Civic Federation and the Merchants' Association of New York, a number of prominent businessmen sponsored conferences and memorialized Congress to support federal distribution of immigration. In most cases their motive was negative, to "relieve the congestion of our eastern coal cities," as the Pittsburgh Chamber of Commerce phrased it. On the other hand, Southern associations such as the Montgomery Commercial Club wanted distribution only if it brought those immigrants "from the North of Europe . . . who are seeking opportunities in the agricultural sections of this country," and they soon realized that Northern businessmen saw the South as "a disposal plant for the sewage of immigration."[7]

A number of employers, led by the NAM, advocated instead the repeal or loosening of the law banning the importation of contract labor. This, they explained, would enable employers to select only the most desirable Europeans. For a brief moment after December 1906, when Secretary of Commerce and Labor Oscar Straus ruled that importation by the state government was legal, these businessmen believed their campaign won. Business journals congratulated the Secretary, the NAM joyfully spread the news to its members, and, among others, the large iron manufacturers around Birmingham paid the Southern Immigration and Industrial Association to arrange for importations. Two months later Attorney General Charles Bonaparte overruled Straus. Organizations such as the Southern Immigration and Industrial Association suddenly collapsed for lack of funds. After denouncing Bonaparte, the journals and the NAM pleaded once again for repeal of the law, and a few less patient employers, including R. G. Rhett, readjusted their plans for importation in hopes of evading the law.[8]

Until it became clear that the federal government would accept neither distribution nor contract labor, most businessmen just complained about those immigrants already arrived. During the latter part of the progressive period urban businessmen from the East and Midwest talked more often about solving the problem immediately at hand. One alternative, which the National Liberal Immigration League popularized, recommended a period of ten years or more before a newcomer could become a citizen. To a few businessmen this in turn suggested postponing naturalization indefinitely until an immigrant could prove his assimilation complete. Even more appealing, a number of businessmen decided to go after the immigrant and see to it that he became Americanized — "by tactful measures if possible, but if not by force," the Home Market Club of Boston added. Led first by the Eastern magnates who in 1909 sponsored the North

American Civic League, the movement rapidly spread among moderately prosperous businessmen as well. Before 1914 the Cleveland and Boston Chambers of Commerce had inaugurated Americanization programs; then under the stimulus of preparedness patriotism, business groups throughout the East and Midwest sent their task forces after the hyphenate American. A system of night-school education established by the Detroit Board of Commerce and publicized by the United States Chamber of Commerce became their favorite device, and despite the resistance which civic-minded businessmen met from some immigrants and employers, the Americanizers boasted enthusiastically about the results. Still their ambivalence remained. On the one hand, many worried about a deluge of Europe's unfit after the war. On the other, as organized labor profited from the rising demand for workers, some of these same businessmen longed for the day when "our immigration safety valve" would operate again.[9]

The valuation businessmen placed upon themselves provided a third method of modifying "the people." Business, they enjoyed telling one another, brought out the best in a man, and in partial proof, they pointed to the rapidly improving business morality of their own times. A representative for the NAM reported that businessmen everywhere were responding to intelligent criticism by adopting a new and higher code of ethics. Now they realized, as a president of the Alabama Bankers Association said, that "our present problem [is] to industrialize our society without commercializing our souls." "By RIGHT DOING," declared William G. Thomas of the Memphis Merchants' Exchange, "the Exchange [will] revolutionize the commercial life of the city." Businessmen disavowed the unscrupulous techniques of the nineteenth century. Railroad executives, apologizing for the practices of the Gilded Age, heralded the arrival of a new era in railroad morality, and even the staid *Wall Street Journal* ridiculed "the king of petroleum, John D. Rockefeller, who is also prince of financial concentration, duke of trusts, earl of banks, marshal of railroads, knight of the golden fleece of billions, and decorated with the brass medal of the Order of Ida M. Tarbell."[10]

Today, business spokesmen declared, the avidity of a Russell Sage and the secretiveness of a Henry Havemeyer were anachronisms. Businessmen of all types described their philanthropies with self-satisfaction: the Board of Trade of Williamsport, Pennsylvania, was as proud of its $5,000 donation to sufferers from the San Francisco earthquake of 1906 as the New York Chamber of Commerce was of its $782,000; and the president of the Merchants' Exchange of St. Louis announced that the association was "recognized as the almoner of the people of St. Louis in dispensing their [sic] benevolences in case of public calamity." Less wealthy businessmen enjoyed talking about the extraordinary benefactions of the very rich, a major reason why Rockefeller's reputation rose among smaller businessmen during the latter part of the progressive era. Moreover, a number of businessmen came to believe that the modern age required an open book as well as an open hand, and under the guidance of men such as George Perkins they tried to demonstrate their honesty by publishing general summaries of their business affairs.[11]

Businessmen demanded that critics take their ethical progress into account. As the attacks of the muckrakers broadened, businessmen of all types spoke out against them. In 1906 David Parry accused "prejudice writing" of fathering socialism, a president of the American Bankers' Association predicted that journals of "sensationalism" would create a panic, and a small businessman from Virginia expressed fervent thanks that the "muckrake men" had not yet infiltrated his state. Later in the era academicians became a favorite target: the NAM, the American Protective Tariff Association, and Elbert Gary agreed that colleges nurtured the many "Isms" which threatened to undermine America's business civilization. Always businessmen reserved a special bitterness for the so-called yellow press. "It is hard for the average man to estimate the dangers of the yellow press," Ferdinand Schwedtman wrote a friend, "unless you come in contact with the low types of humanity who secure out of these sheets all of their knowledge, all of their inspiration, and all of their dissatisfaction with present conditions." In response to what these men regarded as indiscriminate attacks, they defended themselves uncritically: at those moments all businessmen respected "the rights and interests of their competitors, their customers, their employees . . . and the public generally." Elbert Gary, speaking for the nation's magnates, put it another way: "Men in power are more thoughtful in their treatment of those who are more or less dependent. Those holding positions of trust have been brought to recognize fully the rights and interests of their beneficiaries and are giving them more information and better protection. The rich are more liberal and more charitable and the poor are more grateful for what they receive." [12]

But in time, businessmen showed their sensitivity to these attacks. As a well-to-do Kansas banker said, "It is the arrogance of those so deeply intrenched in corporate authority, and the absolute disregard of the rights of the public . . . that have aroused the general hostility and excited the deep seated feeling of wrong." Therefore if the businessman would "trust the people, serve them, love them, educate them," went a popular sentiment of the period, he could "expect hereafter to receive due consideration and fair treatment by the public." In many forms, public relations became an important part of their responses to the progressive movement. The railroads, among the most severely criticized, constructed the most elaborate system which professionals such as Ivy Lee of the Pennsylvania Railroad ran and which required the active participation of prominent executives. In 1916 the major roads established the Railway Executives' Advisory Committee to handle press relations on subjects common to all of them. Large corporations such as Standard Oil, U.S. Steel, and International Harvester also founded or expanded propaganda bureaus and, again, leading executives and publicity agents cooperated in spreading the story of industry's blessings to the nation. Among the less powerful, cotton manufacturers tried to convince the Southern farmer that the grower and the spinner had identical interests.[13]

No group took the subject of public relations more seriously, or managed it more haphazardly, than the nation's small bankers. Once, they believed, bankers had held the confidence of their patrons and the respect of their communities. Now as a Nevada banker said, "the name of bank or banker . . . is synonymous with all that is dishonest, corrupt and criminal." To regain stature, to improve business, and to discourage unfavorable state legislation, small financiers devoted an extraordinary amount of time in their association meetings exhorting each other to woo their customers and win their communities. Convinced that they were "the natural point of gravity" in their towns, they vowed to become more "broad-minded and liberal" so that they could "give advice and direct [their] fellow men." The Oklahoma Bankers Association condensed their campaign into a resolution: "Whereas, Bankers, as a class, have been criticized, and in many cases justly, on account of lack of interest in the public welfare, and Whereas, Much hostile legislation has resulted therefrom, therefore Be it Resolved, That it is the sense of this body that every member of the association be directed in the interest of themselves [sic] and the people at large to show a greater spirit of co-operation in the upbuilding of each local community."[14]

Their scarcely veiled assumption throughout was that, in a society dedicated to economic progress, businessmen should lead. At times of special stress, that assumption became a declaration. According to an advocate of the Aldrich plan, the people had decided upon the National Reserve Association when the business community, enlightened by the nation's bankers, endorsed it. Control by 7,000 national bankers guaranteed freedom from "special interests." Any law to regulate the corporations, decided the Philadelphia Board of Trade, should come from businessmen, who are "best able to judge of its effect upon the welfare of the country." The *Commercial West* bluntly declared that "the voice of the public will be the word spoken through the Chamber of

Commerce of the United States of America with its 600 members of different trade organizations." [15]

Such simple equations between the people and the business community were exceptional. Usually one group of businessmen established its own right to leadership by attacking another. To guide his flock from the evils of the "Wall Street sharks," a president of the North Dakota Bankers Association preached from the country bankers' golden rule: "I most strenuously urge upon bank officials to eschew dealing in options, booming townsites . . . in fact all avenues of wild speculation." A moderately prosperous banker offered another road to leadership: "In an era of . . . great combinations aiming at the restriction if not the entire removal of competition . . . the banks have gone on in the old way . . . wedded to the idea of individuality and independence as a cherished tradition. The more the tendency toward combinations and the restraint of competition affects commerce and industry, the more the banks will inevitably gain favor by contrast. The greater the force of the trust movement in the direction of overcapitalization, the readier the country will be to look upon banks and bankers as champions of independence in business and as safeguards of conservatism." And businessmen battling over progressive legislation regularly traded accusations of populist and monopolist to enhance the justice of their own proposals. [16]

But seldom during these wrangles did true virtue wander outside of the business community. Even to the haters of bigness, the heroes were not statesmen or warriors, but businessmen, often big ones. Among their cries against monopoly, smaller businessmen interspersed remarks about James J. Hill the "modern Jefferson," Andrew Carnegie contributor to "a higher and better civilization," and — a special favorite after the Panic of 1907 — J. Pierpont Morgan the awesome genius of Wall Street. Pride in their own kind also showed in the way businessmen treated the erring colleague. As long as a possibility of innocence remained, businessmen of similar interests and stature defended him without reservation. But once proven guilty, to cleanse themselves, they ostracized him. When the press scolded Charles Schwab in 1902 for gambling on the Riviera, the House of Morgan stood by the president of U.S. Steel; but a year later, when it became known that Schwab had brought friends into an unethical stock transaction, the House forced his resignation and refused him comfort. Five years later, as Schwab returned to business with Bethlehem Steel, George Perkins condescendingly welcomed him like a returning prodigal: "All of us are mighty glad it is turning out so good for you." As scandals in the management of the New York, New Haven and Hartford unfolded during the early months of 1913, spokesmen for the railroads and high finance doggedly maintained that the road's president, Charles Mellen, was not receiving a fair hearing. By the end of the year, with the corruption fully documented, the same sources lashed him unmercifully for a time, then forgot him. After Frank Bigelow's conviction for defalcation, the American Bankers' Association expunged this popular president from its records and banned his name within the association. In each case their critical point emphasized how exceptional the bad ones were. When Thomas Parker, scorning "businessmen who claim to moral leadership," said, "I see precious little difference in the spiritual or moral elevation of the average business man and of the average politician, labor union leader or demagogue," he had obviously lost touch with his colleagues, who claimed national leadership as a natural right.[17]

Businessmen from each segment of the community set as their goal the preservation of classless America. The National Board of Trade, read the resolution of a group of small businessmen, "deplores and deprecates any unnecessary agitation which stirs up class hatred and feeling." Usually the agitators were union leaders and demagogic politicians. "A few years ago," related George Pope of the NAM, "the relations between employer and employe were of the most cordial character. A spirit of co-operation, a desire to assist, a willingness to serve one's employer, was the keynote of industrial life . . . [Why] in the face of laws enacted with the intent of bettering working conditions . . . does the tide of unrest constantly rise? Is it safe for us to assume that the passage of such laws are [sic] the breeder of class consciousness and are slowly but surely compelling the employers by legislative acts to be segregated into a class . . . ?" And despite businessmen's advice, lamented Elbert Gary, "legislation calculated to create classes is urged persistently." [18]

Foreigners, working through the labor unions, had spread this infection throughout America. With "the 'foreign invasion' of the anarchist and socialist, criminals and outcasts from other nations" had come the International Workers of the World — "this baleful organization . . . of European origin" the National Association of Wool Manufacturers called it — and the "un-American institution" of the closed shop. Those born in the United States, a printer from Kentucky told the Senate Committee on Education and Labor in 1904, want "the true 'American' plan (open shop), not the 'European' plan (closed to non-union workmen)." Why had the anthracite miners struck in 1902? "Tens of thousands of the anthracite miners are Poles, Hungarians, Slavs and other foreigners, who can not spell a word of English," explained David Parry. "Many of these men are imbued with anarchistic and socialistic sentiments before they come to America, and they make excellent material for agitators to work upon." And the Lawrence strikers of 1912? All "Italians and other foreign-born operatives," declared the American Protective Tariff League. In the garment industry, one of its spokesmen said, native workers had "laid meekly down before the Jewish labor power," which preached revolutionary socialism. The nation's troubles became clear, said the New York *Journal of Commerce*, once you asked yourself "how many of the most active leaders of labor unionism are of American blood." [19]

Alien influences had penetrated beyond the unions: some businessmen found them in sensational journalism; others in American colleges which, according to the NAM, treated "simon-pure Socialism" as humanitarianism; and still others in the low-tariff movement which, professional protectionists claimed, drew strength from "New York's Foreign Chamber

of Commerce." Even the Chief Executive was not immune.
When Roosevelt took issue with a Supreme Court decision
in 1908, the *Bulletin of the American Iron and Steel Association* remarked, "The President has evidently listened to
Mr. Gompers, who was born in England in 1850." [20]

On occasion businessmen still displayed a bumptious, out-
going pride in their country. When a Britisher challenged
the statement of C. A. Carlisle that the United States had
more wealth than the total from Great Britain, France, and
Germany, the Studebaker executive wrote to Senator Albert
Beveridge, "The truth of the matter is I do not know where
I dug this up myself unless I got it in an inspiration from
some of your talks. I am a firm believer, however, that an
American every day in the week is equal to the whole three
combined . . ." But over the course of the progressive era
their nationalism became increasingly devil-ridden. By the
preparedness years, as businessmen saw foreign influences
sustaining radical causes, fomenting strikes, and subverting
the tariff, nationalism involved the evils of the outside world
far more than the glories of America. And by then, more and
more of them had come to agree with George Pope that
businessmen, as a defense against alien class attacks, must
unite in order "to realize their importance as a class." [21]

The classless society derived much of its importance from
the encouragement it gave to individualism. Businessmen's
maxims explained the development of America as the prod-
uct of exceptional men — usually entrepreneurs — who,
through "self-denial and perseverance," had built "great institutions from the smallest beginnings." "[John D. Arch-
bold's] story is the regular thing," said the *Economist*, "a
poor boy who had the stuff in him and went after the wealth
of the world, which he succeeded in capturing, to the extent
of $100,000,000, maybe." Motivation, explained Herbert
Miles, came from "the element of self-interest, which at-
taches itself to anything and everything where there is legal
opportunity." Selfishness, as it operated through business
leaders, was the mainspring for "the divine law of progress"

because their achievements ultimately spread benefits to all mankind.[22]

As businessmen rationalized social justice from what the *Wall Street Journal* called "The Law of the Wolf-Pack," they also talked of the need to run in a pack. The value in consolidation and cooperation was recognized from the House of Morgan to the corner drug store and practiced above all in the hundreds of business organizations. No group prided itself upon rugged individualism more often than the leaders of the NAM. Yet David Parry's definition of socialism — "delegating to one individual or a small group of individuals the management of the interests of many individuals" — neatly summarized the association's history. It was James Van Cleave who stated that every manufacturer in the country was "an organization man," John Kirby who announced that businessmen lived "in an age of organization," and George Pope who called upon manufacturers to "stand together . . . as a class." A Pennsylvania banker, even more enthusiastic, placed association within the laws of history: man evolved from autocracy to isolated individualism into "the more advanced civilization of the present . . . based upon more altruistic motives . . . and more complete cooperation." Looking about them, few denied an Illinois businessman's conclusion, "Organization is the watchword of progress."[23]

Just as the class consciousness of businessmen never endangered their belief in the classless society, so the new cooperation did not interfere with the old individualism. Behind an ideological defense, businessmen talked about their world as they saw it.

II

Not even the labor unions caused businessmen as much worry as the federal government. Their principles granted the government a strictly limited set of powers and responsibilities which should serve the requirements of business. Failing to do that, government forced business, in Frank

Vanderlip's phrase, "to adjust . . . to law instead of adjusting the law to business." "Government is a minor affair in man's existence," one journal reminded the politicians. "The most important part of man's life is business, and government is important when it maintains order that makes business possible." Therefore, a Georgian announced, "We have the right to demand that business measures be taken out of politics" so that "politics don't [sic] rob the business man of the right to legislative aid suitable for business needs." Out of politics meant into businessmen's hands.[24]

"In all periods of the history of this country," said a Virginia banker, striking a theme common to other business groups as well, "the banks have come to the rescue of the government and sustained its credit." Yet, added another from North Carolina, "the lawmakers, as a class are not friendly to our interests." By meddling in private enterprise, the financier Henry L. Higginson told President Taft, politicians continued "to act in 'restraint of trade'" although the government had not "shown even ordinary ability in handling its own affairs." For the enlightenment of misguided politicians, businessmen laid down two cardinal rules: keep the government out of business; and lighten "the ever growing burden of taxation." If the government followed these principles, it would not "get in the way of progress." [25]

The government too often forgot that "legislation cannot make a stupid person smart or a slothful person industrious." No "philanthropic agency," it must not, warned Howard Elliott, "take away by *law* the freedom of action of the individual and attempt to shift upon numerous and often half digested laws, burdens that the individual should carry himself," or it would stultify the American dream with class legislation. Beyond providing maximum opportunity for each individual to "make the most of that which God gave him," the government should leave free men alone. Businessmen often abbreviated their complaints against the government by saying that there were simply too many laws, a habit Representative William C. Adamson, chairman of the House Committee on the Judiciary, undoubtedly knew as he listened to the car manufacturer Henry Joy advocate a permissive federal trade commission.

Mr. JOY. Mr. Chairman, I would like to say this, for example, that that matter of a trade commission, in my mind, is so closely interwoven with the other allied questions of price maintenance and fair competition —

Mr. CHAIRMAN. In other words, you want to make a whole lot of laws in connection with the establishment of a trade commission?

Mr. JOY. Make what?

Mr. CHAIRMAN. A whole lot of laws — Federal laws — pass new laws by Congress?

Mr. JOY. No, sir; quite the contrary.[26]

A few businessmen, notably those associated with the financial houses of Wall Street, refined and rearranged these maxims in such a way that the government became generically akin to a corporation, another unit in society with interests and scope similar to those of U.S. Steel or Standard Oil. This interpretation lay behind the gentlemen's agreements which Elbert Gary made with the Roosevelt administration as one sovereign power might with another. In 1915, years after the agreements had collapsed, Gary still recommended diplomacy as the way to regulate business: "Few, if any, cases [concerning business practices] have been found which could not have been satisfactorily and properly adjusted by personal and friendly, though persistent, efforts without any open or advertised opposition." An associate of Gary's, Henry Clay Frick, offered his services to Roosevelt as mediator between the federal government and Standard Oil. In the same vein, the *Wall Street Journal* looked forward to "a proper 'balance of power' between the government and the corporations," and another journal advocated a "reconciliation" between the railroads and the government. Later in the progressive era, as the range of the government's activities widened, prosperous businessmen called it an unregulated monopoly, able to tax enemies out of business and, in the case of its parcel post, to set prices which ruined its competitors. From a slightly different perspective, the

Economist described it this way: "A partner in all the leading corporations of the United States, the federal government, which has invested no capital therein . . . is now the most potent influence in the management of their affairs."[27]

Others even more explicitly talked about the government as just another business. Arthur Reynolds, angry at the way the government deposited its funds, told the American Bankers' Association, "The power here conferred upon the Secretary of the Treasury to control money and credit, if attempted by [private bankers], would probably call for a special act of Congress to curtail their activities." California power companies, in an odd constitutional twist, defined the government's status as a landowner in the same fashion. Because "no other proprietor could interfere with the State and its laws," their representative declared, "the United States Government should not attempt to do so." And to James J. Hill, the President and the governors of the states served as a board of directors for that "great economic corporation known as the United States of America."[28]

Certain events during the progressive period required nothing more than a direct application of businessmen's first principles concerning government. Increased taxes, for example, always violated the rules of good government. The corporation tax of 1909, declared the Syracuse Chamber of Commerce, was "novel, unjust, inequitable, discriminatory, inquisitorial and unnecessary," sentiments echoed in business organizations across the country.[29] A very few businessmen, as a diversion, suggested instead an inheritance or income tax, but when they faced a graduated income tax in 1913, businessmen everywhere judged it the most destructive legislation in the nation's history. It promised "constant Government espionage" and placed a premium upon dishonesty. It alternately violated the sacred precepts of the Founding Fathers and spread false ideas about the equality of man. Now improvidence paid. Worst of all, one prosperous businessman lamented, "it immediately arrays ninety-seven per cent. of the people against three per cent. of the people." With repeal apparently out of the question, some businessmen shifted their attack after 1913 to the government's refusal to tax incomes below $4,000. "So far from opposing direct taxes," the *Wall Street Journal* grimly announced in 1915, "this newspaper would like to see them imposed upon every voter, however small his means." [30]

Businessmen dealt with most labor legislation just as easily. Measures to control hours and wages broke the natural laws of economics. Any limitation upon the labor injunction meant flagrant class favoritism, and jury trials in injunction cases placed justice at the disposal of the mob. Commenting on compulsory old-age insurance, the president of the Massachusetts Board of Trade, an organization often receptive to progressive legislation, reminded the government of its proper field: "The State can and should encourage thrift and self reliance; it should encourage the individual to make provision for his own future without the loss of dignity and manliness." And the NAM called compulsory sickness and old-age insurance "a departure from accepted doctrines, contrary to American ideas and detrimental to thrift and economy." [31]

Laws covering employers' liability and workmen's compensation proved more awkward. Some business groups, such as the Philadelphia Board of Trade, consistently opposed them as vicious government interference which held the employer responsible for his workers' "reckless indifference to danger." But a larger number, including the major railroads, the NAM, and moderate organizations such as the Boston and Cleveland Chambers of Commerce, resigned themselves to some laws and concentrated upon defeating the most dangerous ones. More honest than most, the legislative committee for the Philadelphia Trades' League reported on the subject of employers' liability: "Your Committee did not favor the enacting of any legislation of this kind, as a whole, but realized the strong possibility of the passage of some kind of a bill, and used its efforts in helping to secure the wording of the bill as moderate in terms as possible." Employers wanted the laws permissive and the schedule of payments low, and the NAM, under the guidance of the perceptive Ferdinand Schwedtman, designed a "model law" in 1911 to accomplish these purposes. By 1914 the association claimed that twenty-five states had borrowed its formula. But, with the possible exception of a few magnates within the National Civic Federation, none of these businessmen acknowledged liability and compensation laws as a legitimate function of government.[32]

Most businessmen agreed upon a few obligations, other than maintaining law and order, which the government should assume. Federal appropriations for vocational education served the public interest, according to the NAM, the many employers in the National Society for the Promotion of Industrial Education, and an overwhelming majority of the members of the U.S. Chamber of Commerce. So did laws to strengthen the consular service and any other legislation, aside from tariff reform, which encouraged trade and investment abroad. And in language which disparaged the politician and commended thrifty government, a large number of businessmen also recommended an expansion of civil service.[33]

But businessmen differed on almost all other issues of the period, and with disagreement came confusion over principles. From a distance they appeared to be arguing about definitions. Where, for instance, did the natural laws of economics apply? Howard Elliott of the Northern Pacific told the Senate Committee on Interstate Commerce in 1905 that any abuses in the railroad rate structure would correct themselves "through the friction of business," and that regulatory laws would bankrupt the roads by disrupting the free-play of the credit market. A few days before, Edward Bacon had begged the committee for government assistance to equalize the contest between shippers and carriers. Asked what effect a rate law might have upon the credit of the railroads, Bacon had replied, "It seems to me that it is perfectly safe to leave those things to the operation of financial laws." [34]

When did labor legislation become class legislation? If it involved child labor, Southern textile manufacturers believed. At each hint of a federal law, they marched upon

Congress to defend the freedom of Southern children who, these employers maintained, would lose health, education, and industrious habits if they lost their jobs. The NAM and the Merchants' Association of New York, defending the jurisdiction of the states, supported them. But several of the nation's great bankers, touched by the accounts of arrested children in Southern factories, encouraged federal legislation, and many Northern employers, already operating under state child labor laws, asked for national legislation to end the unfair advantage of Southern businessmen. A president of the New England Cotton Manufacturers' Association recommended a federal minimum hour law for the same reason. In rebuttal, a North Carolina textile manufacturer said these proposals were part of "a deep laid scheme, of some of the Northern manufacturers, to put the Southern Mills out of business," and the *Manufacturers' Record,* in part because of the magnates' support for child labor legislation, warned that Northern philanthropy in Southern education would destroy the time-honored institutions of the South.[35]

When did the government enter the domain of private enterprise? Most lumber, mineral, and water power interests west of the Mississippi drew the line before federal conservation projects. They asked Congress to preserve tradition, praising what a representative for Pacific lumber companies called "the good old laws" which allowed private development of the nation's natural resources. But east of the Mississippi business organizations of all varieties supported the extension of federal forest reserves, with several requesting the retirement of all remaining timber land. "I know of no other organization," Gifford Pinchot wrote in 1909 to the National Board of Trade, "whose work in the past has embraced so many different phases of the general scope of the National Conservation Commission's present work." And the Philadelphia Board of Trade, as well as the small businessmen in the Trans-Mississippi Commercial Congress, advocated federal development of the nation's water resources because "private capital has done all it could."[36]

At what point did government assistance become paternalism, stifling individual initiative? Southern businessmen dependent upon cotton decided that the point lay beyond federal assistance in moving the cotton crop. Some wanted the Secretary of the Treasury to deposit federal funds in Southern banks to help finance its distribution. "Why should we not call upon the Government for aid as do the gambling-stricken banks when pressed by frenzied speculation?" demanded an Atlanta banker. Others requested federal warehouses to ease the strain and expense of distribution or, in some cases, to enable the brokers to store their cotton until a better market day. When the war in Europe up-ended the cotton market in 1914, both of these demands grew almost hysterical, and a few suggested that the government force the farmers to plant grain instead of cotton the next year. Prosperous financiers in the North blanched at such invasions of private enterprise.[37]

What constituted a utopian attempt to legislate personal morality? Prohibition, answered the nation's brewers and distillers. Jacob Ruppert, Jr., the New York brewer, even dared to threaten politicians with the labor vote in an effort to defeat a local option bill. Other businessmen demurred. "Every practicable step in the direction of curtailing the liquor traffic and restricting the saloon influence in the present state of human society," one spokesman remarked, "is a step toward a better condition of things." Another called prohibition "a plain business proposition. The [liquor] business is regarded as a drag on the national welfare and prosperity."[38]

Although an outsider could reconstruct a series of intellectual debates, businessmen were otherwise occupied. There were many country bankers who endorsed parcel post at the same time they condemned postal savings, shippers who advocated rate regulation as they denounced the regulation of the laborers' working conditions, merchants who recommended a decentralized banking system while they asked government indulgence for consolidations and price maintenance leagues, and protectionists who demanded a high tariff within a federal policy of laissez faire. In 1914 the Philadelphia Chamber of Commerce, long a promoter of Latin American trade, recommended "a government line of steamers connecting Philadelphia and New York with the principal seaports of South America" minutes after it had condemned government operation of trans-Atlantic merchant ships as socialism.[39]

Despite their tendency to leap from idea to idea, the nature of their interests combined with the nature of the progressive movement brought businessmen back to some responses more often than others. First, as most of them fell behind the pace of reform, they turned increasingly upon the executive, so strengthened by Roosevelt and Wilson, and the federal commissions, which they loosely associated with the executive, as the source of their troubles. Roosevelt, complained a manufacturer shortly before the President left office, "has no right to dictate to or to coerce [Congress and the] courts in the slightest degree, and it certainly is highly socialistic, and, to my mind, outrageous that he should." During Wilson's first administration, the president of the National Association of Cotton Manufacturers announced, "Commission government seems to be the order of the day. It may well be called paternalistic or socialistic." By the time of the New Freedom, charges of "legislation by the executive" and "government by commission" appeared regularly in their attacks against federal policies, and they sometimes coupled these with demands that the government return to the "traditional" balance of power between the President and Congress.[40] A second theme stressed the immutability of the Constitution and the sanctity of the law. Too many of the proposed amendments, such as the ones dealing with an income tax and with the recall of judges, offended them, and more often than not the older Supreme Court precedents pleased them. In particular businessmen wanted to retain the legal controls over labor.[41]

The third, and most important, gave precedence to the federal government over the states. A handful of businessmen favored the national government because they believed it alone could steer America between socialism and plutocracy. Many more of them simply became irritated with the states. If they wanted results, businessmen soon learned that the states could not manage national problems. And if their area of business covered more than one state, they also learned, as the Association of Manufacturers and Distributors of Food Products had by 1903, that one national regulatory law served them better than "the diversified and often conflicting provisions of laws in thirty-six different States." [42]

By the late progressive years businessmen of all varieties were asking the federal government to save them from the states. Big businessmen included exclusive federal jurisdiction in their plans for an interstate trade commission. The small businessmen in the National Association of Hosiery and Underwear Manufacturers resolved: "All legislation affecting manufacturers who compete with manufacturers in other States should have Federal rather than State origin, so that manufacturers everywhere may be placed on an equally competitive basis." Most active by 1916, the major railroad systems used their newly-created Railway Executives' Advisory Committee almost exclusively to request "such legislation or Constitutional changes as will give the National Government the unqualified power to regulate all railroads." "More and more people are coming to believe," declared Frank Trumbull, who was elected spokesman for the large roads, "that what the United States has done for its banking system it can and ought to do for its railroads." Shippers, also tiring of the confusion of state regulation, agreed: "We favor exclusive federal control of [railroad] regulation," began a resolution in 1916 of the National Industrial Traffic League. A final show of disrespect for the states came in the movements for uniform state laws to replace national control, each one a transparent attempt to destroy or minimize regulation. As Edward Moseley, secretary to the Interstate Commerce Commission, acidly remarked, the railroads demanded state legislation on employers' liability at the same time they begged for protection against state rate laws. [43]

But these, too, were themes of convenience. Suspicions of an overweening executive did not inhibit a large number of

businessmen from demanding that Wilson do something —
anything — to stop a strike by the Railroad Brotherhoods in
1916; nor did faith in an unchanging Constitution deter
ninety-five percent of those voting in a U.S. Chamber of
Commerce referendum from favoring an amendment to
authorize the item veto. After the Supreme Court upheld
the corporation tax of 1909, the *Commercial and Financial
Chronicle*, a high priest of court worship, sneered at the
Justices for deciding "that a tax levied solely on income and
measured by income is not an income tax if it is called by
another name." A spokesman for big business, referring to
possible dangers from the Sherman Act, easily disposed of
the sacred character of the law: "When . . . it is deemed
necessary to do something the spirit of which is contrary to
law, ways have to be found to evade the law." The legal
theory most apt to prosperous businessmen came from
William H. Barr, president of the National Founders' Association: "Historically and morally the citizen and his property existed before this government and he created this
government to protect himself and that which was his. He
does not derive his title to his possessions from his government. His rights existed before he formed a government. The
Constitution recognizes but does not create his rights." Finally, while the railroads asked for full federal jurisdiction
over rates, their alter ego, the Railway Business Association,
demanded an end to all rate regulation, both state and
federal.[44]

Three men deserve special attention for their efforts to
modernize the political theory of the business community.
The least attended was Alpheus B. Stickney, president of
the Chicago Great Western, who early in the century told
businessmen that a strong, respected, and truly national government offered the one intelligent solution to America's
national economic problems. At the core of his program, he
placed a government central bank and an Interstate Commerce Commission which would determine a uniform rate
structure for all railroads.[45] Where Stickney spread his interests broadly, Daniel Willard, the personable president of the

Baltimore and Ohio, concentrated upon the relations among the railroads, their users, and the government. After 1911 most railroad executives granted the necessity of federal regulation only to request amendments which would allow greater leeway. Willard asked them to view government supervision as both wise and desirable. "The railroad," he said, "is a semi-public institution," and its executives should conduct themselves as "semi-public officers." Because every citizen had a vital stake in America's transportation system, only federal regulation could "so harmonize all . . . conflicting interests that, in the long run, the greatest good may come to the greatest number." Perhaps alone among prominent businessmen, Willard congratulated Wilson for resolving the railroad crisis of 1916 with the Adamson Act.[46]

Like Stickney and Willard, George Perkins also tried to convince businessmen that political theory had to keep pace with the technological revolution. More than the other two men, Perkins grew with his times. In 1905 he was attempting to bring the executive into a community of interest agreement with the House of Morgan and was brashly defending the right of life insurance executives to use company funds as they pleased. Seven years later, advocating a strong federal government to stand guard over the economy and stiff criminal penalties to check illegal corporate practices, Perkins had matured into a capable exponent of the thesis that businessmen incurred obligations in return for wise government policies.[47]

III

The social theory of the business community resembled in a general way the views of comfortable Americans everywhere. Its major tenets — a restricted definition of the people, a belief in a leadership elite, a denial of classes, and a faith in individualism — all belonged to the standard philosophy of the early twentieth century. It was by their emphasis that businessmen set themselves apart from the dominant spokesmen for middle-class reform. A tone, patronizing or harsh, toward "people" who opposed him, an insistence upon business leadership, an obsession with class attacks, and plaintive defenses of economic individualism distinguished the articulate businessman from the prominent leaders of reform, who combined optimism with a sense of destiny when they talked about the people, its leaders, and limitations on individualism to prevent class strife. The one dogmatized and warned, the other explained and envisioned; the one preserved his ideology regardless of daily contradictions, the other felt his way toward an adjustment of the traditional to the new.

In the same way, the businessmen's theory of government bore only a rough similarity to the dominant progressive conceptions. Although everyone agreed upon a government of limited powers, businessmen usually shrank these powers well below the level common among reformers. Both James J. Hill and Tom Johnson described government as "a great corporation"; but where Hill thought of the balance sheet, Johnson emphasized service. And in the area of the government's purpose, the differences were even more striking. Like Aldrich, businessmen preferred to think of government as a sift rather than as a vehicle for action. Like the least imaginative small-town reformers, businessmen usually expected the government to serve them alone, which by a mysterious alchemy spread benefits to the nation as a whole. That narrow focus and prudent logic, influencing reform-minded as well as conserving businessmen, looked meager beside the public philosophy which led progressivism to its climax under Wilson.

IX

BUSINESSMEN AND THE PROGRESSIVE MOVEMENT

I

The Cleveland progressives who rallied about Tom Johnson early in the century said that they had captured the city from business and had given it to the people. Breaking through a web of privilege, they had overcome the combined opposition of the newspapers, the Chamber of Commerce, and profiteers who milked the city for private gain, in order to provide equitable and humane government. Although their long fight for cheaper urban transportation and a rational property tax justified some exaggeration, their method of exaggerating revealed a particularism in the progressive movement which created a unique problem for businessmen. In their summary, the Johnson forces had excluded support from two Cleveland papers and the work of the Chamber of Commerce for health and housing legislation, urban renewal, and benevolent capitalism.

Early in the progressive era, descriptions of reform acquired a classic form. Progressives, consciously or otherwise, arranged their stories of battle after that ideal type: public men led average Americans against entrenched business privilege to ensure government by and for the people. The simplified version provided a convenient shorthand for proving authenticity, convincing doubters, and communicating with other reformers. But, like any orthodoxy, it could also be a nuisance. Reform-minded politicians such as Roosevelt and Beveridge had incessantly to guard against looking like professional politicians; reform clergymen had to test donations for taints of privilege; and reformers in general had to watch constantly for dubious companions. Well-to-do businessmen especially suffered under these rules. The word "business" automatically connoted special interests, and a profit-seeker, however respectable in his line, could not easily establish himself as a public man. If, as was very often the case, the reformers saw "business interests" as their ultimate enemy, too many businessmen on the side of reform jeopardized its authenticity as a progressive movement. And if, as was very often the case, the reforming businessmen supported only a portion of a general program, they further weakened their claim as progressives. A crusade belonged to the pure. During the progressive era one either stood with the people or with the interests.

Historians inherited the problems of this orthodoxy whenever they used the essential, yet elusive, term "progressive." The first students of progressivism managed to avoid difficulty by concentrating upon results. Men such as Benjamin DeWitt and Charles Beard, writing in or just beyond the period, relied largely upon a list of particular reforms to describe the movement. And in 1931 Harold U. Faulkner summarized the content school of progressive history with *The Quest for Social Justice,* which traced the outstanding changes of the time with scarcely an interpretation.[1]

Next historians turned to the fascinating gallery of men and women who had dominated the movements which these careful, limited studies detailed. Some of the biographies excluded the broad setting of reform altogether. Others adopted the approach which leading reformers themselves had used. As the autobiographies of Roosevelt and LaFollette had selected events to illuminate their authors, so later biographies, in an effort to recreate personalities, construed the movement to fit the man. Admiring associates of Roosevelt, such as Joseph Bucklin Bishop, arranged his words and claims to present him as the great reformer. Henry F. Pringle, on the other hand, found him wanting in honesty, conviction, humane sensitivity, and detachment from big

business. Instead, Pringle elevated Taft for the legislation
which had passed during his administration. Claude G.
Bowers pictured Beveridge as a reformer because he had
fought big business. By implicitly equating progressivism
with the preferences for antimonopoly and social justice of
Brandeis, Alpheus T. Mason raised LaFollette high among
the reformers and dropped Roosevelt.[2]

Three historians broadened this technique to differentiate
among factions within the movement. Although John Chamberlain discovered no reformers with the right combination
of economic wisdom and intellectual toughness to complete
the fight against monopoly capitalism, he recognized LaFollette and a few like him as the most able. Without Chamberlain's reservations, Matthew Josephson also favored the La-
Follette group for its honest battle against big business. And
in his study of the muckrakers, Louis Filler applied roughly
the same criterion — dedication to the strict control of big
business — to set off a hard core of journalists who had continued their exposures after magnates had closed all but one
of their outlets. Like the biographies, these more incisive
studies of the movement did not attempt to define "progressive" and did not search systematically for the participants
in reform.[3]

By the 1940's an abundant literature about reform leaders
gave historians the confidence to write about progressives as
a group. Casual students of the reform era now placed them
in the American tradition: they were moral, liberal, democratic, and optimistic; above all, they wanted to salvage the
individual from an industrial society.[4] At the same time
specialists analyzed the progressive mind. Eric Goldman and
Morton G. White, following the general guide of the disen-
chanted progressive Randolph Bourne, pointed up the corro-
sive and ill-defined relativism upon which progressive think-
ers had relied. David Noble reconstructed a paradox in which
progressives had tried to reconcile an inexorable social
progress with a man-made leap into utopia. Other intellectual
historians tested the reformers against fixed historical definitions of progressive and liberal. Daniel Aaron called the

reformers who dominated the early twentieth century "pseudo-progressives," lacking the courage and humane vision necessary to challenge entrenched business privilege. Louis Hartz and Arthur Ekirch, both using variations of Lockean liberalism, arrived at equally uncomplimentary conclusions. Hartz saw the progressive movement as a sham revolt against the American business system by men who shared an all-pervasive Horatio Alger ethos: progressivism illustrated America's irrational Lockeanism. And Ekirch pictured early twentieth-century reformers as statists, illiberal by eighteenth-century standards.[5]

By holding the progressives in place, these historians could detach themselves from many of the reformers' assumptions and walk around the group pointing out foibles and failures. Richard Hofstadter, employing principles from social psychology, greatly extended the range of the historian's freedom. His study of the progressive personality described a half-recognized feeling among members of the urban middle class that big business, organized labor, and political machines threatened their status in American society. With indifferent results, substantial citizens tried to solve America's urban-industrial problems through reforms which rested upon an outmoded set of Yankee-Protestant values. Finally, George Mowry, drawing upon his own findings as well as those of Hofstadter and others, synthesized the recent investigations in a "progressive profile."[6]

Over the years historians had gradually closed the door to the progressive club. The recognized political and social leaders, along with their intellectual spokesmen, comprised its membership, and the common characteristics among these men and women supplied its defining quality. To gain admittance, a latecomer had to pass the progressive-personality test. An examination of Mowry's check list indicates how weak the case is for most reforming businessmen, who did not receive invitations when the club was established. His progressives held optimistic views about mankind and nature which supported their faith in an extensive democracy and a swift, man-made progress. Reform-minded businessmen, insofar as they expressed themselves, distrusted the people, broadly considered, and countered projects for direct democracy with talk about republican restraints. To them social progress was a gradual, delicate process. Mowry's progressives suffered the pangs of status decline. The same held true for a number of businessmen, especially bankers, retailers, and manufacturers in the towns and smaller cities of the South and Midwest, but on balance these men like the country banker Andrew Frame opposed change far more often than they encouraged it. Moreover these townsmen usually did not have the economic security which recent writers have emphasized. On the contrary, both the ideas and impetus for reform came from prospering businessmen on the make, men like Edward Bacon, Herbert Miles, George Reynolds, and George Perkins. And where Mowry's progressives deplored the evil city and idealized rural America, their closest counterparts among businessmen were again the townsmen. The more active urban businessmen had made their peace with the city. The same applies to another trait, a distaste for ostentatious wealth and an attempt to separate good and bad riches: reform-minded businessmen usually did not question how the wealthy had acquired and spent their money. Nor did these businessmen, for all of their booster and boomer spirit, display the missionary zeal of Mowry's progressives.

In a few instances, reform-minded businessmen qualify under his provisions. By and large, they were youthful; they came from a middle-class; they had been standpatters a decade earlier; they considered the new immigrants socially dangerous; they feared organized labor as well as organized capital; and they abhorred the word "class." But they score far higher on Mowry's conservative test.[7] They often doubted man's virtuousness; emphasized the slowness of social progress; believed that leaders, not the masses, initiated that progress; respected the inequalities among men; generally held the judiciary in deep regard; and above all had faith in the fundamental soundness and justice of the American business system. And a glance back through recent literature yields similar results. Reforming businessmen were not the statists Ekirch describes, they had little in common with the patricians whom Aaron discusses, they dreamed none of the utopias which Noble's progressives outlined, they did not subscribe to the optimistic pragmatism of Goldman's reformers, they distrusted the muckrakers, and they considered LaFollette a dangerous radical. By unanimous verdict, then, the large majority of them belong with the enemies of the progressives.

Yet how much light do we cast either upon reform-minded businessmen or upon the progressive period by calling these men who worked diligently for several important progressive causes nonprogressives? And how will we deal with other groups currently outside the progressive pale as we learn more about their roles in reform? We have scant information about the relationship between populism and progressivism. The Democratic party between 1900 and 1910 is a historical blur. If Woodrow Wilson's support in 1916 represented the purest coalition of progressives, as Arthur Link maintains, the movement by then relied largely upon rural, small town America, where Wilson's voting strength lay. We know very little concerning organized labor and local reform. Hofstadter's provocative suggestions about the legal profession during the reform era remain a challenge. Until we have solved these and similar problems, reforming businessmen can anticipate company in limbo.[8]

The way to reopen the question of the progressives is to start with content rather than with people. Historians generally agree that, despite its diffuseness, the progressive movement did center about certain broad social, political, and economic issues: to provide the underprivileged with a larger share of the nation's benefits; to make governments more responsive to the wishes of the voters; and to regulate the economy in the public interest. Insofar as a man contributed to the solution of these problems, he was a progressive.

Rarely did businessmen try to improve the lot of low-income Americans. With few exceptions they opposed independent unions and fought against labor legislation. Social

insurance laws were an anathema, and private welfare capitalism, still in its infancy, affected middle-income employees
far more than unskilled workers. Their participation in
Americanization programs and their support for prohibition
belonged in the realm of social control rather than social
meliorism. And in almost all cases those who were more
than casual philanthropists had retired from business affairs.
The only important contribution which businessmen made to
the social welfare movement came as a by-product of their
zeal for civic improvement. As they scrubbed and polished
their cities, some of them did assist in improving local housing and health codes.

Although businessmen wanted to purify democracy, they
opposed extending it. In general they continued the Mugwump tradition, declaiming against local bosses and corrupt
legislators, and encouraging civil service. At cries for direct
primaries, direct election of senators, or the initiative, referendum, and recall, articulate businessmen took shelter from
the mob under principles of regulated democracy.

But questions of economic regulation aroused a very
different response: at least one segment of the business community supported each major program for federal control. In
this area businessmen exercised their greatest influence on
reform and laid their claim as progressives.

II

As a factor in the making of progressivism, businessmen
held a number of advantages. They had more money than
any other group to invest in the men and causes they liked.
Besides wealth, they enjoyed the most extensive organization
among private groups in America. And if their profession did
not widen social horizons, it extended their vision nationally
more naturally than did any other occupation. Before most
Americans had found their bearings at the turn of the century, businessmen had ideas about reform and the means to
implement them.

But they faced peculiar disadvantages as well. A generalized distrust of "business" and specific complaints about par-

ticular groups of businessmen gave them a bad reputation during a reform era. Politicians learned that programs identified with business had less than average chances of success, and that too close an affiliation with prosperous businessmen jeopardized their future. Other groups also viewed an avowedly business campaign with more than normal suspicion. Further weakening their political position, the vigor and abusiveness of their intramural fights both increased their notoriety and consumed their strength.

Finally, businessmen found accommodation even more difficult than did other groups early in the century: they were the most prickly of a sensitive lot. Too accustomed to dominance in their communities, too certain of their superior knowledge in economic affairs, they acted alone rather than compromise with those whom they considered lesser and ignorant Americans. Big businessmen, the first to recognize the wisdom of adjustment, had the most to learn and had not progressed far enough by the end of the era. Moderately prosperous industrialists actually deteriorated as compromisers during the middle years when organizations such as the NAM and the Illinois Manufacturers' Association said no to almost every proposal for reform. Although other businessmen displayed more talent for accommodation than this, the over-all record was poor.

During the first phase of progressivism, their tactical advantages gave businessmen a lead in the debate over national economic reform which often held for several years afterward. Until 1904 business shippers and the carriers monopolized the struggle over rate regulation, and until 1911 they still ranked as the major forces. To 1912 no one except bankers had offered systematic proposals for financial reorganization, and no one had equaled the idea behind the Hepburn amendments as a practical alternative to the Sherman Act. Businessmen applied the most persistent pressure for and against tariff reform to the eve of the Payne-Aldrich Act; after that, while professional protectionists continued to uphold the tariff, Republican progressives carried on the businessmen's program for a scientific tariff commission. In these areas, the most serious limitations on their power until the Panic of 1907 were internal rivalries and national inertia. Nineteen hundred and eight was the watershed. The rapid movement of middle-income groups into national reform posed the first important challenges to their leadership, and as hard times took the glamor from reform, businessmen turned increasingly arrogant and rigid. Tariff revisionists, instead of compromising after 1908, gave up their reform movement. Midwestern city bankers entered an alliance with Wall Street behind a politically impossible financial plan. Only the shippers saw their legislative fight to a finish in 1910, and only the businessmen advocating a permissive trade commission offered a new program with a chance of success. Meanwhile, the established business powers in the East had fallen on the defensive within the Republican party. Although still fairly successful in defeating laws which they did not like, they also killed bills with the touch of their name.

These diverse strands formed a peculiar pattern of influence early in the Wilson years. On the one hand, the full range of progressive groups, including newly arrived businessmen from the West and South, were competing for national favors, and the businessmen from the East and Midwest now faced their most complex problems of maneuver and compromise. On the other hand, the more prosperous businessmen, by arriving first and proposing consistently, had so conditioned the debates over economic legislation that their programs continued to set legislative limits well after 1912, when these businessmen lacked the political power to impose them. This was least evident, although not absent, in the case of the Underwood tariff, which depended very little upon general principles; it was most obvious in the case of the Federal Reserve Act, which Congress largely built from the alternatives bankers had already suggested. And both the Federal Trade Commission and the regulation of agricultural exchanges also demonstrated this lingering influence from the formative years. By the time Congress had resolved the issues which established businessmen had once dominated, they had regained sufficient poise and power to act on their own once again. During 1916 they won, among other concessions, the favor of the FTC, the initiation of the Webb-Pomerene bill, and the passage of the Rainey and Kern Acts.

Whether or not businessmen realized it, certain principles of strategy governed their record during the progressive era. Where they rode a wave of other people's hostility, they enjoyed their easiest victories. Entering the twentieth century, almost every articulate American held some grudge against the railroads: they were either too strong, too arrogant, too expensive, or too irresponsible. Emotions alone never enacted legislation against an ensconced political power. But because of this climate, the determined shippers could depend upon encouragement from a host of middle-income groups not directly involved in questions of freight rates. And a politician looking for a likely reform issue could do no better than support the organized drive for rate regulation.

Where businessmen adopted a conciliatory approach, they maximized their chances of success. In 1913 Senator Owen and Representative Glass assumed that any new financial system would require the approval of the bankers. So inclined, Owen secretly proffered a hand of cooperation to Vanderlip and Benjamin Strong. Vanderlip slapped it away with a vitriolic public letter denouncing everything Congress had thus far done toward a bill. Meanwhile George Reynolds brought a majority of Midwestern city bankers into an attitude of cooperation toward Congress and impressed this fact time and again upon both Glass and Owen. Disregarding the question of specific influences upon particular portions of the final bill, the Federal Reserve Act most closely approximated the long-standing ambitions of the Midwestern city bankers and bore the least resemblance to the expressed desires of Wall Street.

From 1909 to 1914 the NAM compiled an exceptionally pure record of opposition to reform legislation. Faced with the prospect of measures to limit working hours, reform the tariff, and regulate corporations, the association demanded no laws at all; it received the Eight-Hour Act of 1912, the Underwood tariff, and the Clayton and Federal Trade Commission Acts, without appreciably affecting any one of them. Ferdinand Schwedtman, who had repeatedly warned his colleagues that "if we [in the NAM] want to last in politics and in legislative work we must be more constructive," accounted for the one exception. Under his direction the association drew up a model bill for workmen's compensation, which influenced the laws of many states and was also reflected in the federal bill Senator George Sutherland of Utah sponsored.[9]

Where businessmen had the tightest and best established organizations, they enjoyed the greatest opportunities to affect progressive legislation. Big businessmen had organized within the political parties rather than among themselves, and strategic location explained their ability to delay and modify so many reform measures. Through their representatives, they could introduce bills and amendments almost at will, and concrete proposals, as the Wilson years demonstrated, were committing. As the men who filled the party purses, they set boundaries even when they could not dictate legislation. As a result Congress did not attempt to control the insurance companies, pulled teeth from the measures regulating foods and drugs, delayed railroad and tariff laws despite a rising public clamor, and modified both the Clayton and Trade Commission bills toward the wishes of the magnates. Organization also enabled moderately prosperous businessmen to establish their claims early in the century and to keep their demands before Congress. And weakness in organization relegated small businessmen to the cheering sections during most of the progressive era. They applauded antitrust activities, but they did not share in the decisions. Even during the Wilson years, only the country bankers asking for rural credits and the retailers requesting a permissive trade commission exercised a noticeable influence on reform legislation; in both cases these groups were exceptionally well organized for small businessmen, and they profited as well from powerful support outside their ranks.

In all, the business community was the most important single factor — or set of factors — in the development of economic regulation. And a significant portion of this influence supported reform. Until 1908 businessmen deserve Arthur Link's commendation as the "backbone" of the major movements for national regulation, and some, notably the conciliationist city bankers and the shippers in the National Industrial Traffic League, contributed to reform throughout the era.[10] In 1916 the stanchest defenders of the Federal Reserve system were the member bankers, of the Interstate Commerce Commission the shippers, and of the Federal Trade Commission an assortment of merchants and manufacturers. Moderately prosperous businessmen from the Midwestern cities comprised the bulk of the reforming businessmen. After them came the shippers elsewhere in the nation who eventually joined the fight for rate control; a very few big businessmen, such as George Perkins, who contributed to the movement for a trade commission; the country bankers, particularly from the South, who influenced financial legislation during Wilson's administration; and a variety of importers and exporters from the East and South who applied pressure for tariff revision. These men were progressives. They stood apart from the majority of reformers not because they selected (others picked and chose) or because their reforms expressed self-interest (others identified the general welfare with their needs) but because of their narrow public philosophy. Progressive businessmen singularly lacked a grand social vision. Placing reform on a business basis, they represented — to borrow a phrase from Richard Hofstadter — the hard side of progressivism.

III

On the surface the progressive movement had changed businessmen considerably less than they had the movement. They had not untangled their confusion over politics and political action. The close correlation between the roll of the business cycle and the rise and fall of their reform impulses illustrated how much they still longed for stability. After sixteen years their predispositions about American society sounded much the same. And an era of bitter battles had not altered the broad outlines of business disunity.

Yet important, if subtle, changes had occurred in businessmen. Years of discussion about reform had given them a fresh awareness of American society. First reflected in the phenomenal growth of local, boosting organizations dedicated to civic improvement, it soon broadened to include national questions as well. Many city associations joined the United States Chamber of Commerce so that they could express themselves on national issues and still have the energy for local problems. A new spirit was abroad when businessmen did not have time for all of their public affairs. They had also grown more sensitive to public criticism, which during the progressive period so often prefaced regulatory legislation. "If businessmen cannot be honest from principle," warned a member of the Memphis Merchants' Exchange, "let them be so through fear of public condemnation." [11] For reasons of prudence and pride, businessmen began to sell themselves along with their products. And this livelier interest in what was happening in America led businessmen to talk increasingly about the nation as a whole rather than about a locality or section.

Years of involvement with the federal government also left a mark. A number of previously strange regulations had become part of life by 1916, and these if nothing else made businessmen more conscious in their daily affairs of the government's existence. From their experiences with government supervision, business leaders had learned to spot more quickly the possible advantages from federal action. In 1905 only Elbert Gary and a very few other magnates had thought to win the Bureau of Corporations to their side; after 1914 businessmen everywhere rushed to cooperate with the Federal Trade Commission. In general the progressive move-

ment had forced them to define more carefully what they
wanted.

More alert to the world about them, businessmen gradually
acquired a new attitude toward one another. At the turn of
the century none of them had talked about a business community. But as wave after wave of business groups matured
and entered national affairs, some of their leaders began to
discuss the need for a general business spokesman, leading
eventually to the U.S. Chamber of Commerce. Although the
Chamber fell short of the ideal, the goal remained. The recession of 1914 produced, along with a consensus against reform,
an unprecedented number of statements that American business was on trial and that American business would not
tolerate such abuse. When disunity returned after 1914, it
lacked its former bite. In part businessmen were relaxing
after the battles. Most articulate bankers now operated
within a common and accepted structure. Shippers had won
their legislation, and as long as these controls remained in-
tact, they would assist the railroads in a drive for exclusive
national regulation. Recession and fears of postwar dumping
had narrowed the differences between the professional protectionists and the revisionists; and as cooperative understandings spread throughout the community, smaller businessmen complained less often about collusion among giant
corporations. Moreover, after their experiences with the
Sherman and Clayton Acts, many more businessmen had lost
faith in a stern antitrust statute. Finally, a deepening aversion to organized labor drew big businessmen and the employer associations closer together in their fight against the
unions. Always vague, never binding, their new fellow feeling indicated that after years of debate businessmen recognized each other as kin even if they could not love every
brother.

IV

Out of the progressive experience run lines of continuity
connecting the business community of that day with the

business community of ours. Despite a growing tolerance of organized labor and a broadening conception of the people, the protective ideology has remained substantially the same.[12] Attacks upon private enterprise are un-American, and demands for closer regulation of the economy shameless demagoguery. Although successful businessmen have far greater respect for the power of the federal government, many of them still describe its leadership, financial operations, and services by analogy to a corporation; and "get the government out of business" is still the chamber of commerce war cry. Every four years business spokesmen implore their audience to enter politics, to save America through a businessman's government, and between elections they bemoan the pall of politics over the American economy. The public heroes of businessmen have continued to come primarily from their own community.

If businessmen have used ideology as a buffer against frighteningly rapid change, it has served them well. Beneath a rigid public philosophy, prosperous businessmen in the twentieth century have adjusted to an America in flux more quickly and more effectively than any other segment of society. Thoughtlessly accepting perpetual Republicanism during the progressive era, many business leaders had forgotten to hedge against political mishaps. Since then they have preserved their connections with both parties far more carefully. Even during the darkest days of the New Deal, leading businessmen did not break with important Democrats, and the leverage they retained brought concessions during and after Roosevelt's second administration. Considering the greater stress of the 1930's, their record surpassed that of businessmen from 1910 to 1914. Of course the fact that both parties in an age of mass communication have had to include many more businessmen in their financial base than a Hanna ever required has lightened the task.

A number of business leaders also learned during the progressive years the cost of arrogance toward officeholders. Excepting certain frantic moments of the New Deal, a considerably more suave approach has since characterized their dealings with prominent politicians. Tact has cemented natural alliances between legislators and businessmen back home to procure lucrative government contracts, and between federal commissioners and their charges to regularize regulation within an industry. Again, the deep involvement of many congressmen in business activities and their continuing interest in business-connected jobs upon retirement have eased the problems of diplomacy.

Political tact is only part of a broad canopy which has spread over business affairs. As public relations, born of a concern over progressive attacks, has grown from the ballyhoo of the Twenties to the qualitative techniques of our time, it has become increasingly essential in the minds of business leaders and therefore increasingly entwined with business operations. Now no significant policy emerges without a protective coating of public relations. In part this demonstrates the ability of an enterprise to sell its own indispensability. But more important, the expansion of public relations reflects a prudent desire among prominent businessmen to dress well on all occasions so that they will never again stand naked as "interests" or "economic royalists."

This keener appreciation of public forces provides one index to a remarkable success story, the ability of prosperous businessmen to protect their positions of leadership in America's twentieth-century society in transition. Capitalizing upon a sudden worship of productivity in 1917, businessmen comprised most of the "public men" who directed the national mobilization of World War I. Here was the America of Herbert Croly's dreams, a corporate society led by the federal government, only Bernard Baruch had replaced Theodore Roosevelt. After paying for the campaign which elected Warren Harding and a Republican Congress, business leaders held the initiative among the heirs of progressivism early in the Twenties.

Rather than frontally attacking the middle-income groups — businessmen, professionals, agriculturalists, and skilled laborers — who had challenged them during the progressive era, big business leaders gradually incorporated or neutralized them. In the late progressive years, big businessmen had started cooperating with erstwhile enemies such as the NAM; during the Twenties they joined organizations such as the U.S. Chamber of Commerce and the American Bankers' Association, which they had disdained before. And a more elaborate and permissive federal government, serving as a clearinghouse for business compromise, widened the new communities of interest. Despite continued in-fighting, especially among functional competitors and among those of varying sizes, harmony characterized the business community in this period of prosperity.

Some of the professionals who had made a livelihood from progressivism now found employment with big business. Others, including many teachers and clergymen, discovered anew that their jobs and community standing often depended upon the tolerance of successful businessmen. Through mediators such as Herbert Hoover and Senator Arthur Capper, alert business leaders recognized the wisdom of selective assistance to organized agriculture, a policy which blunted its reform thrust through most of the decade. Following the grim postwar battles which deflated the unions, company paternalism, not skull-cracking, typified labor relations during the 1920's. For a time this approach undermined old unions and forestalled new ones so successfully that most crafts would gladly have accepted a niche within industry, as the Railroad Brotherhoods did, if only their organizations had commanded sufficient respect. One after another, the progressive groups had been brought into a loose and complex system which shared the advantages of industrialism without taking from the most prominent businessmen the important perquisites of leadership. And as this network of relationships materialized, businessmen were also transforming progressive government into a mechanism for self-regulation.

Even economic collapse after 1929 did not destroy the system, despite a widespread belief that "business" was responsible for the worst features of the depression. Considering the pressures of hard times, former progressives remained remarkably passive while successful businessmen worked with President Hoover to strengthen the self-regulatory system of the 1920's. As Hoover turned increasingly negative, more flexible business leaders, well before Franklin Roosevelt's inauguration, proposed the central idea of what would be the National Recovery Administration. Welcoming a change under Roosevelt and the New Deal, they supplied the NRA with its basic substance, the codes. And such men as Edward Filene and John Fahey, reminders of the liberal origins of the U.S. Chamber, ably served the New Deal in minor capacities. When the New Deal after 1935 alienated most successful businessmen, the bulk of the old progressive groups either joined business leaders in protecting the establishment or sought neutral ground. Buttressed by this support and saved by such timely concessions as swift recognition of unionism in Big Steel, prominent business leaders resourcefully defended their power against both the dispossessed and the federal government.

Again a world war enabled business leaders to recoup their losses. By effectively controlling the mobilization process and by winning most of the credit for America's phenomenal wartime productivity, they regained an initiative which they have held through the years of cold war, with its continued emphasis upon productivity and technological advance. Across the nation capitalism and freedom are considered synonymous. Once more prominent businessmen have adjusted rapidly enough to secure their positions of leadership. A prompt acceptance of industrial unions has given labor a larger share of America's plenty without power over broad industrial or national policy. Systematically organized agriculture, which business leaders will not seriously oppose, enjoys latitude in determining the subsidies it will receive and little power in any other area of public policy. By providing Negroes with wider employment and desegregated facilities, major corporations have championed the so-called moderate approach in race relations. Only a greatly enlarged government bureaucracy competes with successful businessmen for national leadership, and this competition is real only to the degree that the two are distinct forces. The great blend of our time has so intermixed business and government that a practical, precise separation of the two is no longer possible.

In spite of the advantages which a dominant economic position and an inside view of technological progress have given business leaders, they have also laid a claim to brilliance by the success of their accommodation. With so few signs of domestic upheaval at the beginning of the 1960's, any elite would take pride in the record of America's durable business leadership. In the end, it was these men who benefited most from the progressive movement, which their predecessors once feared would destroy them.

BIBLIOGRAPHY

The important sources for this study fall into four categories: document collections; congressional hearings; publications of business organizations; and journals and newspapers addressed to businessmen. It is these sources as a whole which underpin the conclusions in the study. The absence as well as the presence of reactions among businessmen, the volume and intensity of these reactions, gradual changes in their tone and content, and the interplay of responses among groups of businessmen require generalizations which no particular set of references gathered into a note can possibly explain. And what is true of business materials is even more true for the work of many scholars, notably Samuel Hays, Richard Hofstadter, and George Mowry, whose findings have had an incalculable influence upon the author.

Document Collections

A few collections contain exceptionally rich material concerning a wide range of subjects.

Records of the Department of Commerce. National Archives.
Records of the Federal Trade Commission. National Archives.
Papers of George W. Perkins. Columbia University.
Papers of Theodore Roosevelt. Library of Congress.
Papers of William Howard Taft. Library of Congress.
Papers of Woodrow Wilson. Library of Congress.

The collections in a second tier hold valuable material on one or two problems and a smattering of material in other areas.

Papers of Nelson W. Aldrich. Library of Congress. Tariff and finance 1908–1911.
Papers of Albert J. Beveridge. Library of Congress. Tariff 1907–1909.
Chamber of Commerce of the United States Archives. Washington, D.C.
Papers of Carter Glass. University of Virginia. Finance 1912–1914.
Records of the Interstate Commerce Commission. National Archives. Railroad rates 1910–1914.

Papers of James Laurence Laughlin. Library of Congress. Finance 1911–1912.

Papers of George von Lengerke Meyer. Massachusetts Historical Society. Postal savings and parcel post 1908–1910.

National Association of Manufacturers of the United States of America Archives. New York.

Papers of John C. Spooner. Library of Congress. Railroad regulation 1902–1906.

Papers of Daniel A. Tompkins. University of North Carolina. National Association of Manufacturers 1901–1906.

Papers of Frank A. Vanderlip. Columbia University. Finance 1906–1914.

Most of the collections contain only scattered information.

Papers of Thomas H. Carter. Library of Congress.

Papers of W. Bourke Cochran. New York Public Library.

Records of the Department of Labor. National Archives.

Records of the Food and Drug Administration. National Archives.

Papers of Joseph B. Foraker. Historical and Philosophical Society of Ohio.

Papers of David R. Francis. Missouri Historical Society.

Papers of James R. Garfield. Library of Congress.

Papers of Charles S. Hamlin. Library of Congress.

Papers of Alonzo Barton Hepburn. Columbia University.

Records of the House of Representatives of the United States. National Archives.

Papers of Henry Lee Higginson. Harvard School of Business.

Papers of Gilbert M. Hitchcock. Library of Congress.

Papers of Philander C. Knox. Library of Congress.

Merchants' Exchange of St. Louis Collection. Missouri Historical Society.

Papers of John Mitchell. Catholic University of America.

Papers of Charles Nagel. Yale University.

Papers of Francis Newlands. Yale University.

Papers of Elihu Root. Library of Congress.

Records of the Senate of the United States. National Archives.

Papers of James Schoolcraft Sherman. New York Public Library.

Papers of Oscar S. Straus. Library of Congress.

Papers of Daniel A. Tompkins. Library of Congress.

Papers of John Sharp Williams. Library of Congress.

Congressional Hearings

Although the research for this study includes some reports of congressional committees, executive departments, and federal agencies, and a miscellany of other government publications, congressional hearings stand by themselves as an outstanding source for the relationship between businessmen and reform. The following list covers almost all of those hearings from 1901 to 1916 relating to reform measures and should be of general value to scholars working in this period.

House Committee on Agriculture. 59 Congress, 1 Session. Hearings on the So-Called "Beveridge Amendment." Washington, 1906.

——— 61 Congress, 2 Session. Prevention of "Dealing in Futures" on Boards of Trades, etc. Washington, 1910.

——— 62 Congress, 2 Session. Cotton and Grain Antioption Bills, Hearings on Bills to Prohibit Interference with Commerce. Washington, 1912.

——— 63 Congress, 2 Session. Regulation of Cotton Exchanges, Hearings Regarding Various Bills Relative to the Regulation of Cotton Exchanges. Washington, 1914.

——— 63 Congress, 2 Session. Uniform Grading of Grain, Hearings on H.R. 14493. Washington, 1914.

House Committee on Banking and Currency. 59 Congress, 2 Session. Hearings on Currency Legislation. Washington, 1906.

——— 60 Congress, 1 Session. Hearings and Arguments on Proposed Currency Legislation. Washington, 1908.

——— 60 Congress, 1 Session. Hearings and Arguments on Senate Bill No. 3023. Washington, 1908.

House Subcommittee of Committee on Banking and Currency. 62 Congress, 3 Session. Money Trust Investigation. 3 vols. Washington, 1912–1913.

——— 62 Congress, 3 Session. Banking and Currency Reform, Hearings. Washington, 1913.

House Committee on Interstate and Foreign Commerce. 57 Congress, 1 Session. Hearings on the Bills to Amend the Interstate Commerce Law. Washington, 1902.

——— 57 Congress, 1 Session. Hearings on the Pure-Food Bills. Washington, 1902.

——— 58 Congress, 3 Session, House Document No. 422. Hearings on Bills to Amend the Interstate-Commerce Act. Washington, 1905.

——— 59 Congress, 1 Session. Hearings on the Pure-Food Bills. Washington, 1906.

——— 59 Congress, 2 Session. Hearings on H.R. 10840, to Provide for the Investigation of Controversies Affecting Interstate Commerce. Washington, 1907.

——— 59 Congress, 2 Session, House Document No. 522. Regulating Interstate Commerce in Certain Cases. Washington, 1907.

——— 60 Congress, 1 Session. Hearings on the Bills Relating to Routing Shipments and Railroad Freight Rates. Washington, 1908.

———— 60 Congress, 1 Session. Hearings Providing for the Inspection and Grading of Grain. 4 vols. Washington, 1908.

———— 61 Congress, 2 Session. Hearings on Bills Affecting Interstate Commerce. 2 vols. Washington, 1910.

———— 61 Congress, 2 Session. Hearings on Grain Inspection and Grading Bills. Washington, 1910.

———— 61 Congress, 3 Session. Hearings on the Bills H.R. 29866 and H.R. 27275 Net Weights and Contents of Packages. Washington, 1911.

———— 62 Congress, 2 Session. Hearings on H.R. 25596 and H.R. 25576 Regarding the Review of Decisions of Interstate Commerce Commission by the Commerce Court. Washington, 1912.

———— 62 Congress, 2 Session. The Pure Food and Drug Act, Hearings. Washington, 1912.

———— 63 Congress, 2 Session. Interstate Trade Commission, Hearings. Washington, 1914.

House Committee on Investigation of United States Steel Corporation. 62 Congress, 2 Session. United States Steel Corporation, Hearings. 53 parts. Washington, 1911–1912.

House Committee on the Judiciary. 58 Congress, 2 Session. Anti-Injunction Bill, Complete Hearings. Washington, 1904.

———— 59 Congress, 1 Session. Hearings in Relation to Anti-Injunction and Restraining Orders. Washington, 1906.

———— 60 Congress, 1 Session. Hearings on the So-Called Anti-Injunction Bills and All Labor Bills. Washington, 1908.

———— 62 Congress, 2 Session. Injunctions, Hearings. Washington, 1912.

———— 62 Congress, 2 Session. Trust Legislation, Hearings. 9 parts. Washington, 1912.

———— 62 Congress, 2 Session. United States Chamber of Commerce, Hearings on H.R. 24798 and H.R. 25106. Washington, 1913.

———— 62 Congress, 3 Session. Employers' Liability and Workmen's Compensation, Hearings on H.R. 20487 (S. 5382). Washington, 1913.

———— 63 Congress, 2 Session. Trust Legislation, Hearings. 3 vols. Washington, 1914.

House Subcommittee No. 3 of Committee on the Judiciary. 60 Congress, 1 Session. An Act to Regulate Commerce, etc., Hearings on House Bill 19745. Washington, 1908.

House Committee on Labor. 57 Congress, 1 Session. Eight Hours for Laborers on Government Work, Hearings. Washington, 1902.

———— 58 Congress, 2 Session. Eight Hours for Laborers on Government Work, Hearings. Washington, 1904.

———— 59 Congress, 1 Session. H.R. 11651 — Eight Hours for Laborers on Government Work, Hearings. Washington, 1906.

—— 62 Congress, 2 Session. Congressional Regulation of Injunctions, Hearings on Pending Anti-Injunction Bills. Washington, 1912.

—— 63 Congress, 2 Session. Child-Labor Bill, Hearings on H.R. 12292. Washington, 1914.

—— 64 Congress, 1 Session. Child-Labor Bill, Hearings on H.R. 8234. Washington, 1916.

House Subcommittee No. 1 of Committee on Labor. 60 Congress, 1 Session. H.R. 15651 Eight Hours for Laborers on Government Work, Hearings. Washington, 1908.

House Committee on the Merchant Marine and Fisheries. 59 Congress, 1 Session. Development of the American Merchant Marine and American Commerce, Hearings on Senate Bill No. 529 — the Shipping Bill of the Merchant Marine Commission. Washington, 1906.

—— 61 Congress, 2 Session. American Merchant Marine in Foreign Trade, etc., Hearings. Washington, 1910.

—— 63 Congress, 1 Session. Investigation of So-Called Shipping Combine, Hearings on H.Res. 587. Washington, 1913.

—— 64 Congress, 1 Session. Creating a Shipping Board, a Naval Auxiliary, and a Merchant Marine, Hearings on H.R. 10500. Washington, 1916.

House Committee on the Post-Office and Post-Roads. 61 Congress, 2 Session. Parcels Post, Hearings. Washington, 1910.

—— 61 Congress, 2 Session. Postal Savings Bank, Hearings. Washington, 1910.

House Subcommittee No. 2 of Committee on the Post-Office and Post-Roads. 60 Congress, 2 Session. Postal Savings Banks, Hearings. Washington, 1909.

House Committee on the Public Lands. 58 Congress, 2 Session. Hearings on S. 5054, an Act to Provide for the Disposal of Timber upon Public Lands. Washington, 1904.

House Committee on Rules. 63 Congress, 2 Session. Grain Exchanges, Hearings on H.Res. 424. Washington, 1914.

House Committee on Ways and Means. 60 Congress, 2 Session. Tariff Hearings. 53 parts. Washington, 1908–1909.

—— 62 Congress, 3 Session, House Document No. 1447. Tariff Schedules, Hearings. 26 parts. Washington, 1913.

Senate Committee on Agriculture and Forestry. 60 Congress, 1 Session. Federal Grain Inspection, Hearings. Washington, 1908.

Senate Subcommittee of Committee on Agriculture and Forestry. 63 Congress, 3 Session. Standardization of Grain Grades, Hearings on H.R. 17971. Washington, 1915.

Senate Committee on Banking and Currency. 63 Congress, 1 Session. Hearings on H.R. 7837 (S. 2639). 4 vols. Washington, 1913.

—————— 63 Congress, 2 Session. Regulation of the Stock Exchange, Hearings on S. 3895. Washington, 1914.

Senate Subcommittee of Committee on Commerce. 64 Congress, 1 Session. Creating a Shipping Board, a Naval Auxiliary, and a Merchant Marine, Hearings on H.R. 15455. Washington, 1916.

Senate Committee on Education and Labor. 57 Congress, 1 Session, Senate Document No. 141. Eight Hours for Laborers on Government Work, Hearings. Washington, 1903.

—————— 58 Congress, 2 Session. Senate Bill 489. Eight Hours for Laborers on Government Work, Arguments. Washington, 1904.

—————— 62 Congress, 2 Session. Eight-Hour Law, Hearings on H.R. 9061. Washington, 1912.

Senate Committee on Interstate Commerce. 59 Congress, 1 Session, Senate Document No. 243. Regulation of Railway Rates, Hearings on Bills to Amend the Interstate Commerce Act. 5 vols. Washington, 1906.

—————— 61 Congress, 2 Session. Court of Commerce, Railroad Rates, etc., Hearings on Bills S. 3776 and S. 5106. Washington, 1910.

—————— 62 Congress, 2 Session. Hearings Pursuant to S.Res. 98. 3 vols. Washington, 1912.

—————— 63 Congress, 2 Session. Interstate Trade, Hearings on Bills Relating to Trust Legislation. 2 vols. Washington, 1914.

—————— 64 Congress, 1 Session. Interstate Commerce in Products of Child Labor, Hearings on H.R. 8234. Washington, 1916.

Senate Subcommittee of Committee on the Judiciary. 60 Congress, 1 Session. Amendment of Sherman Antitrust Law, Hearings on the Bill (S. 6331) and the Bill (S. 6440). Washington, 1908.

—————— 62 Congress, 3 Session. Limiting Federal Injunctions, Hearings on H.R. 23635. Washington, 1913.

—————— 63 Congress, 1 Session. Maintenance of a Lobby to Influence Legislation, Hearings. 4 vols. Washington, 1913.

—————— 63 Congress, 1 Session. Appendix, Maintenance of a Lobby to Influence Legislation. 4 vols. Washington, 1913–1914.

—————— 64 Congress, 1 Session. Nomination of Louis D. Brandeis, Hearings on the Nomination of Louis D. Brandeis to Be an Associate Justice of the Supreme Court of the United States. Washington, 1916.

Senate Committee on Manufactures. 58 Congress, 2 Session. Hearings on the Bill (S. 198) for Preventing the Adulteration, Misbranding, and Imitation of Foods, Beverages, Candies, Drugs, and Condiments. Washington, 1904.

—————— 60 Congress, 1 Session. Hearings on Bills S. 42 and S. 3042. Washington, 1908.

Senate Subcommittee of Committee on Post Offices and Post Roads. 62 Congress, 1 Session. Parcel Post, Hearings under S.Res. 56. 5 vols. Washington, 1912.

Senate Subcommittee of Committee on Privileges and Elections. 62 Congress, 3 Session. Campaign Contributions, Testimony Pursuant to S.Res. 79. 2 vols. Washington, 1913.

Senate Committee on Public Lands. 61 Congress, 2 Session. Public and Private Rights in the Public Domain No. 1, Hearings on the Bill S. 4733. Washington, 1910.

Senate Select Committee to Investigate Wages and Prices of Commodities. 61 Congress, 2 Session. Investigation Relative to Wages and Prices of Commodities, Hearings. Washington, 1910.

Senate Special Committee. 63 Congress, 3 Session. Maintenance of a Lobby to Influence Legislation on the Ship Purchase Bill, Hearings Pursuant to S.Res. 543. Washington, 1915.

Hearings before the Commission on Employer's Liability and Workmen's Compensation Appointed under Joint Resolution of the Senate and House of Representatives of the United States. Washington, 1911.

Hearings before the Merchant Marine Commission. Washington, 1904.

Publications of Business Organizations

Over one thousand volumes of the proceedings and annual reports of business associations form the broadest base for this study. The American Bankers' Association and forty-one state associations of bankers account for 358 volumes; eighty-seven commercial and industrial organizations account for another 708. Of the latter organizations, fifty-five are local, representing forty cities in twenty-five states, six are state, four are regional, and twenty-two are national. Thirty-four of the 106 local, state, and regional associations of businessmen clearly belong to the East, thirty-one to the Midwest, twenty-three to the South, and seven to the Far West. Supplementing these volumes are the reports of business meetings in such periodicals as *Financial Age* and *Iron Age*; the official journals of certain business associations; the itemized votes on the referenda of the U.S. Chamber of Commerce; and a variety of pamphlets and collected addresses, most of which were originally speeches before business groups.

Periodicals and Newspapers

Journals and newspapers directed to business readers comprise the weakest of the major sources. The text indicates those rare cases where conclusions depend heavily or exclusively upon editorial opinion; otherwise the material from the press fills corners and cracks in the study. Forty-one business journals and two business newspapers were systematically exploited. Eleven journals and four newspapers addressed to a general audience were used for selected problems.

NOTES

CHAPTER I. A SETTING FOR PROGRESSIVISM

1. Edward C. Kirkland, *Dream and Thought in the Business Community, 1860–1900* (Ithaca, 1956), p. 10 and *passim*. See also Thomas C. Cochran, *Railroad Leaders, 1845–1890* (Cambridge, Mass., 1953), pp. 160–172, 190, 193.

2. *Annual Report of the Chicago Board of Trade, 1905*, pp. xv–xvi; Russel B. Nye, *Midwestern Progressive Politics; A Historical Study of Its Origins and Development, 1870–1958* (East Lansing, 1959), p. 12.

3. *Financial Age* (New York), 6:273 (Sept. 1, 1902).

In this study, the East is a region radiating out from Boston, New York, and Philadelphia which includes New England and the states along the Atlantic to Maryland; the Midwest a region, with Chicago as its nucleus, which includes Ohio, Indiana, Illinois, Michigan, Wisconsin, Minnesota, Iowa, North and South Dakota, Kansas, Nebraska, and Missouri; the South a region based upon the coastal states from Virginia to Texas and including Arkansas, Tennessee, and Kentucky; and the Far West is California, Oregon, and Washington. Arizona, New Mexico, and Nevada on occasion represent areas subsidiary to the Far West; Idaho, Montana, Wyoming, Utah, Colorado, and Oklahoma to the Midwest; and West Virginia to the East. An excellent discussion of the Midwest as a region in the sense used here is found in Nye, *Midwestern Progressive Politics*, pp. 3–15.

4. Richard E. Cunningham to Carter Glass, Jan. 3, 1914, Papers of Carter Glass, University of Virginia; *Annual Report of the San Francisco Chamber of Commerce, 1904*, pp. 32–34.

5. Joseph G. Pyle, *The Life of James J. Hill* (2 vols., New York, 1916–1917), I, 453–454. See also William T. Hutchinson, *Cyrus Hall McCormick* (2 vols., New York, 1930–1935), II, 594–600; James H. Eckels, *The Financial Power of the New West* (Chicago, 1905); C. Vann Woodward, *Origins of the New South, 1877–1913* (Baton Rouge, 1951), pp. 422–423.

6. *Official Proceedings of the Trans-Mississippi Commercial Con-*

gress, 1902, p. 244; House Committee on Labor (58 Cong., 2 sess.), *Eight Hours for Laborers on Government Work, Hearings* (Washington, 1904), p. 344. See also Lee Benson, *Merchants, Farmers & Railroads; Railroad Regulation and New York Politics, 1850–1877* (Cambridge, Mass., 1955), chap. viii.

7. George E. Mowry, *The California Progressives* (Berkeley and Los Angeles, 1951), pp. 19, 21–23; Festus P. Summers, *William L. Wilson and Tariff Reform* (New Brunswick, N.J., 1953), pp. 67–68, 80; Harold F. Williamson, *Edward Atkinson; The Biography of an American Liberal* (Boston, 1934), p. 79; *Constitution of the American Free Trade League and List of Officers* (n.p., n.d.); Benson, *Merchants, Farmers & Railroads,* pp. 49–50 and *passim;* John A. Garraty, "The United States Steel Corporation Versus Labor: The Early Years," *Labor History* (New York), 1:3–38 (Winter, 1960).

CHAPTER II. AN AGE OF ORGANIZATION

1. *American Industries* (New York), vol. V, no. 5 (Oct. 15, 1906), p. 10; *Proceedings of the National Association of Manufacturers of the United States of America, 1911,* p. 66 (hereafter cited *NAM Proceedings*). See also *Commercial and Agricultural Organizations of the United States* (Washington, 1913), Sen. Doc. no. 1109, 62 Cong., 3 sess.

2. *Why Should I Be a Member of the Chicago Association of Commerce* (n.p., 1911); *Year Book of the Syracuse Chamber of Commerce, 1907–1908,* pp. 20–21; *Proceedings of the California Bankers' Association, 1909,* p. 69.

3. *Cleveland Chamber of Commerce, 1902,* pp. 94–98; *1903,* pp. 105–106; *1904,* pp. 77–79; *1906,* p. 112; *1908,* pp. 122–124; *1912,* pp. 66–70.

4. Clarence E. Bonnett, *Employers' Associations in the United States; A Study of Typical Associations* (New York, 1922); Albert K. Steigerwalt, Jr., "The National Association of Manufacturers: Organization and Policies, 1895–1914," Ph.D. dissertation (MS), University of Michigan, 1952; Gordon M. Jensen, "The National Civic Federation: American Business in an Age of Social Change and Social Reform, 1900–1910," Ph.D. dissertation (MS), Princeton University, 1956.

5. *Manufacturers' News* (Chicago), 5:5 (Aug. 20, 1914).

6. *Detroit Board of Commerce Report, 1904,* p. 12; *Chicago Commerce,* 4:10 (Aug. 14, 1908). See also *Annual Report of the Chicago Association of Commerce, 1914,* p. 96.

7. *Annual Report of the Mobile Chamber of Commerce and Business League, 1913,* p. 17; *Indianapolis Chamber of Commerce Annual Year Book and Directory, 1914,* pp. 16, 24; *Annual Report of the Baltimore Chamber of Commerce, 1911,* p. xii; *Annual Report of the Boston Chamber of Commerce, 1901,* p. 36, *1909,* pp. 14–16; *Year*

Book of the Springfield, Mass., Board of Trade, 1911, p. 9; *Bulletin of the American Iron and Steel Association* (Philadelphia), 46:119 (Dec. 31, 1912).

8. *Iron Age* (New York), 81:1534–1535 (May 14, 1908).

9. Oscar S. Straus to Gustav H. Schwab, Oct. 6, 1908, Records of the Department of Commerce, National Archives (hereafter cited D.Com. Records), File 66419; *Cotton* (Atlanta), 14:208–210 (June 1907); *Transactions of the National Association of Cotton Manufacturers, 1912*, pp. 121–137; *Proceedings of the American Cotton Manufacturers' Association, 1916*, pp. 107–108.

10. *Commercial West* (Minneapolis), 27:8 (May 22, 1915); *Proceedings of the American Bankers' Association, 1907*, pp. 83–107 and *1913*, pp. 202–217 (hereafter cited *ABA Proceedings*); *Proceedings of the California Bankers' Association, 1913*, pp. 76–82.

11. *Financial Age*, 32:718 (Oct. 23, 1915); *Financier* (New York), 84:1255 (Sept. 19, 1904) and 108:484 (Aug. 19, 1916); *Texas Bankers Record* (Austin, Dallas), 5:11–16 (May 1916); *Commercial West*, 4:11–12 (Nov. 15, 1902) and 8:7–8 (Oct. 21, 1905); House Committee on Banking and Currency (60 Cong., 1 sess.), *Hearings and Arguments on Senate Bill no. 3023* (Washington, 1908), p. 183.

12. Senate Committee on Education and Labor, *Eight Hours for Laborers on Government Work, Hearings*, Sen. Doc. no. 141, 57 Cong., 1 sess. (Washington, 1903), p. 23. See also Milton Rubincam, "David MacLean Parry (1852–1915)," mimeographed copy in Mr. Rubincam's possession, 1956.

13. *American Trade* (New York), 5:81 (Apr. 1, 1902); *NAM Proceedings, 1902*, pp. 11–35, 111–114, 120; Marshall Cushing to Frederick E. Matson, Feb. 6, 1904, *Correspondence of the National Association of Manufacturers*, no. 380, Records of the Senate of the United States, National Archives (hereafter cited *Corres NAM*).

14. *NAM Proceedings, 1903*, pp. 167–168. See also *ibid.*, pp. 133–135, 165–175, 228–237; Memoranda concerning NAM convention of 1903 (ca. May 1903), Papers of Daniel A. Tompkins, University of North Carolina.

15. *NAM Proceedings, 1905*, pp. 268–279 and *1906*, pp. 135–137; Parry to Tompkins, Dec. 15, 1905, and Cushing to John M. Maxwell, Dec. 18, 1905, Tompkins Papers, University of North Carolina; E. B. Pike circular letter, May 1, 1906, Papers of Daniel A. Tompkins, Library of Congress.

16. Parry to Field Men, Aug. 1902, *Corres NAM*, no. 8; Cushing to Men Behind the Guns, Aug. 25, 1902, *ibid.*, no. 9; *NAM Proceedings, 1903*, p. 165, *1908*, p. 141, and *1909*, p. 130; *Board of Directors and Executive Committee Minutes of the National Association of Manufacturers* (Sept. 14, 1906), Archives of the National Association of Manufacturers, New York (hereafter cited *NAM Board Minutes*); Steigerwalt, "National Association of Manufacturers," pp. 240–241.

17. Cushing to Ferdinand C. Schwedtman, Aug. 18, 1906, in Senate Subcommittee of Committee on the Judiciary (63 Cong., 1 sess.), *Appendix, Maintenance of a Lobby to Influence Legislation* (4 vols., Washington, 1913–1914), I, 787–788 (hereafter cited U.S. Senate, *Appendix, Lobby*). See also John Kirby, Jr., to W. J. Blakeney, Nov. 8, 1907, *ibid.*, I, 1117–1118; *NAM Board Minutes* (Mar. 8, 1913); *NAM Proceedings, 1912*, p. 40.

18. Memorandum for Field Men (ca. Sept. 1903), *Corres NAM*, no. 144. See also James A. Emery to Henry B. Joy, Apr. 28, 1910, U.S. Senate, *Appendix, Lobby*, III, 3559–3560.

19. *NAM Board Minutes* (May 23 and July 19, 1907); M. M. Mulhall to James W. Van Cleave, June 3, 7, 8, 22, 1907, U.S. Senate, *Appendix, Lobby*, I, 964–970, 986–988; Van Cleave circular letter, Nov. 1, 1907, Tompkins Papers, University of North Carolina.

20. Schwedtman to Kirby (copy), Sept. 14, 1908, Papers of Joseph B. Foraker, Historical and Philosophical Society of Ohio, Cincinnati; Schwedtman to Herbert E. Miles, Oct. 31, 1908, U.S. Senate, *Appendix, Lobby*, II, 2315–2316; Van Cleave to Kirby, Aug. 27, 1909, *ibid.*, III, 3100–3101; Schwedtman to J. P. Bird, Feb. 14, 1911, *ibid.*, IV, 3776; Schwedtman to Miles, Mar. 15, 1911, *ibid.*, IV, 3805–3808.

21. Tompkins to Van Cleave, Dec. 12, 1907, U.S. Senate, *Appendix, Lobby*, II, 1208; Senate Subcommittee of Committee on the Judiciary (60 Cong., 1 sess.), *Maintenance of a Lobby to Influence Legislation, Hearings* (4 vols., Washington, 1913), IV, 3720 (hereafter cited U.S. Senate, *Lobby Hearings*). See also *NAM Proceedings, 1903*, pp. 13–87, 114–130, *1904*, pp. 14–32, and *1906*, pp. 131–134; *Bulletin no. 1 of the Citizens' Industrial Association of America* (Indianapolis, 1903), pp. 3–5, 14; *NAM Board Minutes* (Feb. 1, 1907); Mulhall to Van Cleave, June 7, 1907, U.S. Senate, *Appendix, Lobby*, I, 965–968.

22. Van Cleave to Cushing, July 25, 1906, U.S. Senate, *Appendix, Lobby*, I, 745–746; Van Cleave to James Couzens, Mar. 16, 1908, *ibid.*, II, 1456–1457; U.S. Senate, *Lobby Hearings*, IV, 3949, 4416. See also Albion G. Taylor, *Labor Policies of the National Association of Manufacturers* (Urbana, 1927), pp. 29–34; Schwedtman to Emery, Apr. 12, 1909, *Corres NAM*, no. 136; *Synopsis of Proceedings of the National Metal Trades Association, 1909*, pp. 15–24, *1911*, pp. 14–21, and *1912*, pp. 11–19.

23. Steigerwalt, "National Association of Manufacturers," pp. 224–238; *NAM Proceedings, 1914*, p. 20 and *1915*, p. 19; *NAM Board Minutes* (Sept. 19, 1913).

24. *NAM Proceedings, 1916*, p. 215; *Fourth Yama Conference on National Industrial Efficiency, 1916; Iron Age*, 98:1178 (Nov. 23, 1916). For an example of the working arrangement among the lobbyists, see Senate Committee on Education and Labor (62 Cong., 2

sess.), *Eight-Hour Law, Hearings on H.R. 9061* (Washington, 1912), p. 148.

25. Schwedtman to Frank C. Nunemacher, Feb. 28, 1907, Tompkins Papers, University of North Carolina; *American Industries,* vol. II, no. 6 (Nov. 2, 1903), p. 8; *Journal of the American Bankers' Association* (New York), 7:951–952 (June 1915); Cushing to Schwedtman, Oct. 9, 1906, U.S. Senate, *Appendix, Lobby,* I, 826–828; Ralph M. Easley to Tompkins, Mar. 21, 1907, Tompkins Papers, Library of Congress.

26. Van Cleave to Elbert H. Gary, Jan. 4, 1910, U.S. Senate, *Appendix, Lobby,* III, 3369–3370. See also Schwedtman to Cushing, Oct. 1, 1906, Mar. 26, 1907, *ibid.,* I, 824, 929; Cushing to August A. Busch, Mar. 5, 1904, *Corres NAM,* no. 439; *Protectionist* (Boston), 19:339–340 (Nov. 1907).

27. William H. Barr to Frank A. Vanderlip, Dec. 12, 1916, Papers of Frank A. Vanderlip, Columbia University.

28. Couzens to Van Cleave, Feb. 24, 1908, U.S. Senate, *Appendix, Lobby,* II, 1387.

29. Horace Wilson to George von L. Meyer, Dec. 5, 1908, Papers of George von Lengerke Meyer, Massachusetts Historical Society; Josiah Marvel to Oscar Strouse, Dec. 8, 1906 and Marvel to Oscar O. Straus, Nov. 21, 1907, Papers of Oscar S. Straus, Library of Congress. See also Lee Benson, *Merchants, Farmers & Railroads; Railroad Regulation and New York Politics, 1850–1877* (Cambridge, Mass., 1955), pp. 21–23; *Proceedings of the National Board of Trade, 1901,* pp. xvi–xvii, *1905,* p. ix, and *1911,* pp. xix–xx; Bernard J. Rothwell to Charles Nagel, Dec. 24, 1910, D.Com. Records, File 66419.

30. *National Council of Commerce: Proceedings, 1907,* pp. 8–9, 14–16, 25–33; Straus to Schwab, Dec. 2, 1907, D.Com. Records, File 66419; *Bulletin of the National Association of Wool Manufacturers* (Boston), 38:44–52; Memorandum, Mar. 21, 1912, Tompkins Papers, Library of Congress; *Annual Report of the Boston Chamber of Commerce, 1912,* pp. 26–27; Earl O. Shreve, *The Chamber of Commerce of the United States of America* (New York, 1949), p. 11.

31. Benjamin S. Cable to Mr. Stauffer, Dec. 3, 1910, D.Com. Records, File 66419. See also William McCarroll-Nagel correspondence, *ibid.; National Council of Commerce: Proceedings, 1908,* pp. 23–26; Harwood L. Childs, *Labor and Capital in National Politics* (Columbus, 1930), pp. 9–14.

32. Frederick P. Fish to Nagel, Nov. 29, 1909, D.Com. Records, File 66419. See also Rothwell to Nagel, Dec. 24, 1910, *ibid.;* Nagel to James A. McKibben, July 12, 1909, Papers of Charles Nagel, Yale University; *Chamber of Commerce News* (Boston), 2:1–3 (Apr. 29, 1912).

33. *American Industries,* vol. XI, no. 8 (Mar. 1911), p. 13; Nagel

to Philander C. Knox, Aug. 22, 1911, Albert A. Baldwin to Harry A. Wheeler, Apr. 12, 1912, John Fahey to Baldwin, Apr. 18, 1912, and Wheeler to Baldwin, Apr. 19, 1912, D.Com. Records, File 70503; *Cleveland Chamber of Commerce, 1912,* pp. 159–160; *Minutes of the Chamber of Commerce of the United States, 1912,* pp. 1–6 (hereafter cited *CC Minutes*).

34. Nagel to Charles D. Hilles, Apr. 3, 1912 and Baldwin to Nagel, Apr. 16, 1912, D.Com. Records, File 70503; *Cleveland Chamber of Commerce, 1913,* pp. 144–146.

35. Wheeler to William Howard Taft, July 30, 1912, Papers of William Howard Taft, Library of Congress; *NAM Board Minutes* (Feb. 21, 1913). See also *Board of Directors and Executive Committee Minutes* (July 10–12, 1912 and Mar. 17, 1915), Archives of the Chamber of Commerce of the United States, Washington, D.C. (hereafter cited *CC Board Minutes*); Fahey to Woodrow Wilson, Oct. 8, 1914, Papers of Woodrow Wilson, Library of Congress; E. H. Goodwin to William C. Redfield, June 12, 1913, D.Com. Records, File 70503; *Nation's Business* (Washington), vol. I, no. 7 (Jan. 28, 1913), p. 3.

36. *Nation's Business,* vol. II, no. 2 (Feb. 16, 1914), p. 10. See also *ibid.,* vol. I, no. 7 (Jan. 28, 1913), pp. 2, 4; Senate Committee on Banking and Currency (63 Cong., 1 sess.), *Hearings on H.R. 7837 (S. 2639)* (4 vols., Washington, 1913), III, 2519-2533.

37. New York *Evening Post,* Nov. 22, 1913; *CC Minutes, 1914,* pp. 208, 215–216;*Fourth Yama Conference on Industrial Efficiency, 1916.* See also *CC Board Minutes* (Oct. 20, 1914); *NAM Board Minutes* (Oct. 27, 1916).

38. Washington *Herald,* Apr. 23, 1912; *CC Board Minutes* (July 10–12, 1912); *CC Minutes, 1914,* pp. 22-34, and *1915,* pp. 19–32; *Manufacturers' Record* (Baltimore), 64:50 (Aug. 21, 1913) and 69:39 (Feb. 24, 1916).

39. National City Bank of New York to Wheeler, July 12, 1913 and Wheeler to National City Bank, July 13, 1913, Vanderlip Papers. See also Wallace D. Simmons circular letter, Jan. 10, 1914, Wilson Papers; *Akron Chamber of Commerce Yearbook, 1913,* p. 19; *Year Book of the Newark Board of Trade, 1915–1916,* pp. 48–49.

40. *Nation's Business,* vol. I, no. 16 (Oct. 15, 1913), p. 2; House Committee on the Merchant Marine and Fisheries (64 Cong., 1 sess.), *Creating a Shipping Board, a Naval Auxiliary, and a Merchant Marine, Hearings on H.R. 10500* (Washington, 1916), pp. 20–22, 456; Senate Special Committee (63 Cong., 3 sess.), *Maintenance of a Lobby to Influence Legislation on the Ship Purchase Bill, Hearings Pursuant to S.Res. 543* (Washington, 1915), pp. 412–442.

41. *CC Board Minutes* (June 23, 1914, Feb. 5, 1916); Goodwin to Redfield, Dec. 30, 1913 and Redfield to Goodwin, Dec. 30, 1913,

D.Com. Records, File 69743; Goodwin to Redfield, Jan. 11, 1916, *ibid.*, File 70503.

42. Arthur J. Eddy, *The New Competition* (New York, 1912), Foreword and *passim.*

CHAPTER III. THE EASY YEARS

1. *American Industries*, vol. I, no. 19 (May 15, 1903), pp. 5–6; *Wall Street Journal* (New York), Dec. 9, 1902; A. G. Bodden to John C. Spooner, Jan. 20, 1903, Papers of John C. Spooner, Library of Congress. See also *Commercial and Financial Chronicle* (New York), 82:258 (Feb. 9, 1901); New York *Journal of Commerce and Commercial Bulletin*, Mar. 1, 1901.

2. Herbert E. Miles to James Garfield, July 2, 1906, Records of the Federal Trade Commission, National Archives (hereafter cited FTC Records), File 4440; Ross E. Parks to Theodore Roosevelt, July 13, 1906, *ibid.*, File 4435; A. H. Dutton to Theodore Roosevelt, Oct. 14, 1907, *ibid.*; E. D. Beebe correspondence, *ibid.*, File 3123; J. M. Denty to Theodore Roosevelt, May 5, 1906, *ibid.*, File 4137; Kelso and Anglin correspondence, *ibid.*, File 4138; Strohmeyer and Arpe. Co. to Secretary of Commerce, Feb. 8, 1906, *ibid.*, File 2906.

3. Arthur M. Johnson, "Theodore Roosevelt and the Bureau of Corporations," *Mississippi Valley Historical Review* (Cedar Rapids), 45:571–590 (Mar. 1959); Ralph W. and Muriel E. Hidy, *Pioneering in Big Business, 1882–1911* (New York, 1955), pp. 639 ff.

4. Memorandum of Interview with E. H. Gary, Oct. 6, 1911, FTC Records, File 1940–1; John B. Walker, "Pierpont Morgan, His Advisors and His Organization," *Cosmopolitan* (New York), 34:243–248 (Jan. 1903); Roosevelt to Perkins, June 26, 1903, Papers of George W. Perkins, Columbia University.

5. Memorandum on White House Conference, Nov. 2, 1905 and Gary to Garfield, Nov. 10, 1905, FTC Records, File 2605. See also Garfield to Gary, Oct. 27, 1905, *ibid.*, File 2604–1–1.

6. Perkins to Oscar S. Straus, Dec. 18, 1906 and Cyrus McCormick to Garfield, Dec. 28, 1906, *ibid.*, File 4902–2; Memoranda on First and Second International Harvester Conferences, Jan. 18, 19, 1907, *ibid.*, File 4902–1.

7. Perkins to J. P. Morgan, June 25, 1906 and June 1, 1908, Perkins Papers. See also Herbert Knox Smith to McCormick, Aug. 8, 1907, *ibid.*; Edgar A. Bancroft to Perkins, Feb. 4, 1908, *ibid.*; Gary to Roosevelt, Mar. 15, 1907, Papers of Theodore Roosevelt, Library of Congress; Perkins to Roosevelt, June 10, 1908, Perkins Papers.

8. *Economist* (Chicago), 34:564 (Oct. 14, 1905); *Proceedings of the Washington [State] Bankers' Association, 1905*, p. 75. See also *Proceedings of the National Board of Trade, 1905*, p. 42 and *passim*; *Annual Report of the Philadelphia Board of Trade, 1905*, pp. 24–25;

undated memorandum (ca. Oct. 1905), Tompkins Papers, University of North Carolina.

9. House Committee on Agriculture (59 Cong., 1 sess.), *Hearings on the So-Called "Beveridge Amendment"* (Washington, 1906), p. 5. See also Oscar E. Anderson, Jr., *The Health of A Nation; Harvey W. Wiley and the Fight for Pure Food* (Chicago, 1958), chaps. vii–ix; House Committee on Interstate and Foreign Commerce (57 Cong., 1 sess.), *Hearings on the Pure-Food Bills* (Washington, 1902), pp. 13–15, 611–615; Senate Committee on Manufacturers (58 Cong., 2 sess.), *Hearings on the Bill* (S. *198*) *for Preventing the Adulteration, Misbranding, and Imitation of Foods, Beverages, Candies, Drugs, and Condiments* (Washington, 1904), pp. 9–10.

10. Parry to Van Cleave, Jan. 25, 1906, U.S. Senate, *Appendix, Lobby*, I, 530; *NAM Proceedings, 1907*, pp. 205–207, 228. See also Van Cleave to Tompkins, June 25, 1906, Tompkins Papers, Library of Congress; Tompkins to Van Cleave, June 30, 1906, *ibid.; NAM Board Minutes* (Sept. 14, 1906); *Proceedings of the National Board of Trade, 1906*, p. 271; *Members' Annual of the Los Angeles Chamber of Commerce, 1906*, p. 19.

11. Perkins to Morgan, June 25, 1906, Perkins Papers; E. D. Titus to Joseph Foraker, Dec. 29, 1906, Foraker Papers.

12. *Proceedings of the Washington* [*State*] *Bankers Association, 1907*, pp. 14–28; *Proceedings of the National Board of Trade, 1904*, p. 89. See also *ibid., 1908*, pp. 270–271; David Parry to Albert J. Beveridge, Nov. 25, 1905, Papers of Albert J. Beveridge, Library of Congress; *NAM Proceedings, 1906*, pp. 34–39.

13. Kent T. Healy, "Development of a National System of Transportation," *The Growth of the American Economy*, Harold F. Williamson, ed., (New York, 1944), pp. 532–533; William Z. Ripley, *Railroads: Rates and Regulation* (New York, 1912), chap. xiv.

14. *Annual Report of the Chicago Board of Trade, 1901*, pp. lxxiv–lxxv; *Railway Age* (Chicago), 50:280–282 (Sept. 8, 1905); Bacon to Spooner, Dec. 2, 23, 1901, Spooner Papers; House Committee on Interstate and Foreign Commerce (57 Cong., 1 sess.), *Hearings on the Bills to Amend the Interstate Commerce Law* (Washington, 1902), pp. 124–138; *Annual Report of the San Francisco Board of Trade, 1902*, pp. 14–15; *Commercial and Financial Chronicle*, 74:291–292 (Feb. 8, 1902).

15. A. J. Cassatt to Roosevelt, Apr. 1, 1901, Roosevelt Papers. See also James J. Hill, *Addresses* (n.p., n.d.), "Address Delivered June 4, 1902"; House Committee on Interstate and Foreign Commerce (57 Cong., 1 sess.), *Hearings on the Bills to Amend the Interstate Commerce Law* (Washington, 1902), pp. 364, 395–396; Chester McA. Destler, "Opposition of American Businessmen to Social Control During the 'Gilded Age,'" *Mississippi Valley Historical Review*, 39:666–667 (Mar. 1953).

16. Bacon to Spooner, June 26, July 3, 1902, Jan. 3, 24, Feb. 9, 1903, Spooner Papers; Robert Eliot to Spooner, Apr. 2, 1902, Jan. 23, 1903, *ibid.; Commercial West*, 5:9 (Apr. 4, 1903); I. L. Sharfman, *The Interstate Commerce Commission; A Study in Administrative Law and Procedure* (4 parts, New York, 1931–1937), I, 36–37.

17. *Proceedings of the Interstate Commerce Law Convention, 1904*, pp. 24-38 and *passim;* Bacon to Roosevelt, Aug. 23 and Sept. 18, 1905, Roosevelt Papers. By 1904 commercial and industrial firms outnumbered the grain interests within the convention. Bacon assumed that Roosevelt favored a law which would allow the ICC to fix maximum rates effective immediately and would strictly limit judicial review. To gain this, Bacon subordinated his demands for ICC control over private cars, demurrage, and other means of special privilege, which never concerned Roosevelt. John M. Blum, *The Republican Roosevelt* (Cambridge, Mass., 1954), chap. vi.

18. James F. Paney to George J. Tausey, Feb. 17, 1905, Records of the Merchants' Exchange of St. Louis, Missouri Historical Society; *Annual Report of the Boston Chamber of Commerce, 1905*, p. 21; Senate Committee on Interstate Commerce, *Regulation of Railway Rates, Hearings on Bills to Amend the Interstate Commerce Act*, Sen. Doc. no. 243, 59 Cong., 1 sess. (5 vols., Washington, 1906), IV, pp. 3254–3255; Albert K. Steigerwalt, Jr., "The National Association of Manufacturers: Organization and Policies, 1895–1914," Ph.D. dissertation (MS), University of Michigan, 1952, p. 175; Bacon to Parry, Jan. 3, 1905, in Papers of Francis Newlands, Yale University; *NAM Proceedings, 1905*, pp. 34-69, 114–115, 214–215.

19. Milwaukee *Sentinel*, Oct. 17, 1905; Chicago *Tribune*, Oct. 25, 26, 1905; New York *Times*, Oct. 27, 1905; *Proceedings of the Federal Rate Regulation Association, 1905*, pp. 3–18, 22–28, 51–52; *Proceedings of the Interstate Commerce Law Convention, 1905*, pp. 11–12, 18–19, 60, 66, 99–100.

20. Parry to Albert J. Beveridge, Nov. 21, 1905, Beveridge Papers; E. B. Pike circular letter, Dec. 8, 1905, F. H. Stillman to Parry, Dec. 20, 1905, and Parry to Tompkins, Jan. 3, 1906, Tompkins Papers, University of North Carolina; H. C. Frick to Roosevelt, Oct. 27, 1905, Roosevelt Papers.

21. *Manufacturers' Record*, 47:446 (June 1, 1905); Senate Committee on Interstate Commerce, *Regulation of Railway Rates, Hearings*, Sen. Doc. no. 243, 59 Cong., 1 sess. (5 vols., Washington, 1906), I, 486–491.

22. *Ibid.*, II, 983–984, 1517, and IV, 3270–3283; House Committee on Interstate and Foreign Commerce, *Hearings on the Bills to Amend the Interstate Commerce Law*, pp. 239–263; F. D. Underwood to Spooner, Feb. 9, 1906, Spooner Papers; A. A. Burnham to Foraker, Jan. 20, 1905, Foraker Papers; *Proceedings of the National Board of*

Trade, 1906, pp. 29, 32–33; *Annual Report of the Commercial Exchange of Philadelphia, 1907,* p. 32.

23. *American Industries,* vol. I, no. 15 (Mar. 16, 1903), p. 5; *Financial Age,* 18:1204 (Nov. 30, 1908). See also House Committee on the Merchant Marine and Fisheries (59 Cong., 1 sess.), *Development of the American Merchant Marine and American Commerce, Hearings on Senate Bill no. 529* (Washington, 1906), pp. 274–275; Kenneth W. Hechler, *Insurgency; Personalities and Politics of the Taft Era* (New York, 1940), p. 92; New York *Journal of Commerce and Commercial Bulletin,* Feb. 16, 1901.

24. Frank F. Tripp to Henry L. Higginson, Apr. 2, 1906, Papers of Henry Lee Higginson, Harvard School of Business.

25. Edward Younger, *John A. Kasson; Politics and Diplomacy from Lincoln to McKinley* (Iowa City, 1955), pp. 364–369.

26. *Proceedings of the National Reciprocity Convention, 1901,* pp. 5, 8, 142, and *passim.* See also New York *Times,* Nov. 20, 21, 1901; Washington *Post,* Nov. 20, 21, 1901.

27. *Annual Report of the Boston Chamber of Commerce, 1901,* pp. 18–19; *Annual Report of the Corporation of the Chamber of Commerce of the State of New York, 1902–1903,* pp. 89–90 (hereafter cited *NY Chamber of Commerce*). See also *National Reciprocity* (Chicago), vol. I, no. 1 (Sept. 1902), pp. 1–2, 36; no. 3 (Nov. 1902), pp. 27–32; no. 4 (Dec. 1902), pp. 3, 7–8.

28. *American Economist* (New York), 36:38 (July 28, 1905); Chicago *Tribune,* Aug. 17, 18, 1905; American Reciprocal Tariff League circular letter, undated (ca. Jan. 1906), Spooner Papers; *Proceedings of the National Board of Trade, 1906,* pp. 265–266; *National Boot and Shoe Manufacturers' Association Proceedings, 1906,* pp. 28–30; *Cotton,* 12:4–5 (Oct. 15, 1905).

29. *Manufacturers' Record,* 48:83 (Aug. 10, 1905). See also *National Reciprocity,* vol. I, no. 1 (Sept. 1902), cover; *American Economist,* 30:5 (July 4, 1902) and 37:30 (Jan. 19, 1906); *Protectionist,* 12:596–598 (Apr. 1901) and 17:161–170 (Aug. 1905); *Annual Report of the San Francisco Chamber of Commerce, 1902,* p. 8.

30. Younger, *Kasson,* pp. 374–379; *Annual Statement of the Merchants' Exchange of St. Louis, 1902,* p. 20; *Proceedings of the National Board of Trade, 1903,* p. 234; *St. Paul Chamber of Commerce, 1902–1903,* p. 2.

31. *The Baltimore Plan for the Creation of a Safe and Elastic Currency* (Baltimore, 1894); Senate Committee on Banking and Currency (63 Cong., 1 sess.), *Hearings on H.R. 7837 (S. 2639)* (4 vols., Washington, 1913), III, 3014–3015; H. H. Hanna to Spooner, Jan. 19, 1901, Spooner Papers.

32. Andrew Frame to Roosevelt, Aug. 26, 1903, Roosevelt Papers; *Proceedings of the Kansas Bankers' Association, 1902,* p. 73.

33. *ABA Proceedings, 1902,* pp. 132–134. See also *ibid., 1901,* pp.

149–156 and *1902*, pp. 99–113, 144, 175–176; *Iron Age*, 67:28–29 (Jan. 24, 1901).

34. *Proceedings of the Minnesota Bankers' Association, 1902*, pp. 142–143; *Proceedings of the Iowa Bankers' Association, 1902*, pp. 78–84; *Commercial West*, 5:12 (Aug. 22, 1903).

35. Frame to Spooner, Dec. 31, 1901, Spooner Papers. See also Jacob H. Schiff to Nelson W. Aldrich, Jan. 22, 1902, Papers of Nelson W. Aldrich, Library of Congress; H. C. Fahnestock memorandum, Mar. 25, 1903, Roosevelt Papers; J. W. Stillman to Roosevelt, Aug. 14, 1903, *ibid.*; *Commercial West*, 5:15 (Mar. 7, 1903).

36. *ABA Proceedings, 1906*, pp. 142–155, 165–199, *1907*, pp. 109–113, 145–153; House Committee on Banking and Currency (59 Cong., 2 sess.), *Hearings on Currency Legislation* (Washington, 1906); *Proceedings of the Minnesota Bankers' Association, 1907*, p. 194; *Financial Age*, 16:1167 (Nov. 4, 1907).

37. *Wall Street Journal*, Sept. 29, 1905; *ABA Proceedings, 1903*, pp. 9–15, 163; *Proceedings of the Kansas Bankers' Association, 1903*, pp. 138–142.

38. *Financial Age*, 8:265–267 (Aug. 17, 1903). See also *Report of the Currency Commission to the American Bankers' Association and Remarks by Hon. A. B. Hepburn* (New York, 1907), pp. 1–3; *NY Chamber of Commerce, 1906–1907*, pp. 15–37, 40–57; Charles A. Conant, *A History of Modern Banks of Issue* (6th ed., New York, 1927), pp. 437–440; Paul Morton to William Loeb, Jr., Nov. 12, 1907, Roosevelt Papers. For meaningless recommendations from other businessmen, see *Official Proceedings of the Trans-Mississippi Commercial Congress, 1906*, p. 274; *Report of the Board of Trade of the City of Baltimore, 1906*, p. 41; *NAM Proceedings, 1903*, pp. 138, 194–198.

CHAPTER IV. UNCERTAINTY

1. *Financial Age*, 8:572–574 (Oct. 5, 1903) and 16:1123 (Oct. 28, 1907); *Proceedings of the Chicago Traffic Club, 1907*, p. 2; *American Industries*, vol. VI, no. 4 (Oct. 1, 1907), pp. 13–15.

2. *Proceedings of the Arizona Bankers' Association, 1908*, pp. 37, 78–91; *Report of Proceedings of the South Carolina Bankers' Association, 1908*, pp. 20–28; Senate Committee on Banking and Currency (63 Cong., 1 sess.), *Hearings of H.R. 7837 (S. 2639)* (4 vols., Washington, 1913), II, 1947–1948; Andrew J. Frame, *Panic Panaceas* (n.p., 1904; reissued 1907). See also *Proceedings of the Alabama Bankers Association, 1908*, pp. 95–101.

3. *Financial Age*, 18:944–945 (Oct. 19, 1908). See also *Proceedings of the Colorado Bankers' Association, 1909*, pp. 91–92.

4. Frame, *Panic Panaceas*; *Financial Age*, 18:83 (July 13, 1908) and 9:1096–1097 (June 27, 1904).

5. Undated memorandum, 1911, Perkins Papers; *Wall Street Journal*, Aug. 17, 1907. See also *Annual Report of the Philadelphia Board*

of Trade, 1907, pp. 52–54; Paul Morton to Roosevelt, Nov. 3, 1907, Roosevelt Papers.

6. *Financier,* 91:13–14 (Jan. 6, 1908). See also George E. Mowry, *The Era of Theodore Roosevelt, 1900–1912* (New York, 1958), p. 219.

7. *Economist,* 38:220 (Aug. 10, 1907) and 40:132 (July 25, 1908); New York *Journal of Commerce and Commercial Bulletin,* Aug. 6, 1907 and July 27, 1908; *Financial Age,* 16:361 (Aug. 12, 1907) and 18:189 (July 27, 1908); William M. Wood to George Meyer, Nov. 18, 1907, Meyer Papers.

8. *Proceedings of the National Board of Trade,* 1908, pp. 6–11; *Financial Age,* 18:83 (July 13, 1908); *Commercial and Financial Chronicle,* 86:1248–1249 (May 23, 1908). See also *Proceedings of the New York State Bankers Association,* 1908, pp. 9–17; William W. Finley, *Addresses and Statements, 1907–1913* (2 vols., Washington, n.d.), I, "Address at the 'Prosperity Convention,' Baltimore, March 3, 1908."

9. *Rand McNally Bankers' Monthly* (Chicago), 36:78–80 (Feb. 1908); *Chicago Commerce,* 3:3 (Mar. 6, 1908). See also George W. Perkins to Morgan, May 22, 1908, Perkins Papers; Frank A. Vanderlip to George E. Roberts, Dec. 23, 1907, Vanderlip Papers; House Committee on Banking and Currency (60 Cong., 1 sess.), *Hearings and Arguments on Proposed Currency Legislation* (Washington, 1908), pp. 82–86.

10. Perkins to Morgan, Mar. 16, 1908, Perkins Papers. See also Perkins to Morgan, Apr. 21, 1908, *ibid.;* Belle C. and Fola LaFollette, *Robert M. LaFollette* (2 vols., New York, 1953), I, 244–256; *Wall Street Journal,* May 16, 1908.

11. *Proceedings of the Iowa Bankers' Association,* 1908, pp. 18–25; *Proceedings of the North Dakota Bankers' Association,* 1908, pp. 16–22; *Proceedings of the Minnesota Bankers' Association,* 1908, pp. 9–16. See also *Proceedings of the Missouri Bankers' Association,* 1908, pp. 189–190; *Proceedings of the Kansas Bankers' Association,* 1908, pp. 77–93. A country banker from Ft. Madison, Iowa, memorialized his frozen deposits in doggerel four years later (*Financier,* 98:1606 [Oct. 21, 1911]):

> By the currency embargo, Illinois, Illinois;
> By the nerve of great Chicago, Illinois, Illinois;
> In the panic of 1907,
> We recall in 1911,
> And the memory smells to heaven, Illinois.

12. *Bulletin of the Merchants' Association of New York* (Mar. 19, 1908); *Annual Report of the Philadelphia Trades' League,* 1908, pp. 101–108; *Bulletin of the National Association of Credit Men,* 7:517 (July 1908) and 9:574–575 (July 1909).

13. Vanderlip to Roberts, Dec. 23, 1907, Vanderlip Papers. See also Perkins to Morgan, July 23, 1908, Perkins Papers; Nathaniel W. Stephenson, *Nelson W. Aldrich: A Leader in American Politics* (New York, 1930), chap. xxiv; *Commercial West*, 12:7–8 (Jan. 25, 1908).

14. Perkins to Morgan, July 14, 1908, Perkins Papers; Roberts to Vanderlip, Aug. 26, 1908, Vanderlip Papers; Warburg to Aldrich, Dec. 24, 1909 and A. J. Frame to Aldrich, Sept. 20, 1909, Aldrich Papers; *ABA Proceedings, 1909*, pp. 69–80; *Northwestern Banker* (Des Moines), 14:28 (Oct. 1909). Examples of the opposition to a central bank are *Proceedings of the Alabama Bankers Association, 1910*, pp. 22–24; *Proceedings of the California Bankers' Association, 1910*, pp. 229–238.

15. *NY Chamber of Commerce, 1911–1912*, pp. 146–151, 163–167. *Proceedings of the National Board of Trade, 1911*, pp. 184–207. New York *Times*, Jan. 18, 19, 1911. *The National Citizens' League for the Promotion of a Sound Banking System: The Origins of the League* (Chicago, 1911); *Journal of the American Bankers' Association*, 3:643–648 (May 1911).

16. *Commercial Club of Chicago Year-Book, 1914–1915*, p. 73; *The National Citizens' League: Constitution and By-Laws* (Chicago, 1911); *National Citizens' League . . . Origins*. See also Chicago *Tribune*, Apr. 27, 1911; *Chicago Commerce*, 7:18 (Dec. 22, 1911); James Laurence Laughlin, *The Federal Reserve Act: Its Origin and Problems* (New York, 1933), p. 79. A sample of its support is *ABA Proceedings, 1911*, pp. 380–381; *Annual Report of the Richmond Chamber of Commerce, 1912*, p. 9; *Philadelphia Chamber of Commerce Annual Report, 1912*, p. 103; *Annual Report of the New Orleans Board of Trade, 1912*, p. 12; Elbert H. Gary, *Addresses and Statements, 1904–1926* (7 vols., Boston, 1927), I, "Remarks Made May Fourth, Nineteen Hundred and Eleven."

17. Memorandum, May 21, 1912, Tompkins Papers, Library of Congress. See also *NAM Proceedings, 1912*, pp. 275–281; *Official Proceedings of the Trans-Mississippi Commercial Congress, 1911*, pp. 233, 260; *Bulletin of the National Association of Credit Men*, 12:642–650 (July 1912); *Proceedings of the North Dakota Bankers' Association, 1911*, pp. 130–133.

18. House Subcommittee of the Committee on Banking and Currency (62 Cong., 3 sess.), *Money Trust Investigation* (3 vols., Washington, 1912–1913), I, 106–111 and *passim; Proceedings of the California Bankers' Association, 1913*, pp. 42–48; A. E. Stillwell circular letter, Feb. 6, 1912, Vanderlip Papers; *Proceedings of the Alabama Bankers' Association, 1913*, p. 129; *Savannah Board of Trade Annual Report, 1912–1913*, p. 5.

19. *ABA Proceedings, 1912*, pp. 183–184.

20. Laughlin to Wallace D. Simmons, Jan. 15, 1914, James Laurence Laughlin Papers, Library of Congress. For Laughlin's views on

the Aldrich plan, see statement by Laughlin (ca. 1911), *ibid.;* Laughlin to James B. Forgan, Aug. 13, 1911, quoted in Laughlin, *Federal Reserve Act,* p. 48. For dissension within the league, see *Financier,* 100:474–475 (Aug. 10, 1912); Laughlin, *Federal Reserve Act,* pp. 44–47; Laughlin circular letter, Oct. 2, 1912, Laughlin Papers; H. Parker Willis to Carter Glass, Nov. 29, Dec. 7, 1912, Glass Papers; F. Cyril James, *The Growth of Chicago Banks* (2 vols., New York, 1938), II, 801–803.

21. House Subcommittee of Committee on Banking and Currency (62 Cong., 3 sess.), *Banking and Currency Reform, Hearings* (Washington, 1913), pp. 337–340, 383–384, 447–451; James G. Cannon, *Clearing House and Currency* (Syracuse, 1913).

22. Interview with E. H. Gary, Oct. 6, 1911, FTC Records, File 1940–1; Memorandum of Aug. 28, 1907, Perkins Papers.

23. House Committee on Investigation of United States Steel Corporation (62 Cong., 2 sess.), *United States Steel Corporation, Hearings* (53 parts, Washington, 1911–1912), IV, 167. See also Gary to Elihu Root, Nov. 7, 1907 and Root to Gary, Nov. 11, 1907, Papers of Elihu Root, Library of Congress.

24. Low to Roosevelt, Apr. 11, 1908, FTC Records, File 5589. See also *Proceedings of the National Conference on Trusts and Combinations, 1907,* pp. 454–455, 465; Ralph Easley to Perkins, Feb. 21, 1908, Perkins to Morgan, Feb. 27, Mar. 16, 1908, and Francis Lynde Stetson to Perkins, Mar. 10, 1908, Perkins Papers; Gordon M. Jensen, "The National Civic Federation: American Business in an Age of Social Change and Social Reform, 1900–1910," Ph.D. dissertation (MS), Princeton University, 1956, p. 277; House Subcommittee No. 3 of Committee on the Judiciary (60 Cong., 1 sess.), *An Act to Regulate Commerce, etc., Hearings on House Bill 19745* (Washington, 1908), pp. 3–6.

25. James Emery, *An Analysis of the Proposed Amendments to the Sherman Anti-Trust Act* (New York, 1908); *NAM Proceedings, 1908,* pp. 106–119, 278–280, 296–297; *Annual Report of the Indianapolis Board of Trade, 1908,* p. 63.

26. House Subcommittee of Committee on the Judiciary, *Commerce, etc., Hearings,* pp. 153–164, 167–178; Senate Subcommittee of Committee on the Judiciary (60 Cong., 1 sess.), *Amendment of Sherman Antitrust Law, Hearings on the Bill (S. 6331) and the Bill (S. 6440)* (Washington, 1908), pp. 60–62; Petition from New York Board of Trade and Transportation, Apr. 8, 1908, FTC Records, File 5589. See also Jensen, "National Civic Federation," pp. 285–286.

27. Perkins to J. P. Morgan, Jr., Nov. 10, 1908, Perkins Papers. See also Henry F. Pringle, *The Life and Times of William Howard Taft; A Biography* (2 vols., New York, 1939), I, 347, 355.

28. Memorandum, Aug. 22, 1912, D.Com. Records, File 64606; William H. Baldwin to Garfield, Nov. 28, Dec. 3, 1906, FTC Records,

File 3641; Luther Conant, Jr., to H. K. Smith, Dec. 25, 1908, *ibid.*, File 2604–1–1; Perkins to Smith, July 3, 1911, *ibid.*, File 4902–2; Smith to Perkins, July 8, 1911, Perkins Papers.

29. Pringle, *Taft*, II, 655–666; *American Industries*, vol. X, no. 1 (Aug. 15, 1909), p. 15 and no. 3 (Oct. 1909), pp. 23–24; *NAM Proceedings, 1910*, pp. 81–107, 249–253.

30. New York *Times*, May 16, 1911; New York *Journal of Commerce and Commercial Bulletin*, June 5, 1911; Memorandum for Mr. Roosevelt, Mar. 11, 1912 and Memorandum, July 13, 1911, Perkins Papers. See also *Report of the Illinois Manufacturers' Association, 1911*, pp. 3–23; *Proceedings of the New Jersey Bankers' Association, 1912*, pp. 86–92. Apparently Wickersham would have accepted an agreement if U.S. Steel had voluntarily dissolved. Wickersham to Taft, Sept. 7, 1911, Taft Papers.

31. *Proceedings of the American Iron and Steel Institute, 1910*, pp. 33–42; Gary, *Addresses*, I, "Remarks Made December 10th, 1908"; Interview with E. H. Gary, Oct. 13, 1911, FTC Records, File 1940-1. See also Information Furnished to the Department of Justice Concerning the Steel Investigations, FTC Records, File 6518–8–16 and Interview with E. H. Gary, Oct. 6, 1911, *ibid.*, File 1940–1.

32. J. P. Bird to James A. Emery, Oct. 19, 1911, U.S. Senate, *Appendix, Lobby*, IV, 3940–3942; Senate Committee on Interstate Commerce (62 Cong., 2 sess.), *Hearings Pursuant to S.Res. 98* (3 vols., Washington, 1912), I, 499, 500, 515–524, 693–695, 703–704, 1091–1092. See also *ibid.*, I, 912–938, II, 2321, 2353–2355, 2380–2382, III, 2708–2715; Arthur E. Suffern, *Conciliation and Arbitration in the Coal Industry of America* (Boston, New York, 1915), p. 170.

33. William C. Brown, *Address* (New York, 1908); Perkins to Morgan, Apr. 21, 1908, Perkins Papers. See also Roosevelt to Perkins, July 23, 1908 and Perkins to Gary, July 28, 1908, *ibid.; Annual Report of the Philadelphia Board of Trade, 1907*, pp. 50–52; *Report of the Trades' League of Philadelphia, 1907*, pp. 53–56; *Annual Report of the Cincinnati Chamber of Commerce and Merchants' Exchange, 1907*, p. 42; *NAM Proceedings, 1908*, pp. 144–152; *Members' Annual of the Los Angeles Chamber of Commerce, 1909*, p. 26.

34. James C. Lincoln, *The National Industrial Traffic League* (Chicago, 1908); Edward F. Lacey, "The National Industrial Traffic League: Organization and Development," Bureau of Railway Economics Library (MS); House Committee on Interstate and Foreign Commerce (61 Cong., 2 sess.), *Hearings on Bills Affecting Interstate Commerce* (2 vols., Washington, 1910), I, 395–398.

35. *Proceedings of the Traffic Club of Pittsburgh, 1910*, p. 7. See also House Committee on Interstate and Foreign Commerce, *Hearings on Bills Affecting Interstate Commerce, passim*.

36. Perkins to Morgan, May 31, June 4, 1910, Perkins Papers; *Bulletin of the American Iron and Steel Association*, 44:59 (July 1,

1910); New York *Times,* June 7, 8, 1910; Railroad Rate Agreement, Taft Papers.

37. *Annual Dinner Railway Business Association, 1910,* pp. 8–16; Perkins to Morgan, June 7, Oct. 17, 1910, Perkins Papers.

38. Resolutions of the Chicago Shippers Convention, May 17, 1910, Records of the Interstate Commerce Commission, National Archives, ICC Docket no. 3400; C. D. Chamberlain to Judson C. Clements, Sept. 21, 1910, *ibid.;* Louis D. Brandeis, *Brief on Behalf of Traffic Committee of Commercial Organizations of the Atlantic Seaboard* (Washington, 1911), *ibid.,* ICC Investigation and Suspension no. 3; Testimony, Aug. 29, 1910, *ibid.,* ICC Investigation and Suspension no. 4.

39. *NAM Proceedings, 1910,* pp. 8–15; *Commercial West,* 18:9 (Oct. 1, 1910). See also *Decisions of the Interstate Commerce Commission of the United States* (Washington), 20:243–399 (1911); Alpheus T. Mason, *Brandeis: A Free Man's Life* (New York, 1946), chap. xx.

40. *Annual Dinner Railway Business Association, 1909,* pp. 30–34. See also *Railway Age,* 45:2–3 (Jan. 1908); Perkins to Morgan, July 31, 1908 and Perkins to Roosevelt, Aug. 3, 1908, Perkins Papers.

41. Finley, *Addresses,* II, 279 and *passim; Railway Business Association Bulletin no. 1* (New York, 1910), pp. 2–3. See also Brown, *Address* (Columbus, 1911); *Traffic World and Traffic Bulletin* (Chicago), 6:193–194 (July 30, 1910); *Railway Age-Gazette,* 57:894 (Nov. 13, 1914); Eric F. Goldman, *Two-Way Street: The Emergence of the Public Relations Counsel* (Boston, 1948), chap. i; *American Industries,* vol. XIII, no. 6 (Jan. 1913), p. 20; *NAM Board Minutes* (May 17, 1909 and May 16, 1910).

42. *National Industrial Traffic League: Proceedings, July, 1912,* pp. 18, 26–30. See also *Report of the Boston Chamber of Commerce, 1910,* p. 29; *Annual Report of the Philadelphia Board of Trade, 1911,* pp. 11–24; *Manufacturers' News,* vol. I, no. 21 (July 18, 1912), pp. 5–6; *Annual Report of the San Francisco Chamber of Commerce, 1909,* p. 67; *Annual Statement of the Merchants' Exchange of St. Louis, 1912,* p. 31; *Annual Report of the New Orleans Board of Trade, 1905,* pp. 126–133.

43. Beveridge to Miles, Oct. 9, 1907, Beveridge to Parry, Nov. 29, 1907, and Beveridge to Van Cleave, Jan. 10, 1908, Beveridge Papers. See also Miles circular letter, Aug. 1, 1907, Tompkins Papers, University of North Carolina; *NAM Proceedings, 1907,* pp. 31–47, 163–173, 209–215; *American Industries,* vol. VI, no. 1 (Aug. 15, 1907), p. 16.

44. Van Cleave to Beveridge, Jan. 14, 1908, Beveridge Papers; Miles to James S. Agar, Van Cleave, William Corwine, Mar. 13, 1908, U.S. Senate, *Appendix, Lobby,* II, 1441–1443.

45. Perkins to Morgan, Mar. 16, 1908, Perkins Papers; Beveridge to Miles, Mar. 16, 1908, Beveridge Papers. Cf. Claude G. Bowers, *Beveridge and the Progressive Era* (Boston, 1932), pp. 268–276.

46. Miles to Beveridge, Feb. 26, 1908 and Riesenberg to Beveridge, Nov. 21, 1908, Beveridge Papers. See also Beveridge to Miles, Dec. 21, 1908 and Miles to Beveridge, June 14, 1909, *ibid.*; *American Industries*, vol. VII, no. 22 (July 1, 1908), pp. 15, 31 and vol. IX, no. 14 (Mar. 1, 1909), pp. 5–8, 28; *American Economist*, 42:269–270 (Dec. 4, 1908) and 43:52–53 (Jan. 29, 1909).

47. Parry to Beveridge, May 14, 1909, Beveridge Papers. See also House Committee on Ways and Means (60 Cong., 2 sess.), *Tariff Hearings* (53 parts, Washington, 1908–1909), pp. 3774–3841, 4073–4103; Bowers, *Beveridge*, pp. 352–353, 362–364.

48. *Bulletin of the American Iron and Steel Association*, 52:36 (Apr. 15, 1908). See also *American Economist*, 39:56 (May 31, 1907) and 39:306 (June 26, 1908); *Protectionist*, 19:441–445 (Jan. 1908), 20:557–558 (Mar. 1909) and 21:105 (June 1909).

49. Miles to Beveridge, Mar. 4, 1908, Beveridge Papers; *American Industries*, vol. VIII, no. 6 (Nov. 1, 1908), p. 18. See also Miles to F. C. Schwedtman, Jan. 11, 1908, U.S. Senate, *Appendix, Lobby*, II, 1275–1276; F. C. Schwedtman to James P. Bird, Nov. 10, 1908, *ibid.*, II, 2361–2364; Charles M. Jarvis to John Kirby, Jr., Jan. 20, 1909, *ibid.*, II, 2606–2607; *American Economist*, 42:294 (July 3, 1908); *Report of the Massachusetts State Board of Trade, 1909*, p. 34; *ABA Proceedings, 1909*, pp. 69–80.

50. W. F. Wakeman to Aldrich, Oct. 26, 1909, and Gary to Aldrich, July 12, 1909, Aldrich Papers. See also *American Economist*, 42:4 (July 3, 1908); *Report of the Massachusetts State Board of Trade, 1909*, p. 34; *ABA Proceedings, 1909*, pp. 69–80.

51. *NAM Proceedings, 1910*, p. 43; *Wall Street Journal*, Feb. 4, 1910. See also *Protectionist*, 21:663 (Apr. 1910); Senate Select Committee (61 Cong., 2 sess.), *Investigation Relative to Wages and Prices of Commodities, Hearings* (Washington, 1910); *Iron Age*, 85:810 (Apr. 7, 1910); *Economist*, 43:849–850 (Apr. 31, 1910).

52. Charles M. Pepper to Charles D. Hillis, May 1, 1911, Taft Papers. See also James J. Hill, *Highways of Progress* (New York, 1910), pp. 85–101; *Detroit Board of Commerce Report, 1910*, pp. 21–22; *Year Book of the Board of Trade of Newark, 1910–1911*, pp. 62–63; *Cleveland Chamber of Commerce, 1911*, pp. 53–54; *Proceedings of the American Manufacturers' Export Association, 1911*, p. 52.

53. Henry T. Wills, *Scientific Tariff Making* (New York, 1913), p. 193; *American Industries*, vol. XI, no. 4 (Nov. 1910), pp. 9–10. See also Miles to Roosevelt, Feb. 2, 1912, Roosevelt Papers; *Bulletin of the National Association of Wool Manufacturers*, 42:52–53 (1912); *Annual Report of the Philadelphia Board of Trade, 1912*, pp. 15–17.

54. *Financial Age*, 22:609–610 (Sept. 19, 1910); *Proceedings of the Missouri Bankers Association, 1910,* pp. 31–35; *Report of the Annual Convention of the South Dakota Bankers' Association, 1910,* pp. 26–31.

55. *Proceedings of the National Board of Trade, 1908,* pp. 33–34. See also House Committee on the Post-Office and Post-Roads (61 Cong., 2 sess.), *Postal Savings Bank, Hearings* (Washington, 1910), pp. 3–107; Kenneth W. Hechler, *Insurgency; Personalities and Politics of the Taft Era* (New York, 1940), pp. 159–162.

56. *Official Proceedings of the Trans-Mississippi Commercial Congress, 1907,* pp. 232–240; *Annual Meeting of the Ohio State Board of Commerce, 1904,* pp. 191–195. See also American League of Associations circular letter (ca. 1910), Taft Papers; Thomas E. Watson to George Meyer, Sept. 2, 1907, Meyer Papers; *Bulletin of the Merchants' Association of New York* (Mar. 17, 1908); *Members' Annual Los Angeles Chamber of Commerce, 1910,* p. 28; House Committee on the Post-Office and Post-Roads (61 Cong., 2 sess.), *Parcels Post, Hearings* (Washington, 1910), pp. 15–25, 163–178, 219–232, 299–306.

CHAPTER V. DILEMMA AND MYTH IN POLITICS

1. *Proceedings of the National Business Congress, 1911,* pp. 23–33; U.S. Senate, *Lobby Hearings*, 4:4074; J. P. Morgan, Jr., to George W. Perkins, Oct. 28, 1907, Perkins Papers; *NAM Proceedings, 1912,* pp. 71 ff. See also *Proceedings of the Oklahoma Bankers' Association, 1903,* pp. 34–37; George W. Mueller to John C. Spooner, Feb. 27, 1906, Spooner Papers; *Wall Street Journal,* Oct. 15, 1912.

2. *Proceedings of the National Board of Trade, 1901,* p. 228; A. A. Burnham to Spooner, July 21, 1904, Spooner Papers; Gary, *Addresses,* I, "Remarks Made May Fourth Nineteen Hundred and Eleven." See also *Proceedings of the Trans-Mississippi Commercial Congress, 1904,* pp. 69–70; *Financial Age,* 17:16 (Jan. 6, 1908); *Cotton,* 66:91–93 (Jan. 1912).

3. *Proceedings of the Montana Bankers Association, 1911,* pp. 15–21; *American Industries,* vol. IX, no. 22 (July 1, 1909), pp. 5–9. See also *Wall Street Journal,* Jan. 10, 1910; E. C. Kirkland, *Dream and Thought in the Business Community, 1860–1900* (Ithaca, 1956), pp. 117–118.

4. *Wall Street Journal,* Feb. 14, 1906 and July 28, 1908; M. A. Coolidge to Joseph P. Tumulty, Nov. 20, 1919, Wilson Papers; *Banker and Tradesman* (Boston), 42:643 (Sept. 24, 1910) and 41:829 (Apr. 2, 1910). See also *Financial Age,* 18:333 (Aug. 17, 1908); *Economist,* 40:622–623 (Oct. 24, 1908); *Protectionist,* 22:387–388 (Dec. 1910); *Proceedings of the Washington [State] Bankers Association, 1909,* pp. 34–41, *1910,* pp. 27–29.

5. Taft to Busch, Nov. 5, 1912, Taft Papers; Beveridge to Taft, Nov. 22, 1909, Beveridge Papers; Charles Taft to Charles D. Hillis, Feb. 12, 1912, Taft Papers.

6. Elkins to Stillman, Apr. 1, 1908, Vanderlip Papers; James S. Sherman to George J. Gould, Oct. 14, 1906, Papers of James Schoolcraft Sherman, New York Public Library; Fairbanks to George Perkins, Apr. 4, 1906, Perkins Papers; Gary to Vanderlip, May 11, Vanderlip Papers.

7. Mark Sullivan, *Our Times; The United States 1900–1925* (6 vols., New York, 1926), I (*The Turn of the Century*), p. 77; Platt to Nelson W. Aldrich, Aug. 17, 1903, Aldrich Papers; Aldrich to Morgan, Aug. 5, 1909, typed copy of telegram in Beveridge Papers; House Subcommittee of Committee on Banking and Currency (62 Cong., 3 sess.), *Money Trust Investigation* (3 vols., Washington, 1912–1913), I, 430–454; Frick to Philander C. Knox, Nov. 11, 1901, Papers of Philander C. Knox, Library of Congress; Jerome J. Wilbur and Ailes Files, Vanderlip Papers.

8. Utica Association of Credit Men leaflet, Dec. 12, 1913, Glass Papers; "Confidential Memorandum" (undated), *Corres NAM*, no. 258; "To the Boys on the Firing Line," Mar. 8, 1904, *ibid.*, no. 446. See also *ibid.*, nos. 12–75; Joseph B. Foraker to M. M. Mulhall, Dec. 9, 1908, Foraker Papers.

9. Van Cleave to George H. Barbour, May 4, 1908, U.S. Senate, *Appendix, Lobby*, II, 1607–1608; Van Cleave to Carl R. Lindenberg, July 27, 1908, *ibid.*, II, 1870–1871; Charles M. Jarvis to Van Cleave, June 22, 1908, *ibid.*, II, 1738; Kirby to Joseph G. Cannon June 22, 1908, *ibid.*, II, 1739; Henry F. Pringle, *The Life and Times of William Howard Taft; A Biography* (2 vols., New York, 1939), I, 350–351; Van Cleave to Foraker, July 14, 1908 and Foraker to Van Cleave, July 16, 1908, Foraker Papers.

10. Kirby to Taft, Feb. 15, 1912, Charles D. Hillis to Kirby, Feb. 17, 1912, and Kirby circular letter, July 31, 1912, Taft Papers. See also *American Industries*, vol. XIII, no. 1 (Aug. 1912), pp. 31–32 and no. 3 (Oct. 1912), pp. 7, 21; *NAM Board Minutes* (May 19, 1913).

11. *American Industries*, vol. VII, no. 2 (Mar. 1, 1908), cover; Van Cleave circular letter, Sept. 9, 1908, U.S. Senate, *Appendix, Lobby*, II, 1987; Van Cleave to H. E. Miles, Feb. 2, 1909, *ibid.*, III, 2522–2523. See also *Bulletin of the National Council for Industrial Defense, no. 7* (New York, 1912); Van Cleave to Tompkins, Aug. 15, 1908, Tompkins Papers, University of North Carolina.

12. Miles to F. C. Schwedtman, Jan. 19, 1909, U.S. Senate, *Appendix, Lobby*, III, 2543–2544; Kirby to Taft, Jan. 9, 1912, *ibid.*, IV, 3995. See also Schwedtman to Charles M. Jarvis, Mar. 11, 1909, *ibid.*, III, 2705–2706.

13. John A. Garraty, *Henry Cabot Lodge; A Biography* (New York, 1952), p. 266; U.S. Senate, *Lobby Hearings*, II, 2177–2338.

14. Henry Cabot Lodge to Roosevelt, Apr. 18, 1903, Roosevelt Papers. See also Wilbur F. Wakeman to Charles A. Moore, July 6, 1903 and Moore to Roosevelt, Aug. 1, 1903, *ibid.; American Economist*, 41:76 (Feb. 14, 1908); Wakeman to J. S. Sherman, May 7, 1908, Sherman Papers.

15. William Loeb., Jr., to O. S. Straus, Oct. 14, 1908, D.Com. Records, File 67631; Gilson Gardner to Lee S. Overman, James A. Reed, June 7, 1913, Records of the Senate of the United States, File 63A–F15.

16. Miles to Garfield, Oct. 16, 1906, FTC Records, File 7021–1. See also Charles Nagel to Miles, June 21, 1909, Nagel Papers; *ABA Proceedings, 1904*, pp. 293–294; John V. Farwell to Charles D. Norton, Nov. 1, 1910, Taft Papers.

17. Bacon to Roosevelt, Aug. 15, 1905, Roosevelt to Bacon, Aug. 18, 1905, and Bacon to Roosevelt, Aug. 23, 1905, Roosevelt Papers; F. C. Nunemacher to Taft, Aug. 24, 1908, Taft to George Meyer, Aug. 25, 1908, and Meyer to Taft, Sept. 2, 11, 1908, Meyer Papers.

18. *Rand McNally Bankers' Monthly*, 37:1–8 (July 1908). See also *Proceedings of the North Dakota Bankers' Association, 1907*, pp. 11–22, *1908*, pp. 99–100; *Report of the South Dakota Bankers' Association, 1908*, pp. 30–50; *Transactions of the Arkansas Bankers' Association, 1907*, pp. 15–16; *Manufacturers' Record*, 54:40 (July 23, 1908).

19. C. B. Landis to Roosevelt, Aug. 27, 1908 and Meyer to Taft, Sept. 2, 1908, Meyer Papers. See also Taft to Meyer, Aug. 27, Sept. 5, 1908, Thomas P. Beal to Meyer, Sept. 8, 1908, and Hepburn to Meyer, Sept. 15, 1908, *ibid.; ABA Proceedings, 1908*, pp. 286–305.

20. Taft to J. B. Reynolds, Aug. 29, 1912, Taft Papers. See also Cobb to Taft, Jan. 14, 28, Mar. 3, May 1, June 16, 1911 and Taft to Cobb, May 4, 1911, *ibid.;* Henry T. Wills, *Scientific Tariff Making* (New York, 1913), pp. 169, 213–217; *American Industries*, vol. XI, no. 12 (July 1911), pp. 24–25; Miles to F. C. Schwedtman, Feb. 21, 1910, U.S. Senate, *Appendix, Lobby*, III, 3470–3472.

21. *American Industries*, vol. X, no 12 (July 1910), pp. 7, 10–13. See also Kirby to H. C. Loudenslager, Nov. [?], 1909, U.S. Senate, *Appendix, Lobby*, II, 3307; W. C. Brown to Kirby, Dec. 18, 1911, *ibid.*, IV, 3944; Howard Elliott to Kirby, Dec. 18, 1911, *ibid.*, IV, 3982–3983; Kirby to Elliott, Dec. 20, 1911, *ibid.*, IV, 3983; *Proceedings of the National Business Congress, 1911*.

22. *Wall Street Journal*, June 24, 1901; *Freight* (New York), 12:305 (Nov. 1911); *Bankers Magazine* (New York), 76:817 (June 1908); James M. Swank to Marshall Cushing, Jan. 25, 1905, U.S. Senate, *Appendix, Lobby*, I, 471; *American Industries*, vol. V, no. 8 (Dec. 1, 1906), p. 10. See also *American Economist*, 42:235 (Nov. 13, 1908) and 47:126–127 (Mar. 10, 1911). No business journal was avowedly Democratic; many were Republican.

23. Lamont to W. Bourke Cochran, Apr. 26, 1904, Papers of W. Bourke Cochran, New York Public Library. Lamont was professionally Democratic and therefore not representative. See also N. F. Thompson to Marshall Cushing, Mar. 15, 1904, U.S. Senate, *Appendix, Lobby,* I, 552; *Official Proceedings of the Trans-Mississippi Commercial Congress, 1902,* pp. 244–248.

24. Senate Subcommittee of Committee on Privileges and Elections (62 Cong., 3 sess.), *Campaign Contributions, Testimony Pursuant to S.Res. 79* (2 vols., Washington, 1913), I, 63, 867–869, 931 and II, 1078, 1101–1103; Daniel A. Tompkins to A. B. Farquhar, Jan. 11, 1909, Tompkins Papers, University of North Carolina.

25. *American Industries,* vol. VII, no. 1 (Aug. 15, 1908), p. 15; W. F. Wakeman to Charles A. Moore, July 6, 1903, Roosevelt Papers; Kirby to Miles, Sept. 25, 1912, U.S. Senate, *Appendix, Lobby,* IV, 4121. See also *American Economist,* 34:229 (Nov. 11, 1904) and 38:76 (Aug. 17, 1906).

26. *Financial Age,* 12:1214 (Dec. 11, 1905); *Commercial West,* 11:8 (June 15, 1907); *Annual Report of the Little Rock Board of Trade, 1905,* pp. 91–95.

27. *Annual Report of the Chicago Board of Trade, 1904,* p. xv; *Proceedings of the Alabama Bankers Association, 1905,* p. 60; *Financial Age,* 8:224–226 (Aug. 10, 1903); *Annual Report of the San Francisco Board of Trade, 1904,* p. 40; *American Industries,* vol. V, no. 9 (Dec. 15, 1906), pp. 5–7.

28. *Annual Report of the Savannah Board of Trade, 1908–1909,* p. 9; *Financial Age,* 19:436 (Mar. 8, 1909); *Bulletin of the American Iron and Steel Association,* 43:76 (Aug. 10, 1909); Miles to F. C. Schwedtman, Sept. 25, 1909, U.S. Senate, *Appendix, Lobby,* III, 3161–3162; *Freight,* 10:373 (Dec. 1909). See also *American Industries,* vol. X, no. 4 (Nov. 1909), pp. 7–8; *Wall Street Journal,* Mar. 7, 1910; James M. Swank to Foraker, Oct. 26, Nov. 2, 1910, Foraker Papers.

29. *American Industries,* vol. VIII, no. 7 (Nov. 15, 1908), p. 5; *Wall Street Journal,* Nov. 11, 1910; *Banker and Tradesman,* 42:1041 (Nov. 12, 1910). See also *American Industries,* vol. XI, no. 5 (Dec. 1910), p. 7; *Commercial and Financial Chronicle,* 91:1286–1288 (Nov. 14, 1910); *Economist,* 44:789–790 (Nov. 12, 1910).

30. *American Economist,* 45:271 (June 10, 1910); *Commercial West,* 21:8–9 (Jan. 13, 1912). See also A. J. Frame to Spooner, Sept. 8, 1904, Spooner Papers; New York *Journal of Commerce and Commercial Bulletin,* Oct. 18, 1911; *Wall Street Journal,* Feb. 12, 1912.

31. C. C. Hanch to Kirby, Aug. 28, 1911, U.S. Senate, *Appendix, Lobby,* IV, 3923–3924. See also *Financier,* 99:721 (Mar. 2, 1912); New York *Journal of Commerce and Commercial Bulletin,* Mar. 7, June 24, 1912.

32. *Wall Street Journal,* Apr. 24, May 11, 1912; *Commercial West,*

21:9 (May 4, 1912) and 22:9 (Aug. 17, 1912); *Economist*, 48:12 (July 6, 1912); *Manufacturers' Record*, 62:45–46 (Nov. 14, 1912); James Emery to Kirby, July 17, 1912, U.S. Senate, *Appendix, Lobby*, IV, 4080–4081.

33. *Economist*, 48:210 (Aug. 10, 1912); Munsey to Roosevelt, Aug. 16, 1912, Roosevelt Papers; Miles to C. Edwin Michael, Oct. 28, 1912, Taft Papers. See also B. F. Harris to Frank Harper, Aug. 13, 1912, Roosevelt Papers.

34. Memorandum of letter from Cyrus H. McCormick, Jan. 18, 1912 and Memoranda of letters from John V. Farwell and Franklin MacVeagh, Mar. 13, 1912, Taft Papers; Perkins to William B. McKinley, Apr. 29, 1910, Morgan, Jr., to Perkins, Aug. 19, 1912, and Mary Kihm to Perkins, Mar. 3, 1913, Perkins Papers; John A. Garraty, *Right-Hand Man; The Life of George W. Perkins* (New York, 1960), pp. 282–283.

35. James A. Emery to Kirby, Nov. 7, 1912, U.S. Senate, *Appendix, Lobby*, IV, 4126–4129; *NAM Proceedings, 1913*, pp. 57–84; *CC Minutes, 1913*, p. 156. Later President Harry Wheeler of the U.S. Chamber delivered the congratulatory resolution to Wilson as if it had been adopted at the annual meeting. *CC Board Minutes* (Apr. 25, 1913). See also *Savannah Board of Trade Annual Report, 1912–1913*, pp. 9–10; *Report of the New York Produce Exchange, 1912–1913*, pp. 33–47; *Bulletin of the National Association of Wool Manufacturers*, 42:383–386 (1912).

CHAPTER VI. THE DEMOCRATS

1. *Bulletin of the National Association of Wool Manufacturers*, 42:271–274 (1912). See also New York *Journal of Commerce and Commercial Bulletin*, Oct. 1, 1913.

2. *American Economist*, 51:16 (Jan. 10, 1913) and 52:137 (Sept. 19, 1913); *Protectionist*, 14:633–635 (Mar. 1913); *Annual Report of the Philadelphia Board of Trade, 1913*, pp. 20–23; *Bulletin of the National Association of Wool Manufacturers*, 43:109–112 (1913); *Proceedings of the North Dakota Bankers' Association, 1913*, pp. 13–17. For a comparison between North and South in the same industry see *Proceedings of the American Cotton Manufacturers' Association, 1913*, pp. 85–89, 126–127. See also Perkins to Hiram Johnson, Sept. 19, 1913, Perkins Papers; *Commercial West*, 24:7 (Oct. 11, 1913); *Annual Report of the Massachusetts State Board of Trade, 1914*, pp. 16–22.

3. Vanderlip to Owen, July 14, 1913, Vanderlip Papers; W. D. Simmons circular letter, Jan. 10, 1914, Laughlin Papers. See also *Journal of the American Bankers' Association*, 6:133–136 (Sept. 1913); Paul M. Warburg, *The Owen-Glass Bill; Some Criticisms and Suggestions* (n.p., July 15, 1913); Warburg-Glass correspondence, Dec. 1913, Box 18, Glass Papers; Glass to Albert S. Burleson, Apr. 16, 1914, *ibid.*

4. *Financial Age*, 28:344 (Aug. 30, 1913); *ABA Proceedings, 1913*, pp. 54–65. See also *Economist*, 49:974 (May 10, 1913); James B. Forgan, *Review of Proposed Banking and Currency Bill* (Chicago, 1913).

5. House Subcommittee of Committee on Banking and Currency, (62 Cong., 3 sess.), *Banking and Currency Reform, Hearings* (Washington, 1913), p. 258; Reynolds to Glass, June 7, 1913, Glass Papers. See also A. Barton Hepburn to Glass, Dec. 19, 1912, H. Parker Willis to Glass, Dec. 31, 1912, Jan. 18, 1913, and Reynolds to Glass, Apr. 18, July 7, 1913, *ibid.*; Senate Committee on Banking and Currency (63 Cong., 1 sess.), *Hearings on H.R. 7837 (S. 2639)* (4 vols., Washington, 1913), I, 53; House Subcommittee of Committee on Banking and Currency (62 Cong., 3 sess.), *Money Trust Investigation* (3 vols., Washington, 1912–1913), III, 1654 ff.

6. *Proceedings of the Oklahoma Bankers' Association, 1913*, p. 88; MacFerran to Wilson, Sept. 4, 1913, Wilson Papers; Senate Committee on Banking and Currency, *Hearings on H.R. 7837*, II, 1549, 2083, 2096. See also M. M. Taylor to Glass, Dec. 29, 1913 and J. H. Tregoe to Glass, July 3, 1914, Glass Papers; *Proceedings of the Alabama Bankers Association, 1913*, pp. 29–36; *Oregon State Bankers Association Proceedings, 1913*, pp. 12–14.

7. Glass to Frame, July 11, 1913, Glass Papers. See also Senate Committee on Banking and Currency, *Hearings on H.R. 7837*, I, 680–681 and II, 2247–2334.

8. *American Industries*, vol. XII, no. 11 (June 1913), p. 7; J. J. Littlejohn to Wilson, June 16, 1914, Wilson Papers. See also Wheeler to J. L. Laughlin, Aug. 19, 1913, *ibid.*; Memorandum on Currency Bill, Apr. 23, 1913, Tompkins Papers, Library of Congress; John W. Craddock to Glass, July 23, 1913 and Wheeler to Glass, Aug. 8, 1913, Glass Papers; Senate Committee on Banking and Currency, *Hearings on H.R. 7837*, III, 2070 and IV, 2532–2533; *Nation's Business*, vol I, no. 13 (July 15, 1913), pp. 4–6, no. 16 (Oct. 15, 1913), p. 3.

9. Quoted in Cyrus Adler, *Jacob H. Schiff* (2 vols., New York, 1928), I, 287. See also Owen to Vanderlip, May 27, 1913, Vanderlip Papers; New York *Journal of Commerce and Commercial Bulletin*, Aug. 11, 1913; *Proceedings of the Indiana Bankers Association, 1913, passim*. Arthur S. Link, *Wilson: The New Freedom* (Princeton, 1956), chap. vii, is valuable not only for Wilson's opinions but for Democratic and business attitudes as well.

10. Senate Committee on Banking and Currency, *Hearings on H.R. 7837*, I, 5. See also *ibid.*, I, 123 ff; Chicago *Tribune*, Aug. 24, 25, 1913; New York *Times*, Aug. 23, 24, 1913; *Financial Age*, 28:344 (Aug. 30, 1913).

11. Senate Committee on Banking and Currency, *Hearings on H.R. 7837*, II, 1566. See also *ibid.*, II, 1538–1565; McLane Tilton, Jr., to Glass, Sept. 3, 1913, Glass Papers. For support of the Chicago con-

ference, see *Proceedings of the Ohio Bankers Association, 1913,* pp. 160–162; *Proceedings of the Nebraska Bankers Association, 1913,* pp. 100–112; *Year Book of the Newark Board of Trade, 1914,* p. 113.

12. *ABA Proceedings, 1913,* pp. 75–91, 95–99, 101–116; Senate Committee on Banking and Currency, *Hearings on H.R. 7837,* III, 2911 and IV, 2959, 2964–2967. Tentative Report, Oct. 14, 1913, Vanderlip Papers. The weight of business opinion against a government bank is indicated by the hundreds of telegrams in Box 41, Glass Papers.

13. *Report of Proceedings of the South Carolina Bankers' Association, 1914,* p. 21. See also *Bankers Magazine,* 88:151 (Feb. 1914); John V. Farwell to Glass, Dec. 22, 1913, Warburg to Glass, Dec. 23, 1913, and Irving T. Bush to Glass, Dec. 29, 1913, Glass Papers; Thomas A. Reynolds to J. H. Holbrook, Jan. 17, 1914, Vanderlip Papers; Hepburn to F. E. Farnsworth, Apr. 14, 1914, Hepburn Papers; *Proceedings of the South Dakota Bankers' Association, 1914,* p. 142.

14. *Commercial and Financial Chronicle,* 98:1022–1023 (Apr. 4, 1914); *Annual Report of the Cincinnati Chamber of Commerce, 1914,* p. 38; *Massachusetts State Board of Trade: Annual Report, 1914,* pp. 34–35; *Annalist* (New York), 3:583 (May 11, 1914).

15. *ABA Proceedings, 1914,* pp. 151–153; William C. Redfield to Joseph E. Davies, Feb. 7, 1914, FTC Records, File 5589–22; F. C. Bretsynder to Wilson, June 25, 1914, Wilson Papers; *Nation's Business,* vol. II, no. 7 (July 15, 1914), p. 3.

16. *Monthly Bulletin of the American Iron and Steel Institute* (New York), 1:172 (May 1913); *Cleveland Chamber of Commerce, 1915,* p. 155. See also House Committee on the Judiciary (63 Cong., 2 sess.), *Trust Legislation, Hearings* (3 vols., Washington, 1914), II, 1102–1105, 1444–1445; J. Leyden White to J. P. Tumulty, June 18, 1914, Wilson Papers; Chamber of Commerce of the United States *Special Report,* June 2, 1916.

17. House Committee on the Judiciary, *Trust Legislation,* I, 520; Chicago Plan, in Wilson Papers. See also Thomas Creigh to Wilson, June 15, 1914, *ibid.; Nation's Business,* vol. II, no. 2 (Feb. 16, 1914), pp. 22–27; *New Jersey State Chamber of Commerce Annual Report, 1914,* pp. 49–51; House Committee on Interstate and Foreign Commerce (63 Cong., 2 sess.), *Interstate Trade Commission, Hearings* (Washington, 1914), pp. 110–117, 124–133, 138–147.

18. John M. Glenn, *Urge Congress to Adjourn* (Chicago, 1914); *NAM Proceedings, 1914,* p. 127. See also *Nation's Business,* vol. II, no. 6 (June 18, 1914), pp. 5–6; Senate Committee on Interstate Commerce (63 Cong., 2 sess.), *Interstate Trade, Hearings on Bills Relating to Trust Legislation* (2 vols., Washington, 1914), I, 688–694; Clarence A. Cotton to Wilson, May 27, 1914 and D. P. Black to G. S. Graham, July 3, 1914, Wilson Papers; *NY Chamber of Commerce, 1913–1914,*

pp. 176–181, 196–203; *Report of the Boston Chamber of Commerce, 1914*, p. 48.

19. H. C. Barlow to John H. Marble, Oct. 22, 1913, ICC Records, ICC Docket no. 5860; *Railway Age-Gazette*, 55:962–964 (Nov. 21, 1913). See also H. G. Wilson to E. E. Clark, Nov. 22, 1913, F. A. Delano to E. E. Clark, May 12, 1913, M. D. Taylor to Franklin K. Lane, June 3, 1913, J. C. F. Merrill to E. E. Clark, Nov. 26, 1913, and John M. Glenn to J. C. Clements, Jan. 3, 1914, ICC Records, ICC Docket no. 5860; *Annual Report of the Philadelphia Board of Trade, 1914*, pp. 56–68; *Report of the Boston Chamber of Commerce, 1913*, pp. 38–39 and *1915*, pp. 41–42; *Cleveland Chamber of Commerce, 1914*, p. 44.

20. Edwin G. Merrill to Interstate Commerce Commission, Feb. 18, 1914, and Thomas S. Birdseye to Interstate Commerce Commission, Feb. 24, 1914, ICC Records, ICC Docket no. 5860. See also White and Kemble to Interstate Commerce Commission, Feb. 10, 1914, *ibid.*; *Briefs*, vol. vi, *ibid.*, ICC Investigation and Suspension no. 333; E. B. Leigh, *Railway Purchases Measure General Business Prosperity* (New York, 1913). A good summary of the remaining opposition is given in *Decisions of the Interstate Commerce Commission of the United States*, 31:357 (1914).

21. *Ibid.*, 31:425–426; John H. Blessing to Harlan, Apr. 4, 1914, ICC Records, ICC Docket no. 5860. See also Alpheus T. Mason, *Brandeis: A Free Man's Life* (New York, 1946), chap. xxi.

22. James J. Hill, *Addresses*, "The Outlook for Business, December 5, 1914"; *ABA Proceedings, 1914*, pp. 57–68; *Proceedings of the American Cotton Manufacturers' Association, 1914*, pp. 132–139. See also *Transactions of the National Association of Cotton Manufacturers, Apr. 1914*, pp. 115–118; *Iron Age*, 95:310 (Feb. 4, 1915); *Proceedings of the California Bankers' Association, 1914*, pp. 134–148; *American Industries*, vol. XIV, no. 10 (May 1914), p. 7; *Proceedings of the National Wholesale Grocers' Association, 1914*, pp. 105–106.

23. *Proceedings of the New York State Bankers Association, 1914*, pp. 10–24; Simmons Hardware Company circular letter, June 9, 1914, National Association of Manufacturers circular letter, July 30, 1914, Wilson Papers. See also Henry L. Higginson to Elihu Root, June 9, 1914, Root Papers; *Annual Report of the Richmond Chamber of Commerce, 1914*, p. 3.

24. *Proceedings of the American Cotton Manufacturers' Association, 1910*, pp. 115–123, 186–189 and *1913*, pp. 124–125; Memphis Cotton Exchange to John Sharp Williams, Mar. 12, 1914, Papers of John Sharp Williams, Library of Congress.

25. Alexander Berger to Roosevelt, Mar. 6, 1908, FTC Records, File 5598; *Annual Statement of the St. Louis Merchants' Exchange, 1909*, p. 29; Grain Inspection Bill File, Box 37, Root Papers; *Iron Age*, 93:1414 (June 4, 1914).

26. *Nation's Business,* vol. II, no. 8 (Aug. 15, 1915), p. 2; Hepburn to Robert F. Maddox, Aug. 10, 1914, Hepburn Papers; *American Industries,* vol. XV, no. 2 (Sept. 1914), p. 7. See also *Transactions of the National Association of Cotton Manufacturers, 1914,* pp. 33–41; *Financial Age,* 30:269–270 (Aug. 8, 1914).

27. House Committee on the Merchant Marine and Fisheries (64 Cong., 1 sess.), *Creating a Shipping Board, a Naval Auxiliary, and a Merchant Marine, Hearings on H.R. 10500* (Washington, 1916), p. 161. See also Merchant Marine, D.Com. Records, File 72155–18 and National Foreign Trade Council, Jan. 21–22, 1915, *ibid.,* File 71737–1; *Iron Age,* 73:36–37 (June 2, 1904); *NAM Board Minutes* (May 16 and Oct. 13, 1910).

28. J. McD. Price to Wilson, Jan. 25, 1915, Wilson Papers; *Annual Report of the Philadelphia Board of Trade, 1915,* p. 29.

29. *National Industrial Traffic League: Proceedings, Nov. 1915,* pp. 4–5; *Economist,* 53:914 (Nov. 20, 1915). See also U.S. Chamber of Commerce *Special Bulletin, July 9, 1915; Commercial West,* 28:7 (Nov. 6, 1915); *NY Chamber of Commerce, 1914–1915,* pp. 158–199; *Annual Statement of the Merchants' Exchange of St. Louis, 1916,* p. 18; House Committee on the Merchant Marine and Fisheries, *Creating a Shipping Board,* pp. 516–517 and *passim.*

30. *Nation's Business,* vol. IV, no. 2 (Feb. 1916), part II, pp. 63–65. See also *ibid.,* vol. III, no. 4 (Apr. 15, 1915), p. 8; *Report of the Boston Chamber of Commerce, 1915,* pp. 37–38; *Merchants' Association of New York Annual Report, 1915–1916,* p. 27; E. N. Hurley, "Helping Business from Within, Dec. 14, 1915," in Wilson Papers; *Proceedings of the National Wholesale Grocers' Association, 1916,* pp. 38–39; *Iron Age,* 97:1341 (June 1, 1916); *Annual Report of the Federal Trade Commission* (Washington, 1916), p. 13.

31. E. H. Goodwin to Redfield, Dec. 13, 1914, and Redfield to Wilson, Feb. 3, 1915, D.Com. Records, File 72626; *Annual Report of the Federal Trade Commission,* (Washington, 1916), pp. 34–35; *Proceedings of the American Manufacturers' Export Association, 1916,* p. 330; *Proceedings of the American Cotton Manufacturers' Association, 1916,* pp. 148–149; *Annual Report of the Philadelphia Board of Trade, 1916,* pp. 19–20; *Banker and Tradesman,* 53:1051 (May 20, 1916); *Bankers Magazine,* 93:135–136 (Aug. 1916).

32. *Proceedings of the American Iron and Steel Institute, May 1916,* p. 16; *Bulletin of the National Association of Wool Manufacturers,* 46:164 (1916). See also *Manufacturers' Record,* 69:37 (Apr. 20, 1916); *CC Board Minutes* (Nov. 22, 1915); Henry R. Towne to George W. Loft, Dec. 7, 1915, and John V. Farwell to Wilson, Dec. 27, 1915, Wilson Papers; *Banker and Tradesman,* 52:739 (Oct. 16, 1915); *Economist,* 55:634 (Sept. 30, 1916).

33. *American Industries,* vol. XVI, no. 7 (Feb. 1916), pp. 10–11;

Iron Age, 97:788–789 (Mar. 30, 1916); *American Economist*, 56:107 (Mar. 8, 1916) and 56:137 (Mar. 24, 1916).

34. *Texas Bankers Record*, 4:8–15 (June 1915). See also Diary, 2:157–158 (Aug. 12, 1914), Papers of Charles S. Hamlin, Library of Congress; Vanderlip to Gilbert Hitchcock, Sept. 1, 1914, Vanderlip Papers; A. B. Hepburn to J. J. Mitchell, Aug. 14, 1914, Hepburn Papers; *Proceedings of the Tennessee Bankers' Association, 1915*, p. 78; *Proceedings of the Illinois Bankers Association, 1915*, pp. 48–54; *Proceedings of the Minnesota Bankers' Association, 1915*, pp. 15–18.

35. *Proceedings of the Florida Bankers Association, 1915*, pp. 21–37. See also *ABA Proceedings, 1916*, p. 171; *Proceedings of the Wisconsin Bankers' Association, 1913*, p. 162; *Annual Convention of the Michigan Bankers' Association, 1914*, pp. 24–32; Herrick to Vanderlip, June 5, 1914, Sept. 5, 1916, Vanderlip Papers. *Proceedings of the Illinois Bankers Association, 1915*, pp. 89–100.

36. *Proceedings of the Florida Bankers Association, 1916*, pp. 18–20. See also *Bankers Magazine*, 93:1–4 (July 1916); *Financial Age*, 34:344 (Sept. 2, 1916); *Proceedings of the Vermont Bankers' Association, 1915*, pp. 18–26; *Proceedings of the Idaho Bankers Association, 1916*, pp. 30–32; New York *Journal of Commerce and Commercial Bulletin*, Feb. 17, 1916; *ABA Proceedings, 1916*, pp. 219–245.

37. Wilson to Frank Trumbull, Sept. 10, 1914, Wilson Papers. See also *The Railroads' Appeal to the President of the United States, September 9, 1914* (n.p., 1914); *Decisions of the Interstate Commerce Commission*, 32:325–354 (1914).

38. Elliott, *Addresses*, II, "Remarks of December 31, 1914"; *Annual Statement of the Merchants' Exchange of St. Louis, 1915*, pp. 13–14; *National Industrial Traffic League: Proceedings, Aug. 1914*, pp. 29–31 and *Sept. 1915*, pp. 3–4. See also *ibid., Nov. 1914*, pp. 3–7 and *Apr. 1916*, p. 9; *Cleveland Chamber of Commerce, 1915*, pp. 66–68; Benjamin F. Bush, *Why Are Several Large Western Railroad Systems in Receivers' Hands?* (n.p., 1915).

39. *Traffic World* (Chicago), 18:529–530 (Sept. 2, 1916); *Manufacturers' Record*, 70:37–38 (Aug. 24, 1916). See also *Commercial and Financial Chronicle*, 102:782 (Sept. 2, 1916); *Boston News Letter*, Sept. 6, 1916.

40. *Protectionist*, 28:257–258 (Sept. 1916); *Wall Street Journal*, Oct. 14, 1916.

41. *American Industries*, vol. XII, no. 6 (Jan. 1911), p. 9. For other examples of antagonism toward lawyers, see John Claflin to George Perkins, Mar. 14, 1906, Perkins Papers; *Camden Board of Trade Journal*, 1:12 (Mar. 1911); *Manufacturers' News*, 6:8 (Sept. 17, 1914). A rare attack upon the Brandeis nomination is *Commercial and Financial Chronicle*, 102:377–378 (Jan. 29, 1916).

42. Gary to Perkins, undated (Apr. 1916), Perkins Papers; New

York *Journal of Commerce and Commercial Bulletin,* Oct. 19, 1916. See also *ibid.,* Nov. 6, 1916; Arthur S. Link, *Woodrow Wilson and the Progressive Era, 1910–1917* (New York, 1954), pp. 243–244. For comments on Wilson's foreign policy, see *Proceedings of the Vermont Bankers' Association, 1915,* pp. 191–202, 211–212; *Proceedings of the Georgia Bankers Association, 1915,* pp. 66–67; *Financial Age,* 31:740 (May 15, 1915); *Banker and Tradesman,* 52:1147 (Dec. 11, 1915), pp. 11–27.

43. *Protectionist,* 28:472–476 (Dec. 1916); *Financial Age,* 34:828 (Nov. 11, 1916).

CHAPTER VII. LABOR

1. *Commercial and Financial Chronicle,* 75:412 (Aug. 30, 1902); New York *Journal of Commerce and Commercial Bulletin,* Aug. 27, 1902. See also *ibid.,* July 31, 1902; John Mitchell to Daniel Keefe, Sept. 24, 1900, Papers of John Mitchell, Catholic University of America; *Independent* (New York), 53:1895–1898 (Aug. 15, 1901); *Outlook* (New York), 71:321 (May 31, 1902); New York Board of Trade and Transportation Resolutions, June 4, 1902, Roosevelt Papers.

2. *Independent,* 54:2228 (Sept. 18, 1902); Mark Hanna to George Perkins, undated (ca. Aug. 1902), Perkins Papers; *Annual Report of the Philadelphia Board of Trade, 1902,* p. 30; New York *Journal of Commerce and Commercial Bulletin,* Aug. 25, 1902; *Wall Street Journal,* Sept. 30, 1902; *Bankers Magazine,* 65:281–282 (Sept. 1902); William F. King to Roosevelt, Oct. 4, 1902, Roosevelt Papers.

3. *Wall Street Journal,* Oct. 3, 15, 1902; New York *Journal of Commerce and Commercial Bulletin,* Oct. 17, 1902; *Commercial West,* 4:11 (Oct. 25, 1902). A dissent is *Iron Age,* 70:28 (Oct. 23, 1902).

4. *Annual Report of the Denver Chamber of Commerce and Board of Trade, 1903,* p. 17; *American Industries,* vol. V, no. 15 (Mar. 1907), pp. 5–6.

5. The best book on this neglected subject is Marguerite Green, *The National Civic Federation and the American Labor Movement, 1900–1925* (Washington, 1956). See also Arthur Suffern, *Conciliation and Arbitration in the Coal Industry of America* (Boston, 1915); *Annals of the American Academy of Political and Social Sciences* (Philadelphia), vol. XX, no. 1 (July 1902), pp. 19–26.

6. *Report to the President on the Anthracite Coal Strike by the Anthracite Coal Strike Commission,* Sen. Doc. no. 6, 58 Cong., special sess. (Washington, 1903), pp. 64, 75, 76, 78.

7. *Manufacturers' Record,* 46:627 (Jan. 12, 1905); House Committee on Labor (58 Cong., 2 sess.), *Eight Hours for Laborers on Government Work, Hearings* (Washington, 1904), p. 166. See also *Annual Report of the Pittsburgh Chamber of Commerce, 1902,* pp. 54–59; *Transactions of the National Association of Cotton Manufac-*

turers, Apr. 1913, pp. 112–120; *Railway Age,* 36:58–59 (July 18, 1902); New York *Journal of Commerce and Commercial Bulletin,* Sept. 12, 1916.

8. *Rand McNally Bankers' Monthly,* 22:215–217 (Sept. 1901). See also *Financial Age,* 8:572–574 (Oct. 5, 1903) and 7:309 (Feb. 23, 1903); New York *Journal of Commerce and Commercial Bulletin,* May 18, 1901 and June 4, 1909; *Wall Street Journal,* Feb. 22, 1916.

9. *Wall Street Journal,* Apr. 8, 1912; *Annual Meeting of the Hartford Board of Trade, 1902,* pp. 20–22; New York *Journal of Commerce and Commercial Bulletin,* Sept. 16, 1903. See also *Wall Street Journal,* Oct. 24, 1903, May 17, 1913; *Economist,* 30:266–267 (Aug. 29, 1903); *Bankers Magazine,* 65:9–10 (July 1902); *Manufacturers' Record,* 54:53 (Sept. 3, 1908); *Financial Age,* 23:788 (Apr. 29, 1911).

10. *Wall Street Journal,* Jan. 13, 1911, Jan. 3, 1914; *NAM Proceedings, 1905,* p. 195. See also House Committee on Interstate and Foreign Commerce (61 Cong., 2 sess.), *Hearings on Bills Affecting Interstate Commerce* (2 vols., Washington, 1910), I, 234–261; *Annual Report of the Boston Chamber of Commerce, 1907,* p. 35; *Annual Report of the San Francisco Chamber of Commerce, 1907,* p. 7; New York *Journal of Commerce and Commercial Bulletin,* Apr. 13, 1907; *Commercial West,* 7:9–10 (May 13, 1905).

11. *American Industries,* vol. III, no. 2 (Sept. 1, 1904), p. 13; *Railway Age,* 42:770 (Dec. 21, 1906); *Manufacturers' News,* 3:9–10 (May 1, 1913); Julius Rosenwald to Wilson, Mar. 20, 1913, Wilson Papers.

12. *Cotton,* 13:3–4 (Aug. 15, 1906); *Annual Report of the Chicago Board of Trade, 1902,* pp. xiii–xiv; Barbour to Parry, Dec. 26, 1902, *Corres NAM,* no. 80. See also The Gold Medal Camp Furniture & Novelty Manufacturing Co. to Parry, July 1, 1902, *ibid.,* no. 7; *Cleveland Chamber of Commerce, 1914,* pp. 243–257.

13. *Annual Meeting of the National Civic Federation, 1908,* pp. 38–41; Ralph M. Easley circular letter, June 13, 1913, Root Papers; *Bulletins of the United States Bureau of Labor Statistics* (Washington), no. 191 (Mar. 1916), pp. 26–27, 46; *Report of the Boston Chamber of Commerce, 1912,* pp. 46–49; *Official Proceedings of the Trans-Mississippi Commercial Congress, 1904,* p. 163; George Mowry, *The California Progressives* (Berkeley, Los Angeles, 1951), p. 144.

14. Perkins to Morgan, July 23, 1907 and Memorandum, Apr. 1901, Perkins Papers. See also Perkins to Morgan, Apr. 12, 1909, Memorandum for President Corey, Dec. 16, 1909 and George W. Wickersham to Perkins, Feb. 19, 1910, *ibid.;* Elbert H. Gary, *Addresses and Statements* (7 vols., Boston, 1927), I, "Interview of 1904," "Remarks of June 25, 1914"; John A. Garraty, "The United States Steel Corporation Versus Labor: The Early Years," *Labor History,* 1:3–38 (Winter 1960).

15. Gary, *Addresses,* I, "Address of October 19, 1911."

16. Herrick to Perkins, Jan. 2, 1902, Perkins Papers. See also Joseph A. Thatcher to Perkins, Jan. 8, 1903, *ibid.; Wall Street Journal,* Feb. 7, 1903, July 13, 1909, Feb. 22, 1915, Apr. 1, 1916; *Annalist,*.7:537 (Apr. 24, 1916); H. L. Higginson to Elihu Root, Apr. 1, 1910, Root Papers; *Transactions of the National Association of Cotton Manufacturers, Sept. 1912,* pp. 47–54; *Commercial and Financial Chronicle,* 101:882–883 (Sept. 18, 1915); W. L. Park, *The Concern of Railroad Employes in the Existing Railroad Situation* (n.p., n.d.).

17. *Iron Age,* 93:150 (Jan. 8, 1914); *Banker and Tradesman,* 49:211 (Jan. 31, 1914); *Cotton,* 78:269 (May 1914).

18. Paul H. Giddens, *Standard Oil Company (Indiana); Oil Pioneer of the Middle West* (New York, 1955), pp. 333–336; *Iron Age,* 97:440 (Feb. 17, 1916).

19. House Committee on Labor (58 Cong., 2 sess.), *Eight Hours for Laborers on Government Work, Hearings* (Washington, 1904), pp. 22–23; Clarence E. Bonnett, *Employer Associations in the United States: A Study of Typical Associations* (New York, 1922), pp. 454–464; *American Industries,* vol. XVI, no. 1 (Aug. 1915), pp. 23–24.

20. *Synopsis of Proceedings of the National Metal Trades Association, 1909,* pp. 11–16. See also Bonnett, *Employer Associations,* pp. 103–118.

21. *NAM Proceedings, 1901,* p. 20 and *1903,* pp. 165–169. See also Senate on Education and Labor, *Eight Hours for Laborers on Government Work, Hearings,* Sen. Doc. no. 141, 57 Cong., 1 sess. (Washington, 1903), pp. 181, 256.

22. *Proceedings of the Citizens' Industrial Association, 1904,* p. 8; *NAM Proceedings, 1903,* pp. 199–228. See also *American Industries,* vol. I, no. 3 (Sept. 15, 1902), p. 10.

23. *NAM Proceedings, 1903,* p. 17 and *1907,* pp. 31–47; *American Industries,* vol. XIII, no. 11 (June 1913), p. 13 and vol. XIV, no. 5 (Dec. 1913), p. 7. See also Marshall Cushing circular letter, Sept. 25, 1905, Tompkins Papers, University of North Carolina.

24. *NAM Proceedings, 1911,* pp. 65–90; House Subcommittee of Committee on Labor (60 Cong., 1 sess.), *H.R. 15651 Eight Hours for Laborers on Government Work, Hearings* (Washington, 1908), p. 231. See also *Wall Street Journal,* May 15, 1903; *New York Journal of Commerce and Commercial Bulletin,* July 29, 1903; *Economist,* 28:582 (Nov. 1, 1902).

25. Cushing to N. F. Thompson, Mar. 19, 1904, *Corres NAM,* no. 486. See also House Committee on the Judiciary (59 Cong., 1 sess.), *Hearings in Relation to Anti-Injunction and Restraining Orders* (Washington, 1906); House Committee on Labor (57 Cong., 1 sess.), *Eight Hours for Laborers on Government Work, Hearings* (Washington, 1902).

26. A sample of the opposition to eight-hour and anti-injunction laws is *Annual Report of the St. Paul Chamber of Commerce, 1902–*

1903, pp. 7–8; *Annual Report of the Philadelphia Board of Trade*, *1902*, pp. 18–20; *Annual Report of the Cincinnati Chamber of Commerce, 1904*, p. 39; A. A. Burnham to Foraker, Apr. 26, 1906, Foraker Papers; *Annual Report of the Merchants' Association of New York*, *1908*, pp. 23–24; *Annual Report of the San Francisco Chamber of Commerce, 1910*, p. 10; *Cleveland Chamber of Commerce, 1912*, pp. 154–155; Railroad Presidents' open letter to the Senate, July 3, 1912, Taft Papers.

27. *American Industries*, vol. XV, no. 5 (Dec. 1914), pp. 7–9; *Commercial and Financial Chronicle*, 102:1746–1747 (May 13, 1916). See also New York *Journal of Commerce and Commercial Bulletin*, May 21, 1902; *NAM Proceedings, 1907*, pp. 15–16, 31–47; *Illinois Manufacturers' Association Annual Meeting, 1911*, pp. 3–23; Gordon M. Jensen, "The National Civic Federation: American Business in an Age of Social Change and Social Reform, 1900–1910," Ph.D. dissertation (MS), Princeton University, 1956, pp. 304–312.

28. *NAM Proceedings, 1907*, pp. 15–16, 31–47; *American Industries*, vol. VII, no. 14 (Mar. 1, 1908), p. 16. See also *ibid.*, vol. V, no. 7 (Nov. 15, 1906), p. 8 and vol. VII, no. 17 (May 15, 1908), pp. 18–19.

29. William R. Corwine to Roosevelt, Oct. 2, 1902, Roosevelt Papers; *Protectionist*, 14:385–389 (Nov. 1902); *Commercial West*, 5:9 (Aug. 1, 1903); *Wall Street Journal*, July 24, 1903, Apr. 11, 1910.

30. *Synopsis of Proceedings of the National Metal Trades Association, 1910*, pp. 5–9. See also *ibid.*, *1914*, pp. 17–27; *Commercial and Financial Chronicle*, 80:1442–1443 (Apr. 22, 1905) and 86:513–515 (Feb. 29, 1908).

31. *Iron Age*, 91:668–669 (Mar. 13, 1913); *Nation's Business*, vol. I, no. 12 (June 16, 1913), pp. 1, 8–9, vol. II, no. 8 (Aug. 15, 1914), p. 10, and vol. IV, no. 2 (Feb. 1916), part II, pp. 47–52. See also Sundry Civil Bill File, Wilson Papers; *Chicago Commerce*, 9:9 (May 16, 1913); *Annual Report of the Merchants' Exchange of New York, 1913*, p. 21.

32. *American Anti-Boycott Association December Bulletin, 1914; American Industries*, vol. I, no. 21 (June 15, 1903), p. 12. See also *ibid.*, vol. XIV, no. 12 (July 1914), pp. 7–8; David Willcox memorandum, Oct. 3, 1902, Roosevelt Papers; *Wall Street Journal*, Feb. 7, 1906; Senate Committee on Interstate Commerce (62 Cong., 2 sess.), *Hearings Pursuant to S.Res. 98* (3 vols., Washington, 1912), II, 1979–2103; *Nation's Business*, vol. II, no. 7 (July 15, 1914), pp. 8–9.

33. *Wall Street Journal*, Mar. 15, 1916. See also *Nation's Business*, vol. III, no. 3 (Mar. 15, 1915), p. 12 and vol. IV, no. 3 (Mar. 1916), p. 3; *Report of the Boston Chamber of Commerce, 1914*, pp. 36–37; *Annual Report of the Philadelphia Board of Trade, 1915*, pp. 9–12; *Members' Annual Los Angeles Chamber of Commerce, 1914*, pp. 46–47; *American Industries*, vol. XV, no. 9 (Apr. 1915), p. 11.

34. *Commercial and Financial Chronicle*, 99:1783 (Dec. 19, 1914). See also Charles D. Hillis to Taft, Oct. 26, 1912, Taft Papers; Walter Drew to J. P. Tumulty, Oct. 16, 1914, Wilson Papers; *American Industries*, vol. XV, no. 6 (Jan. 1915), pp. 15–17; *Economist*, 53:449 (May 13, 1915); *Iron Age*, 96:474 (Aug. 26, 1915).

35. *CC Minutes, 1916*, p. 205. See also *Nation's Business*, vol. IV, no. 2 (Feb. 1916), part II, pp. 5, 29–34; *Commercial and Financial Chronicle*, 102:368–369 (Jan. 29, 1916); *National Industrial Traffic League: Proceedings, Apr. 1916*, p. 23.

36. *Nation's Business*, vol. IV, no. 7 (July 1916), pp. 2, 4; John V. Farwell to Wilson, July 29, 1916, Harry A. Wheeler to Wilson, Aug. 12, 1916, George Pope to Wilson, Aug. 18, 1916, and R. G. Rhett to Wilson, Aug. 22, 1916, Wilson Papers.

37. *Chicago Commerce*, 12:6 (Sept. 8, 1916); *Wall Street Journal*, Nov. 28, 1916. See also Henry Ford to Wilson, Sept. 1, 1916, Wilson Papers; *National Industrial Traffic League: Proceedings, Nov. 1916*, p. 6; *Greater New York* (New York), 5:1 (Nov. 27, 1916); *Bankers Magazine*, 93:291–293 (Oct. 1916); Festus J. Wade to David R. Francis, Sept. 4, 1916, Papers of David R. Francis, Missouri Historical Society.

38. *Greater New York*, 5:1–5 (Sept. 25, 1916); U.S. Senate, *Lobby Hearings*, IV, 3979–3988. See also Walker D. Hines, *The Needs and Opportunity of the Railroad Situation* (n.p., 1916); Chamber of Commerce of the United States *Yearbook, 1917*, pp. 97–98; New York *Journal of Commerce and Commercial Bulletin*, Aug. 4, 1916.

CHAPTER VIII. PREDISPOSITIONS AND PROGRESSIVISM

1. Ivy Lee, *The Railroads and Human Nature* (New York, 1914); *Financial Age*, 16:1522 (Dec. 30, 1907); Irving T. Bush to J. P. Tumulty, Dec. 15, 1914, Wilson Papers; *Wall Street Journal*, Nov. 24, 1910. See also *ibid.*, Apr. 10, 1912; *Economist*, 25:392 (Apr. 6, 1901).

2. *NAM Proceedings, 1912*, pp. 71–101; *American Economist*, 47:126 (Mar. 10, 1911); *American Industries*, vol. XIII, no. 11 (June 1913), p. 9; *Economist*, 45:1909 (June 17, 1911); *Commercial West*, 13:7–8 (May 30, 1908). See also *Cleveland Chamber of Commerce, 1908*, pp. 69–72; Memorandum on Initiative, Referendum, and Recall, Feb. 24, 1912, Tompkins Papers, Library of Congress; New York *Journal of Commerce and Commercial Bulletin*, June 22, 1909.

3. *Manufacturers' Record*, 56:42 (Sept. 30, 1909). See also *Official Proceedings of the Trans-Mississippi Commercial Congress, 1908*, pp. 118–119.

4. *Iron Age*, 77:1914 (June 14, 1906); *Commercial West*, 10:10 (Oct. 6, 1906); W. W. Finley, *Addresses*, I, "Address of June 21, 1910." See also Senate Committee on Education and Labor (58 Cong., 2 sess.), *Senate Bill 489, Eight Hours for Laborers on Government*

Work, Arguments (Washington, 1904), p. 160; Economist, 40:276–277 (Aug. 22, 1908).

5. American Industries, vol. IX, no. 12 (Aug. 1, 1909), pp. 8–10; Financial Age, 6:425–427 (Sept. 29, 1902) and 13:35 (Jan. 1, 1906); Annual Meeting of the Ohio State Board of Commerce, 1904, pp. 198–199; Proceedings of the National Board of Trade, 1904, p. 34. See also NAM Proceedings, 1908, pp. 191–192.

6. For Southern ambivalence see Annual Report of the Savannah Board of Trade, 1906–1907, pp. 7–8; Charleston [South Carolina] Chamber of Commerce Annual Report, 1914–1915, p. 3; Cotton, 9:5 (Apr. 15, 1904); NAM Proceedings, 1910, pp. 39–53. See also Seattle Chamber of Commerce Annual Report, 1914, p. 10; Nation's Business, vol. II, no. 3 (Mar. 20, 1914), p. 14; Detroit Board of Commerce Report, 1910, pp. 32–33; Proceedings of the American Cotton Manufacturers' Association, 1906, pp. 270–279. For exceptional support for a literacy test, see Annual Report of the Indianapolis Board of Trade, 1906, p. 23; Annual Statement of the Merchants' Exchange of St. Louis, 1912, p. 13.

7. Annual Report of the Pittsburgh Chamber of Commerce, 1911, p. 49; Manufacturers' Record, 47:317 (Apr. 27, 1905); Proceedings of the National Board of Trade, 1907, pp. 52, 246. See also Annual Report of the Philadelphia Trades' League, 1905, pp. 147–149; Jacob H. Schiff to O. S. Straus, Jan. 22, 1907, Straus Papers; CC Board Minutes (Apr. 8, 1914).

8. American Industries, vol. V, no. 11 (Jan. 15, 1907), pp. 1–5 and vol. V, no. 15 (Mar. 15, 1907), p. 8; Manufacturers' Record, 50:569 (Dec. 20, 1906) and 52:44 (Oct. 24, 1907); D. C. Heyward to D. A. Tompkins, Aug. 21, 1907, Tompkins Papers, Library of Congress; Cotton, 14:122–123 (Apr. 1907); NAM Proceedings, 1910, pp. 22–39. Chinese immigration posed a unique problem. Beyond asking the government to admit token immigration in order to end Chinese boycotting, businessmen apparently accepted the exclusion law. See ibid., 1904, pp. 90–92; Official Proceedings of the Trans-Mississippi Commercial Congress, 1905, pp. 167–179.

9. Protectionist, 24:94 (June 1912); Wall Street Journal, Sept. 12, 1916. See also ibid., June 28, 1907; Proceedings of the National Board of Trade, 1902, p. 238; New York Journal of Commerce and Commercial Bulletin, May 23, 1903; Cleveland Chamber of Commerce, 1913, p. 158; Nation's Business, vol. III, no. 12 (Dec. 1915), pp. 2, 18–20; Annual Report of the Cincinnati Chamber of Commerce, 1916, pp. 22–23; Report of the Boston Chamber of Commerce, 1916–1917, p. 43; Edward G. Hartman, The Movement to Americanize the Immigrant (New York, 1948), pp. 38 ff.

10. Proceedings of the Alabama Bankers Association, 1907, pp. 18–22; Annual Statement of the Memphis Merchants' Exchange, 1904,

pp. 15–19; *Wall Street Journal,* Sept. 1, 1905. See also *American Industries,* vol. III, no. 22 (July 1, 1905), p. 8; *Commercial West,* 23:9 (Apr. 12, 1913); *Proceedings of the Traffic Club of Pittsburgh, 1911,* pp. 7–16.

11. *Annual Statement of the Merchants' Exchange of St. Louis, 1902,* pp. 12–13. See also *Wall Street Journal,* July 30, 1906; *Commercial West,* 15:8 (June 5, 1909); *Williamsport Board of Trade Annual Report, 1906,* p. 17; *NY Chamber of Commerce, 1905–1906,* pp. xxxvii–xxxviii; Perkins to W. M. Reay, Aug. 12, 1907, Perkins Papers.

12. *NAM Proceedings, 1906,* pp. 10–27; *ABA Proceedings, 1906,* pp. 14–20; *Financial Age,* 13:1156–1158 (June 25, 1906); F. C. Schwedtman to L. Hayne, Dec. 12, 1907, U.S. Senate, *Appendix, Lobby,* II, 1201; *Proceedings of the American Iron and Steel Institute, Oct. 1913,* pp. 287–294; Gary, *Addresses,* I, "Interview of Jan. 2, 1908." See also *ibid.,* "Address of October 20, 1915"; *Wall Street Journal,* Mar. 29, 1904, Feb. 3, 1911; *American Industries,* vol. XV, no. 12 (July 1915), p. 9; *American Economist,* 47:363 (June 23, 1911).

13. *Proceedings of the Kansas Bankers' Association, 1905,* pp. 168–177; *Wall Street Journal,* Nov. 2, 1915. See also *Proceedings of the American Cotton Manufacturers' Association, 1906,* pp. 82–86.

14. *Proceedings of the Nevada Bankers' Association, 1910,* pp. 11–15; *Financial Age,* 8:224 (Aug. 10, 1903); *Proceedings of the Wisconsin Bankers' Association, 1909,* p. 40; *Proceedings of the Oklahoma Bankers' Association, 1915,* pp. 84–85. See also *Bankers Magazine,* 92:179 (Feb. 1916).

15. *Wall Street Journal,* Jan. 18, 1911; *Annual Report of the Philadelphia Board of Trade, 1914,* pp. 10–18; *Commercial West,* 29:7–8 (June 17, 1916). See also *New York Journal of Commerce and Commercial Bulletin,* Oct. 21, 1913.

16. *Proceedings of the North Dakota Bankers' Association, 1907,* pp. 16–22; *ABA Proceedings, 1902,* pp. 8–12.

17. *Commercial West,* 15:7 (June 12, 1909); *Annual Report of the Pittsburgh Chamber of Commerce, 1900,* pp. 28–29; Perkins to Schwab, Oct. 14, 1908, Perkins Papers; Thomas F. Parker to Van Cleave, Aug. 8, 1907, Tompkins Papers, University of North Carolina. On Morgan, see *Annual Report of the Savannah Board of Trade, 1912–1913,* p. 10; *Proceedings of the Florida Bankers Association, 1913,* pp. 71–72; *Proceedings of the Wisconsin Bankers' Association, 1913,* pp. 46–54. On Schwab, see Schwab to Perkins, July 2, 1903, Perkins Papers. On Mellen, see *Banker and Tradesman,* 47:475 (Mar. 1, 1913) and 48:1299 (Dec. 13, 1913). On Bigelow, see *Commercial and Financial Chronicle,* 80:1694 (Apr. 29, 1905); *ABA Proceedings, 1905,* pp. v–vi, 9–13.

18. *Proceedings of the National Board of Trade, 1908,* p. 270; *Proceedings of the American Iron and Steel Institute, Oct. 1913,* p.

292; *NAM Proceedings, 1914,* pp. 4–15. See also *ibid., 1910,* p. 133; *Annual Report of the San Francisco Board of Trade, 1901,* p. 17; New York *Journal of Commerce and Commercial Bulletin,* July 17, 1906. 19. *NAM Proceedings, 1903,* pp. 13–87, 273–274 and *1913,* p. 194; *Bulletin of the National Association of Wool Manufacturers,* 42:139–141 (1912); New York *Journal of Commerce and Commercial Bulletin,* May 6, 1904 and Aug. 5, 1916; *American Industries,* vol. II, no. 16 (Apr. 1, 1904), p. 5 and vol. XIII, no. 10 (May 1913), pp. 19, 42–43; *American Economist,* 49:29 (Jan. 19, 1912). See also *Official Proceedings of the Trans-Mississippi Commercial Congress, 1905,* p. 103.

20. *American Industries,* vol. XIII, no. 13 (July 1913), p. 11; *American Economist,* 29:16–17 (Jan. 10, 1902); *Bulletin of the American Iron and Steel Association,* 42:33 (Apr. 15, 1908).

21. C. A. Carlisle to A. J. Beveridge, Feb. 8, 1906, Beveridge Papers; *American Industries,* vol. XIV, no. 2 (Sept. 1913), p. 15. See also New York *Journal of Commerce and Commercial Bulletin,* July 23, 1915.

22. *Economist,* 55:1142 (Dec. 9, 1916); *American Industries,* vol. XIV, no. 3 (Oct. 1913), p. 7; H. E Miles to Van Cleave, Aug. 31, 1908, U.S. Senate, *Appendix, Lobby,* II, 1955–1956; *Commercial and Financial Chronicle,* 98:489–490 (Aug. 26, 1911). See also New York *Journal of Commerce and Commercial Bulletin,* May 19, 1903; *Bankers Magazine,* 89:620–621 (Dec. 1914).

23. *Wall Street Journal,* May 7, 1904: *NAM Proceedings, 1907,* p. 84 and *1911,* pp. 65–90; *Proceedings of the Pennsylvania Bankers' Association, 1906,* pp. 15–20; *Proceedings of the Illinois Bankers Association, 1911,* pp. 56–65. See also *Manufacturers' News,* 1:7–8 (Apr. 25, 1912).

24. *Commercial West,* 20:7 (Dec. 16, 1911) and 20:7 (Sept. 23, 1911); *Proceedings of the Georgia Bankers Association, 1911,* p. 14. See also *Annual Report of the Pittsburgh Chamber of Commerce, 1911,* pp. 49–57; *Transactions of the National Association of Cotton Manufacturers, Sept. 1915,* pp. 32–42.

25. *ABA Proceedings, 1908,* pp. 38–48; *Financial Age,* 7:1030–1031 (June 29, 1903); H. L. Higginson to Taft, July 26, 1911, Taft Papers; *Commercial and Financial Chronicle,* 96:1527 (May 31, 1913); Stuyvesant Fish to J. S. Williams, Apr. 31, 1915, Williams Papers.

26. *Banker and Tradesman,* 63:411 (Feb. 25, 1911); *Wall Street Journal,* Jan. 7, 1913; Howard Elliott, *Public Opinion; Its Effect on Business* (n.p., 1912); *NAM Proceedings, 1905,* pp. 194–214; House Committee on the Judiciary (62 Cong., 2 sess.), *Trust Legislation, Hearings* (9 parts, Washington, 1912), I, 393.

27. *Proceedings of the American Iron and Steel Institute, May 1915,* pp. 11–27; *Wall Street Journal,* Feb. 24, 1904; *Railway Age,*

43:373–374 (Mar. 22, 1907); *Economist*, 45:565 (Apr. 1, 1911). See also Frick to Roosevelt, Nov. 30, 1907, Roosevelt Papers; Hill, *Addresses*, "Address Delivered June 4, 1902"; New York *Journal of Commerce and Commercial Bulletin*, Mar. 26, 1914.

28. *ABA Proceedings, 1914,* pp. 57–68; Senate Committee on Public Lands (61 Cong., 2 sess.), *Public and Private Rights in the Public Domain No. 1, Hearings on the Bill S. 4733* (Washington, 1910), pp. 68–69; George E. Mowry, *The Era of Theodore Roosevelt, 1900–1912* (New York, 1958), p. 216.

29. *Year Book of the Syracuse Chamber of Commerce, 1909–1910,* pp. 83–84. See also *NAM Board Minutes* (Feb. 24, 1910); *Annual Report of the San Francisco Chamber of Commerce, 1910,* p. 7; *Annual Statement of the Merchants' Exchange of St. Louis, 1910,* p. 29; *Jacksonville Board of Trade Report, 1910,* p. 23.

30. *Commercial and Financial Chronicle,* 90:76–78 (Jan. 8, 1910); *Proceedings of the American Iron and Steel Institute, May 1913,* pp. 11–20; *Wall Street Journal,* Apr. 26, 1915. See also *ibid.,* Apr. 14, 1913; Memorandum on Federal Taxes, Oct. 17, 1912, Tompkins Papers, Library of Congress; *Report of the Annual Convention of the South Dakota Bankers' Association, 1913,* pp. 37–49; Darwin P. Kingsley to Wilson, Apr. 14, 1913, Wilson Papers.

31. *Massachusetts State Board of Trade: Annual Report, 1909,* p. 18; *NAM Proceedings, 1910,* pp. 234–235.

32. *Annual Report of the Philadelphia Board of Trade, 1915,* pp. 37–39; *Annual Report of the Philadelphia Trades' League, 1907,* pp. 90–91. See also *Hearings before the Commission on Employer's Liability and Workman's Compensation Appointed Under Joint Resolution of the Senate and House of Representatives of the United States* (Washington, 1911), pp. 91–92, 760–761, and *passim; NAM Board Minutes* (May 13, 1911); *Cleveland Chamber of Commerce, 1913,* pp. 160–162; *Annual Report of the Boston Chamber of Commerce, 1911,* p. 52; Gordon M. Jensen, "The National Civic Federation: American Business in an Age of Social Change and Social Reform, 1900–1910," Ph.D. dissertation (MS), Princeton University, 1956, p. 327.

33. *Nation's Business,* vol. IV, no. 6 (June 1916), p. 3; William C. Redfield to Elihu Root, Nov. 9, 1912, Root Papers; *American Industries,* vol. III, no. 21 (June 15, 1905), p. 8 and vol. XVII, no. 1 (Aug. 1916), p. 7; *Year Book of the Syracuse Chamber of Commerce, 1907–1908,* p. 31; *Annual Report of the Pittsburgh Chamber of Commerce, 1912–1913,* p. 25.

34. Senate Committee on Interstate Commerce, *Regulation of Railway Rates, Hearings, Sen Doc.* no. 243, 59 Cong., 2 sess. (5 vols., Washington, 1906), IV, 3279 and III, 1792.

35. L. F. Groves to Wilson, Aug. 2, 1916, Wilson Papers. See also House Committee on Labor (64 Cong., 1 sess.), *Child-Labor Bill,*

Hearings on H.R. 8234 (Washington, 1916), pp. 3–176; Senate Committee on Interstate Commerce (64 Cong., 1 sess.), *Interstate Commerce in Products of Child Labor, Hearings on H.R. 8234* (Washington, 1916), pp. 312, 314; *Philadelphia Chamber of Commerce Annual Report, 1914*, p. 19; *Massachusetts State Board of Trade: Annual Report, 1914*, p. 29; *Transactions of the New England Cotton Manufacturers' Association, 1904*, pp. 101–113; *Iron Age*, 77:432 (Feb. 1, 1906); Claude G. Bowers, *Beveridge and the Progressive Era* (Boston, 1932), pp. 250, 265–266; Cyrus Adler, *Jacob H. Schiff; His Life and Letters* (2 vols., Garden City, 1928–1929), I, 296–298; *Manufacturers' Record*, 46:318 (Oct. 20, 1904).

36. Senate Committee on Public Lands, *Public and Private Rights*, pp. 38–39, 45–46; *Proceedings of the National Board of Trade, 1909*, p. 6; *Annual Report of the Philadelphia Board of Trade, 1902*, p. 21. See also *Official Proceedings of the Trans-Mississippi Commercial Congress, 1901*, pp. 226–252; *Annual Report of the Savannah Board of Trade, 1901–1902*, pp. 4–5; *NY Chamber of Commerce, 1901–1902*, p. 144; F. D. Mitchell to Spooner, Feb. 10, 1905, Spooner Papers; *Annual Report of the Boston Chamber of Commerce, 1907*, p. 33; *NAM Proceedings, 1908*, pp. 251–253; *Cleveland Chamber of Commerce, 1908*, pp. 146–147.

37. *Annual Report of the Little Rock Board of Trade, 1907*, p. 116. See also Tompkins to Wade H. Harris, Aug. 7, 1913, Tompkins Papers, Library of Congress; *Cotton*, 76:187–188 (Mar. 1912); *Financial Age*, 30:604–605 (Oct. 10, 1914); W. H. Armstrong to J. S. Williams, Aug. 6, 1914, Williams Papers; William S. Witham to Glass, Oct. 17, 1914, Glass Papers.

38. New York *Journal of Commerce and Commercial Bulletin*, Sept. 21, 1908; *Bankers Magazine*, 43:516–517 (Dec. 1916). See also *Commercial West*, 25:7–8 (Apr. 18, 1914); J. E. Uihlein to Spooner, Dec. 24, 1904, Spooner Papers; Jacob Ruppert, Jr., to James Sherman, Mar. 13, 1908, Sherman Papers.

39. *Philadelphia Chamber of Commerce Annual Report, 1914*, pp. 17–18.

40. George P. Bent to Tompkins, Feb. 4, 1907, Tompkins Papers, Library of Congress; *Transactions of the National Association of Cotton Manufacturers, Apr. 1915*, pp. 120–120h. See also *Annual Report of the Philadelphia Board of Trade, 1914*, pp. 20–22.

41. *Financial Age*, 21:853–854 (May 9, 1910); *NAM Proceedings, 1912*, p. 260; *Proceedings of the American Iron and Steel Institute, May 1913*, pp. 11–20.

42. Association of Manufacturers and Distributors of Food Products to Spooner, Feb. 23, 1903, Spooner Papers. See also *Commercial West*, 19:7 (Apr. 15, 1911); Mowry, *Era of Theodore Roosevelt*, p. 83.

43. New York *Journal of Commerce and Commercial Bulletin*, June 19, 1914 and May 7, 1915; *Reasonable Regulation of Railroads*

(Philadelphia, 1916); Frank Trumbull, *Railway Service: Is It a National Problem or a Local Issue?* (n.p., 1915); *National Industrial Traffic League: Proceedings, Nov. 1916*, pp. 9–10. See also Railway Executives' Advisory Committee, Press Releases 1–51 (1916), in Bureau of Railway Economics Library; *Hearings . . . Employer's Liability and Workman's Compensation . . .* , p. 16; Moseley to William Loeb, Jr., Mar. 19, 1907, Roosevelt Papers.

44. *Commercial and Financial Chronicle*, 45:258 (Aug. 3, 1912); *Wall Street Journal*, Nov. 21, 1901 and Nov. 15, 1913; *American Industries*, vol. XIV, no. 6 (Jan. 1914), pp. 12–13. See also Chamber of Commerce of the United States *Yearbook, 1917*, pp. 96–97; *Proceedings of the New York State Bankers Association, 1916*, pp. 185–195.

45. *ABA Proceedings, 1901*, pp. 108–121; A. B. Stickney, *The Defects of the Interstate Commerce Law* (n.p., 1905).

46. Daniel Willard, *Address* (Boston, 1913) and *The Railroads and the Public* (n.p., 1915); Memorandum on letter of Willard to Franklin K. Lane, Aug. 30, 1916, Wilson Papers.

47. George W. Perkins, *The Business Problems of the Day* (n.p., 1911); John A. Garraty, *Right-Hand Man; The Life of George W. Perkins* (New York, 1960).

CHAPTER IX. BUSINESSMEN AND THE PROGRESSIVE MOVEMENT

1. Benjamin DeWitt, *The Progressive Movement* (New York, 1915), pp. 3–5 and *passim;* Charles A. Beard, *Contemporary American History, 1877–1913* (New York, 1918), chaps. x–xiii; Harold U. Faulkner, *The Quest for Social Justice, 1898–1914* (New York, 1931).

2. Robert M. LaFollette, *Autobiography* (Madison, Wis., 1913); Theodore Roosevelt, *An Autobiography* (New York, 1914); Henry F. Pringle, *Theodore Roosevelt; A Biography* (New York, 1931) and *The Life and Times of William Howard Taft; A Biography* (2 vols., New York, 1939); Claude G. Bowers, *Beveridge and the Progressive Era* (Boston, 1932); Alpheus T. Mason, *Brandeis: A Free Man's Life* (New York, 1946), pp. 365–375 and *passim.*

3. John Chamberlain, *Farewell to Reform* (New York, 1932), pp. 234, 267–269, and *passim;* Matthew Josephson, *The President Makers; The Culture of Politics and Leadership in an Age of Enlightenment, 1896–1919* (New York, 1940); Louis Filler, *Crusaders for American Liberalism* (New York, 1939).

4. See, for example, Samuel E. Morison and Henry S. Commager, *The Growth of the American Republic* (4th rev. ed., 2 vols., New York, 1950), II, chap. xv; Ralph H. Gabriel, *The Course of American Democratic Thought* (2nd ed., New York, 1956), chap. xxv; Merle Curti, *The Growth of American Thought* (2nd ed., New York, 1951), chap. xxiv; Russel B. Nye, *Midwestern Progressive Politics; A Historical*

Study of Its Origins and Development, 1870–1958 (East Lansing, 1959), pp. 184–189 and *passim;* Carl N. Degler, *Out of Our Past* (New York, 1959), pp. 368–378.

5. Eric F. Goldman, *Rendezvous with Destiny* (New York, 1952); Morton G. White, *Social Thought in America; The Revolt Against Formalism* (New York, 1949); David Noble, *The Paradox of Progressive Thought* (Minneapolis, 1958); Daniel Aaron, *Men of Good Hope; A Story of American Progressives* (New York, 1951), pp. xi–xiv, 245 ff; Louis Hartz, *The Liberal Tradition in America* (New York, 1955), chaps viii–ix; Arthur A. Ekirch, Jr., *The Decline of American Liberalism* (New York, 1955), chap. xi and *passim.*

6. Richard Hofstadter, *The Age of Reform; From Bryan to F.D.R.* (New York, 1955), chaps. iv–vi; George E. Mowry, *The Era of Theodore Roosevelt, 1900–1912* (New York, 1958), pp. 47–58, chap. v. In a different vein, Samuel P. Hays, *The Response to Industrialism, 1885–1914* (Chicago, 1957), to which this writer is particularly indebted, so thoroughly blends progressivism with the rest of American history in the period that a distinguishable progressive movement no longer exists.

7. Mowry, *Era of Theodore Roosevelt,* pp. 38–45.

8. Arthur S. Link, *Woodrow Wilson and the Progressive Era, 1910–1917* (New York, 1954), pp. 238–241; Hofstadter, *Age of Reform,* pp. 155–163. As an example of the confusion which the word creates for an intelligent, casual student of history, Seymour Martin Lipset writes, "[The] Progressive movement [party?] . . . died away without coming to national power." "The Sources of the 'Radical Right.'" *The New American Right,* Daniel Bell, ed. (New York, 1955), pp. 178–179.

9. F. C. Schwedtman to H. E. Miles, May 29, 1908, U.S. Senate, *Appendix, Lobby,* II, 1671.

10. Arthur S. Link, "What Happened to the Progressive Movement in the 1920's?" *American Historical Review* (New York, Washington), 64:836 (July 1959).

11. *Annual Statement of the Memphis Merchants' Exchange, 1904,* pp. 15–19.

12. See, for example, James W. Prothro, *The Dollar Decade; Business Ideas in the 1920's* (Baton Rouge, 1954); Francis X. Sutton *et al., The American Business Creed* (Cambridge, Mass., 1956).

INDEX